" 'Salvation' is at the heart of Christi̶a̶ yet remains a complex and elusive notion. How are we saved? And why do we need to be saved in the first place? Thoughtful people of faith have wrestled with these questions from the very beginning of Christianity. In this exceptional book, Robin Ryan, CP, provides a trustworthy and illuminating account of the various explanations of 'salvation' from its roots in the Scriptures through the course of history until the present day. He provides lucid and informative analyses of the wide diversity of Christian perspectives on salvation, spanning the foundational views of the Patristic era to the ecological and liberationist perspectives of the modern era. But this is not a simple cataloguing of others' opinions. Ryan's keen and clear interaction with these theologies of salvation and his own pastorally rich perspective on salvation and communion make this a singular contribution to contemporary theology—one that will be esteemed by theologians and pastors alike."

> —Donald Senior, CP
> President Emeritus
> Catholic Theological Union

"This very well-researched, sensible, and accessible book covers the major questions to be raised about the salvation brought through Jesus Christ and the Holy Spirit. The divine concern for the whole human family and its environment is as timely a message as ever."

> —Gerald O'Collins, SJ
> Emeritus Professor of the Gregorian University
> Author of *Jesus Our Redeemer: A Christian Approach*
> *to Salvation*

"A clear, balanced, and reliable guide to the many ways that Christians have thought about salvation in Jesus Christ. Robin Ryan's book will help anyone seeking a deeper understanding of what Jesus' life, death, and resurrection mean for us today."

> —Robert Schreiter
> Vatican Council II Professor of Theology
> Catholic Theological Union

"In his latest work, *Jesus and Salvation: Soundings in the Christian Tradition and Contemporary Theology*, Robin Ryan provides an informative and judicious overview of Christian thought on the salvific work of Jesus Christ from the New Testament to the present. Among modern authors, Karl Rahner, Hans Urs von Balthasar, and Edward Schillebeeckx receive the most detailed attention. This well-written book should prove to be of interest and value to serious students of Christology."

> —John P. Galvin
> Ordinary Professor of Systematic Theology
> The Catholic University of America

"This book is a gem. Ryan's comprehensive survey of images, metaphors, and theories of salvation is both a splendid compendium of what has been developed through the centuries of Christian tradition and a groundbreaking study that opens new ways of speaking of Christ's saving activity. It is both highly readable and refreshingly provocative, a must-read for anyone seriously thinking about soteriology."

> —Barbara E. Reid, OP, PhD
> Vice President and Academic Dean
> Catholic Theological Union

Jesus and Salvation

Soundings in the Christian Tradition and Contemporary Theology

Robin Ryan, CP

A Michael Glazier Book

LITURGICAL PRESS
Collegeville, Minnesota

www.litpress.org

A Michael Glazier Book published by Liturgical Press

Cover design by Jodi Hendrickson. Cover image: Dreamstime.

1   2   3   4   5   6   7   8   9

Library of Congress Cataloging-in-Publication Data

Ryan, Robin.
    Jesus and salvation : soundings in the Christian tradition and
contemporary theology / Robin Ryan, CP.
        pages   cm
    "A Michael Glazier book."
    ISBN 978-0-8146-8253-1 — ISBN 978-0-8146-8278-4 (ebook)
    1. Salvation—Christianity—History of doctrines.   2. Jesus Christ—
History of doctrines.   I. Title.

BT751.3.R93   2015
234.09—dc23   2014024559

Contents

Acknowledgments

I wish to express my sincere gratitude to colleagues who generously assisted me in the writing of this book. Donald Senior, CP, professor of New Testament and president emeritus of Catholic Theological Union, offered his consultation for the chapters on the Hebrew and Christian Scriptures. William Palardy, professor of patristics and rector of Pope Saint John XXIII Seminary, provided helpful suggestions for the material on the early church. Stephen Dunn, CP, retired professor at Saint Michael's Faculty of Theology in Toronto, and Anthony Mahowald, Louis Block Professor Emeritus at the University of Chicago, contributed their insights for the chapter on Christ and the cosmos. Elizabeth Johnson, distinguished professor of theology at Fordham University, was a faithful source of encouragement for the entire project and offered her suggestions for the chapter on Christ as universal savior.

In a special way, I wish to extend my gratitude to Paul Zilonka, CP, retired professor of New Testament at Saint Mary's Seminary. Paul was extremely generous in reading every chapter and offering his expert advice. He made this contribution to my work while facing serious physical illness in his own life. Paul reflects the grace of God in Christ through his generous service to others.

Introduction

Talking about Salvation

I n the summer of 2012, I made my first visit to the country of Haiti. I traveled with some colleagues from my Passionist religious community to visit Father Rick Frechette, a Passionist priest and physician who has worked in Haiti for more than twenty years. Frechette initially went to Haiti to establish an orphanage, but he has subsequently led the way in the founding of two hospitals, including the leading pediatric hospital in the country. He has also been involved in the building of a number of primary and secondary schools, as well as projects to provide housing for people who are either homeless or living in woefully substandard housing. Many of these people lost their homes in the devastating earthquake that struck Haiti in January of 2010.

On the second day of our visit, we accompanied Frechette to Cité du Soleil, one of the worst slums in the Western Hemisphere, located outside Port-au-Prince. The area is lined with endless rows of shacks with tin roofs that leak in the rain. It is a bleak place with a history of violence. On that day, however, there was a small celebration taking place in Cité du Soleil. A new bakery was being dedicated there. The bakery had been built to establish a modest business enterprise in the area that would provide a few jobs as well as baked goods for the community. Representatives from a variety of agencies that had collaborated in the project were present, including UNICEF, which had provided some of the funding. There was even a small band comprised of young people from Cité du Soleil, playing patriotic and popular songs under a makeshift canopy.

My travel companions and I stood on the outskirts of this dedication ceremony, listening to lengthy speeches under the hot sun. Small children milled around us, most of them in bare feet and wearing ragged clothes; some asked us for money, using their own forms of "sign language." One little girl, about six or seven years old, decided that she was going to watch this ceremony holding my hand. She wore a tattered pink dress that had frayed lace. She had a beautiful smile. She did not ask me for money or anything else. Because I do not speak Haitian, we were unable to converse except by means of expression and gesture. But we smiled at one another and held hands while watching the ribbon cutting for the new bakery. Occasionally, she would rest her face against my arm. When the ceremony concluded, we exchanged one last smile. She then went off to mingle with her friends.

Anyone who travels to Haiti is bound to be struck by the pervasive poverty in that country and the miserable conditions in which many of the people are forced to live. The faces of the poor remain lodged in the memory long after one has returned to the so-called First World. The Haitian face that has been most prominent in my mind is that of the little girl in the pink dress. What kind of life will she have? Will she ever receive a decent education? Does she have any hope of escaping the desperate situation into which she was born?

This is a book about "soteriology." The term is derived from the Greek word *soteria*, which means "salvation." In Christian thought, soteriology is the study of the saving work of God in and through Jesus Christ. We will explore the biblical testimony about salvation, as well as a number of ancient and modern theological accounts of Christ's saving work. We will see that some soteriological theories are quite complex. Soteriology, however, is not a purely academic pursuit unrelated to the everyday concerns of ordinary people. Whichever soteriological image or theory one adopts, it must always be related to the struggles of ordinary people throughout the world, particularly those who suffer the most. Thus, as I begin this exploration of the Christian tradition about Christ's saving work, I ask how the Christian proclamation of salvation in Jesus Christ relates to the life and concerns of the little girl in the pink dress who lives in Cité du Soleil. What would it mean for her to be "saved" by Jesus Christ? Would salvation for her consist entirely of the hope for and the gift of eternal life with God? How might the church credibly preach the message of salvation in Christ to her and to her neighbors in Cité du Soleil?

Discourse about salvation seems foreign to some people in the contemporary world. On the one hand, there is a tendency in modern society to question the need for salvation. Emboldened by the remarkable scientific and technological advancements of recent years, some people insist that we can find solutions to our own problems, without any assistance from a deity. In fact, to appeal to a saving act from "outside" of humanity represents, they think, an avoidance of human responsibility in the task of solving the world's problems. Gerald O'Collins summarizes the view of such critics in these words: "Whatever our spiritual or other problems, surely we human beings can deal with them and solve them, provided we put our minds to it and make a real effort."[1] In my experience of discussing soteriology with graduate theology students over the years, I have found that a significant number of younger people have difficulty relating to language about "salvation." Students sometimes ask questions like: What is it that I am supposed to be saved from? Do we really need a "savior"? There is a strong sense of human autonomy and self-sufficiency in some people that makes Christian talk about salvation in Christ seem unintelligible.

From a quite different perspective, others object to Christian talk about salvation because of the problematic state of the world. They ask: How can we speak of Christ saving the world when the world seems so "unredeemed"—when there is such strife and deprivation across the globe? These critics particularly object to Christian language about salvation that reflects what theologians call a "realized eschatology," that is, a conception of salvation as a present reality, already transforming the here-and-now. One sometimes encounters such a view of salvation in the prayers of the liturgy. For example, in one of the prefaces for Mass during the Easter season, the priest prays these words: "For, with the old order destroyed, a universe cast down is renewed, and integrity of life is restored to us in Christ."[2] These words can certainly be interpreted to mean that Jesus' death and resurrection had real effects and that integrity of life is found in following Christ. It is through living as a disciple of Jesus that one discovers wholeness of life and an entirely new perspective on the world. Nevertheless, such expressions can also have a triumphalistic ring for those who are painfully aware that the "old order" continues to have adverse effects on the lives of billions of people around the world. The world about which we read daily in our newspapers is in desperate need of rescue and renewal. These critics provide a salutary reminder to Christians that we need to "watch our language" when speaking about salvation in a world where there continues to be massive suffering—where children have to eke out an existence in places like Cité du Soleil.

Australian theologian Denis Edwards identifies four contemporary issues that constitute the context in which Christians today ask about God's salvation: first, the arms race, which takes desperately needed resources from the poor and threatens the very existence of the human family; second, the widespread malnutrition, unemployment, and poverty that mark the lives of billions of people around the globe; third, the exploitation of the earth and the resulting ecological crisis; fourth, the aspirations of women for equality in rights and opportunity.[3] As a kind of postscript, Edwards mentions the issue of salvation in Christ in a world where the majority of people are not Christian. I consider this issue of religious pluralism to be of critical significance for contemporary reflection on the saving work of Christ. Edwards argues that a Christian perspective on salvation must address these pressing issues affecting the entire world. A further issue, discussed by Edwards in other works and linked with the ecological crisis,[4] is the connection between soteriology and our understanding of an evolving universe. How does the saving work of Christ relate, not simply to human history, but to the story of the cosmos? Here soteriology must address the relationship between creation and redemption and, more broadly, the dialogue between theology and science.

Talking about salvation, then, requires careful reflection undertaken in light of the Christian tradition and contemporary human experience. Shallow discourse about being "saved" in Christ, which is often characteristic of fundamentalist Christians, sounds shrill to many people and can actually be an obstacle to Christian proclamation of the Gospel. Believers must ask what salvation in Christ means for the present and the future, for the human family and the cosmos as well as for individuals. And they must ask how salvation in Christ is both *gift* and *call*—how the saving grace of God in Christ evokes human responsibility for the well-being of the human family and the rest of creation.

Christology and Soteriology

In Christian thought, soteriology has traditionally been understood as a dimension of Christology. Christology can be defined as a historical and systematic study of the person and work of Jesus Christ as the object and foundation of Christian faith. According to this definition, Christology encompasses an exploration of both the *person* of Jesus (who he is believed to be) and his *saving work*, that is, what he accomplished that effected salvation for human beings and the world. This is the most complete understanding of Christology. In the early church, the intrinsic relationship between the identity (person) of Christ and his saving work was strongly emphasized. For example, in his defense of the divinity of Christ against the followers of Arius, Athanasius of Alexandria repeatedly stressed that Christ could not give us genuine salvation unless he was truly divine. Since for Athanasius salvation meant participation in the very life of God, he was convinced that only someone who was truly divine could give such a benefit. One cannot "give" what one does not "have." Similar arguments were offered by theologians of the early church regarding the humanity of Jesus. They were convinced that salvation had to come from "our side"—from someone like us. Thus, Jesus must have truly shared in our humanity. As the theological tradition developed, however, Christology sometimes became fragmented, and discussion of the person of Christ was separated from consideration of his saving work. This disjunction was a feature of neoscholastic theology—the theological movement that resulted from a revival of Thomistic thought in the second half of the nineteenth century and extended through the first half of the twentieth century.[6] In this approach Christology—in a more narrow understanding of the term—was a study of the person of Jesus Christ. It was mainly devoted to a theology of the incarnation. In soteriology, one subsequently studied what Christ did to save the world.

Most contemporary theologians oppose such a disjunction between exploration of Christ's person and consideration of his saving work. They point out that study of the New Testament has made it clear that, for the earliest Christian communities, it was the experience of salvation in Jesus that led disciples to ask about his identity. Referring to the first disciples of Jesus, Elizabeth Johnson says, "Their encounter with Jesus in his ministry, death, and new resurrected life in the power of the Spirit unleashed positive religious experiences. They perceived that through Jesus the redeeming God of Israel, the God of boundless *hesed* and *emeth*, of loving-kindness and fidelity, had drawn near to them in an intensely gracious way and moved their lives into a changed direction, symbolized by their new community and its mission."[7] The life-giving experience of God mediated by Jesus led these disciples to inquire: If such a gift flows from him, who must he really be? Thomas Marsh puts it like this: "Jesus is recognized as who he is because he is experienced and seen as the absolute Bringer of Salvation."[8] Thus, while the focus of our inquiry in this book will be on the ways in which the saving work of Jesus Christ has been conceived and articulated, we must keep in mind the intrinsic relationship between Christ's salvific work and his personal identity.

As Christian doctrine developed, the church issued a number of official statements related to the person of Christ. These are teachings of faith that serve as norms for thinking and speaking about Christ. At the Council of Nicea (325 CE), the church officially taught that Jesus Christ, the incarnate Son of God, was truly divine. The Son of God is consubstantial with (*homoousios*: one in being with) the Father. At the First Council of Constantinople (381), the church taught that Christ was truly human, that his humanity was complete and not abbreviated in any way. The Council of Chalcedon (451) officially declared that Christ was one person in two distinct natures, human and divine. Each nature maintains its integrity, but the two natures are united in one person. The Third Council of Constantinople (680–681) defined that Jesus had both a human will and a divine will, though these were always in harmony with one another. These dogmatic definitions resulted from protracted debates. They were made in response to other positions that the church came to reject as incorrect or inadequate conceptions of the identity of Christ.

The church has not promulgated such defined teaching about the saving work of Christ to the same extent that it has about Christ's identity. It teaches that Jesus Christ is the unique savior of the world and that the salvation he effected has implications for all people, and even for the cosmos itself.[9] But the church has not officially taught that there is one specific way in which Christ's saving work must be conceived or explained. We will see that the soteriology of Anselm of Canterbury—known as the theory of satisfaction—achieved widespread recognition in theology, popular preaching, and spirituality and that Anselm's formulation of soteriology retains its influence even today. But it was never officially defined as the only way to conceive of the saving work of Christ. For example, about 170 years after Anselm developed his argument, Thomas Aquinas drew on the theory of satisfaction but also introduced subtle changes into it. The church has tolerated a rather wide-ranging diversity in thinking about soteriology. Gerald O'Collins remarks that "no period of Christianity can claim to have produced a truly unified systematic soteriology."[10] In our exploration of soteriology, we will need to pay attention to this diversity of thought and explore the underlying reasons for differences in approach.

Images and Theories

It is important to distinguish between *images* and *metaphors* employed to speak of Christ's saving work, on the one hand, and *theories* that are constructed to explain it, on the other. For example, the image/metaphor of "ransom" is found in the New Testament to depict Christ's saving work, particularly his death by crucifixion. In a moving section of the First Letter of Peter, the author exhorts the Christians to whom he writes to exhibit reverence in their way of living. He tells them that they were "ransomed" from their old way of life "not with perishable things like silver or gold but with the precious blood of Christ as of a spotless unblemished lamb" (1 Pet 1:18-19). Here the author may be drawing on the Fourth Servant Song from the book of Isaiah in comparing the blood of the crucified Jesus to that of an unblemished lamb (see Isa 53:7, 10). The practice of ransoming was well known in the ancient world. Prisoners of war and slaves could be ransomed in a variety of ways, usually through the payment of money. Thus, ordinary people could readily imagine what it might be like to be ransomed and set free from captivity or slavery. And so in early Christianity ransom served as an intelligible image to express what God had done in Christ to give disciples a new experience of freedom and a fresh start on life. In this case the ransom "price" did not consist of a payment of money but Christ's offering of his very life—signified by his "precious blood."

The author of 1 Peter does not elaborate further on this image. He does not ask, for example, to whom the ransom was paid or how the "transaction" was effected. He simply employs the metaphor as one way of expressing the munificence of God's saving work in Christ and as motivation to his readers to act with reverence for God in every aspect of their lives. Later Christian authors, however, will attempt to develop this ransom metaphor into a theory, speculating about the means of the transaction, to whom the ransom was given, and why it had to be offered in the first place. We will see, for example, that Gregory of Nyssa (among others) argues that the ransom was paid to the devil.

Theologians sometimes distinguish between "first-level" ("first-order") language and "second-level" ("second-order") language.[11] First-level language abounds in image and metaphor. It is the language of proclamation, narrative, poetry, and prayer. The four gospels show that the early communities of disciples employed narrative in their proclamations of faith; they told the story of Jesus, the crucified and risen One. Narrative has its own characteristics and rules, which differ from those of theory. For contemporary believers, the collects and the eucharistic prayers of the liturgy are rich in images and metaphors that are employed to tell the story of God's redeeming action in history and in the present. They reflect the language of proclamation and prayer; they are first-level religious language. Music and art can also be considered as first-level expression. Think of the rich ways in which the redemptive work of God in Christ is articulated in hymns like "Hail Redeemer, King Divine" or in artistic works like the Isenheim Altarpiece of Matthias Grünewald.

Second-level expression is the language of doctrine and theology. Such theological expression often draws on philosophy for purposes of clarification and precision. When images or metaphors are turned into theories and doctrines, one has moved from first-level to second-level expression. Gregory of Nyssa begins to make this move in his elaboration of the biblical language of ransom, as does Anselm of Canterbury in his theory of satisfaction. Anselm employs sophisticated rational argumentation to construct his theory of satisfaction. The distinction between first- and second-level language is not always hard and fast, but there is a real difference. O'Collins puts it like this: the images and metaphors of first-level language "show" God's redeeming action, while theories attempt to "explain" God's redeeming action. Theories attempt to provide a coherent explanation that accounts for all the relevant data at hand. O'Collins emphasizes that theories that attempt to "explain" salvation in Christ cannot take the place of images and metaphors that "show" Christ's saving work.[12] This is true because in speaking about God's redemptive work we are trying to articulate a mystery of faith. The mystery of God's redeeming action is inexhaustibly rich. We will never wrap our minds around it or be able to explain it adequately, though we can make affirmations about it that are true. Even the most subtle and compelling soteriological theory will fall short of capturing the mystery of salvation. So we are always brought back to the language of proclamation, narrative, and prayer in giving testimony to God's saving love in Christ. Anselm of Canterbury taught that theology is a dynamic movement of faith seeking understanding. This dynamism ultimately ends in prayer—prayer that employs words and contemplation that is lovingly silent before the mystery of the God who saves.

One of the reasons for the broad diversity in the Christian soteriological tradition has been the multiplicity of images and metaphors used to "show" God's redeeming action, even within the New Testament itself. Elizabeth Johnson observes that in telling the story of the crucified and risen Jesus early Christians "spoke in financial categories of redemption or release from slavery through payment of a price; in legal categories of advocacy, justification, and satisfaction; in cultic categories of liberation and victory over oppressive powers; in personal categories of reconciliation after dispute; in medical categories of being healed or made whole; in existential categories of freedom and new life; and in familial categories of becoming God's children by birth (John) or by adoption (Paul)."[13] No single image or metaphor could exhaust the mystery of God's saving love in Jesus Christ; many were needed. This multiplicity of biblical images gave rise to diverse theologies of salvation.

"Moments" in the Jesus Story

John Galvin suggests a helpful question to keep in mind when exploring Christian soteriology: Which aspect of the existence of Jesus Christ is viewed as salvific by this author or in this text?[14] The four main points of reference have been: first, the incarnation—the becoming flesh of the Word/Son of God; second, the public life and ministry of Jesus; third, his death by crucifixion; fourth, his resurrection, which also implies his glorification and the gift of the Holy Spirit. Keeping this question in mind will help to shed light on the texts and authors we will study.

a) Some Christian thinkers highlight the salvific significance of the incarnation itself. They propose that the becoming flesh/human of the Son of God was itself transformative of the human situation, and even of the entire cosmos. Certain theologians of the early church will espouse this idea, which is sometimes called "physical redemption." It is based on the notion—inspired by Platonic philosophy—that human nature is a universal in which all people participate. So the becoming human of the Son of God in itself transforms human nature. Since in Christ God shared our life, we are granted a share in the life of God. Human nature has been elevated because in Christ it was assumed by the divine. We will see that some contemporary theologians who address scientific findings about the evolution of the cosmos retrieve this patristic theme in their soteriologies. They speak not only of the elevation of human nature but also of the transformation of the cosmos.

b) Other thinkers elucidate the words and deeds of Jesus in his public ministry as salvific. For example, in his deeds of healing and exorcism, Jesus made the reign of God present in the lives of people who were in dire need. His table fellowship with all kinds of people—rich and poor, saint and sinner—had the effect of bringing these people into communion with God. People who encountered Jesus experienced God's saving presence and action in their lives. A careful reading of the soteriological tradition reveals that this aspect of the existence of Jesus has sometimes been underplayed in depicting his redemptive work. Contemporary liberationist and feminist theologians—among others—argue that more attention should be given to the salvific significance of Jesus' public ministry. They suggest that there has been a tendency in soteriology to move directly from the incarnation to the death of Jesus. This is reflected in the assertion that Jesus "came to die" or that God "sent his Son to die for us." Even in the Nicene Creed, professed at the Eucharist by Christians, there is no mention of the earthly ministry of Jesus. Attention to Jesus' public ministry is particularly important when it comes to the question of the image of God that is reflected in a particular soteriology. If one ignores the public ministry of Jesus and focuses on his death as *the* salvific action of his life, this can result in a distorted notion of God.

It is clear that the death of Jesus has been a key point of reference for identifying the saving work of Christ from the beginning. Even the most critical New Testament scholars—those who accentuate the influence of later Christian belief and practice in shaping the gospel narratives—point out that Jesus' death is understood as salvific in the most ancient strands of the tradition. For example, in 1 Corinthians 15:3-8, Paul quotes an early Christian tradition about the resurrection of Jesus and the appearances of the risen Christ to various individuals and groups. It is a tradition that predates him and that he has received, though he appends his own experience of the risen Jesus at the end. This creedal formula begins by affirming "that Christ died for our sins in accordance with the scriptures." In this early profession of faith, then, the death of Jesus is viewed not simply as a brute fact of history. It is envisioned as a death "for our sins," and it is "in accordance with the scriptures." In other words, it is a death that has salvific significance, and it is in some way integral to the revelation of God's intentions for the world. In popular piety, Christians are accustomed to prayers such as, "We adore you, O Christ, and we praise you, because by your holy cross you have redeemed the world." And the redemptive power of Jesus' death on the cross is articulated often in liturgical prayer. Still, Christian thinkers through the centuries have struggled with how to elucidate the salvific significance of the death of Jesus. What is it about Jesus' death that makes it redemptive? Distinct theologies of the cross have been crafted, giving rise to diverse perspectives on the role that Jesus' death plays in his saving work.

Finally, the resurrection has also been viewed as having redemptive implications. The passage from 1 Corinthians cited above makes it clear that a number of disciples claimed to have encountered Jesus after his death. They experienced him present to them in a transformed state. These experiences led to the fundamental Christian confession that God had acted to raise the crucified Jesus from death. And his being raised from the dead engendered their own hope for resurrection. Through the centuries, certain accounts of soteriology have paid little attention to this key moment in the Jesus story. We will see that Anselm does not integrate the resurrection of the crucified Jesus into his theory of satisfaction. On the other hand, the Christology and soteriology of other authors can be viewed as resurrection-centered. The soteriology of Edward Schillebeeckx is sometimes understood that way. The resurrection of the crucified Jesus is obviously another key "moment" in the existence of Jesus that has soteriological implications.

It is helpful to keep Galvin's question in mind as we explore the soteriological tradition. Typically, Christian authors appeal to some combination of these four aspects of the existence of Jesus in articulating their theology of salvation, though they often place particular emphasis on one of them. Contemporary theologians point out that these "moments" in the Jesus story, while distinct, should never be separated. Thomas Marsh emphasizes this point:

> Attention must be focused, then, on the ministry, death and resurrection of Jesus not as isolated events but as intrinsically connected events which constitute the unfolding character of the continuum this history is. The total meaning of this history, therefore, cannot be found in any one moment of it separated from the others.[15]

In speaking of God's redeeming action in Christ, then, one must attend to the entire Jesus story. For purposes of analysis, however, identifying where various authors place their emphasis is helpful for understanding and evaluating their arguments.

The "From" and the "For" of Salvation

The idea of salvation, or redemption, implies a movement from a negative state to a positive—or at least a more positive—state. Salvation, then, involves being rescued or liberated from some form of evil. The source and nature of the evil from which human beings are saved has been identified in various ways in Christian soteriology. Sometimes it is described simply as "sin." Here sin is understood as something more encompassing than an individual offense against God. It is a power that holds humanity in thrall, as described by Paul in his letter to the Romans (see Rom 7:13-25). Other writers focus on "death" as the evil from which Christ frees us. Human enslavement to death—usually connected with the presence of sin in human history—is overcome by Christ, enabling us to share in his immortality. A number of theologians of the early church spoke of Christ redeeming us from the power of death, making us sharers in his victory over death. We sometimes hear this idea in the liturgy, for example, in the preface for the Epiphany of the Lord: "For today you have revealed the mystery of our salvation in Christ as a light for the nations, and, when he appeared in our mortal nature, you made us new by the glory of his immortal nature."[16]

Some modern theologians describe the "from" of salvation in terms of "alienation."[17] Human beings have become alienated—estranged—from their true selves, one another, and God. We are not who we were meant to be. In particular, the capacity to love ourselves, others, and God has been stunted, and so we live in a state of exile from our true selves. It is Christ who frees us from this alienation, not only by *showing* us what it means to be human, but also by *enabling* us to recover our genuine humanity and, thus, to thrive in life-giving relationships.

At the same time, the Christian concept of salvation does not entail only being rescued "from" some form of evil or negative state. It is also salvation "for"; it entails the capacity and the summons to live as redeemed people. This dimension of soteriology is often referred to as the "benefits" of salvation. Philip Melanchthon, the disciple and colleague of Martin Luther, was famous for speaking of "Christ and his benefits."[18] New Testament authors use a variety of different images to describe what salvation in Christ is "for." For example, Paul employs the language of "adoption" to speak of the new relationship with God that Christ has made possible: "For those who are led by the Spirit of God are children of God. For you did not receive a spirit of slavery to fall back into fear, but you received a spirit of adoption, through which we cry, '*Abba*, Father!'" (Rom 8:14-15). Paul accentuates the freedom that Christians enjoy, a freedom to relate to God with the trust and intimacy that a child has with his or her parent.

The Christian idea of salvation, then, entails more than simply release from a state of negativity. At its deepest level, it is the gift of sharing in the very life of God. We will see this conviction in our examination of patristic theologians, for whom "God's ultimate design is that we become totally united with God, sharing the divine life, light, and love."[19] We will also encounter it in the thought of Karl

Rahner, who adopts the position that the incarnation would have taken place even if there had been no sin. Release from the power of evil and sin is certainly intrinsic to the Christian notion of salvation, but it is not the total meaning of salvation. There is something more happening in the story of salvation; that "more" has to do with God's self-communication, God's gift of self to the human family. As we explore various approaches to soteriology in the Christian tradition, it is helpful to identify what an author depicts humanity as being saved "from" and the way in which he or she describes what we are saved "for."

Soteriology and Other Dimensions of Christian Life and Thought

In my reference to my visit to Haiti, I mentioned that Christian soteriology has relevance for the real concerns of everyday life, especially for those who suffer most acutely in our world. It is also important to note that soteriology is closely related to other dimensions of Christian thought and practice. What is explored and discussed in soteriology connects closely with Christian spirituality and pastoral ministry. If Christian spirituality is ultimately about the life with God that disciples of Jesus experience, the conception of salvation/ redemption in Christ is integral to spirituality. What does it mean to live a "redeemed" life? In the practice of pastoral care, ministers help others recognize and respond to the invitations of grace that are present in their lives. Our understanding of redemption, of what the grace of Christ holds out for us, influences the healing, hope, and direction we share with others.

The references to the liturgy that I have made suggest that soteriology is also closely related to liturgical theology and the practice of liturgy within the life of the church. The celebration of the Eucharist, for example, is replete with affirmations of God's salvation accomplished in Christ. The proclamation of the eucharistic prayers consists of a narration of the story of salvation in the context of praise and thanksgiving. One eucharistic theme that is explicitly soteriological is that of sacrifice.[20] The sacrificial offering of the Eucharist is, of course, intrinsically connected with Jesus' death on the cross. We will see that the concept of sacrifice is integral to the Christian soteriological tradition, though its relevance for today is contested by some thinkers. Is the language of "sacrifice" intelligible to people today and does it inform an authentic Christian spirituality? As we proceed in our exploration, I invite readers to connect the expressions of soteriology found within the tradition with the affirmations about salvation that are made in the celebration of the Eucharist.

A Look Ahead

I will adopt a chronological approach for our study of the development of Christian thought on salvation. The first two chapters will consist of a summary discussion of key soteriological terms and themes in the Hebrew and Christian Scriptures. It is impossible to [...] [...]al testimony to salvation [...] But we will explore salient [...] of God's saving presence [...] the third chapter, reflection [...]s of the early church will [...] exploration of medieval [...] onsider Anselm's theory [...]ring work found in Peter [...]inas, especially as found [...]dress the perspectives on [...]nt Reformers Martin Lu- [...] will engage the thought [...]logians of the twentieth [...]ar, and Edward Schille- [...]thinkers reveal distinct [...] conversation" with one [...]n discussion about the [...] poor and of women will occupy our attention in the sixth chapter. Liberationist and feminist Christologies have challenged some of the assumptions and expressions of traditional soteriology, particularly in light of the suffering of marginalized peoples throughout the world. We will explore some of the key themes found in the work of liberationist and feminist theologians. In the seventh chapter, we will delve into the dialogue between science and theology by examining the relationship between salvation in Christ and the evolution of the cosmos. This discussion

10/22/2016

Lisa

I love you so much! I could see your wonderful mind at work on all these thing discussed by these persons presenting. Don't [...] brilliant mind not help what is to be the future. We need warrior mačkas! mc will necessarily touch on ecology and the future of our endangered planet. In chapter 8, we will address the burning issue of the relation of Christ to other religious traditions. What does the Christian confession of Jesus Christ as the unique and universal mediator of salvation mean in a world where most people are not professing Christians? Finally, in chapter 9, I will glean some principles from our exploration of the tradition and suggest one soteriological model that I believe is relevant for our contemporary world.

Throughout this introduction, I have raised a number of questions for readers to keep in mind as they enter into this theological conversation that spans the ages. Some of these key questions are:

- Which aspect(s) of the existence of Jesus is viewed as salvific by this author or text?

- In the work of this author, what does Christ save us *from*? What does Christ save us *for*?

- What is the image of God that is conveyed in this account of the saving work of Christ?

- What implications does this perspective on soteriology have for Christian life and worship?

- In what way does this soteriology speak to human concerns and aspirations across the globe?

CHAPTER I

The Saving God of Israel

C hristian conceptions of salvation are rooted in the biblical testimony to God's saving action in the history of Israel. Though seemingly obvious, it is important to recall that Jesus himself was a first-century Jew, and he drew on the story of his own people in speaking about the way in which God was offering salvation in and through his ministry. For example, his proclamation of the reign of God tapped into the Jewish belief that God was the ultimate ruler of Israel and of all nations. After Jesus' death and resurrection, his disciples utilized images and metaphors drawn from the Scriptures of Israel to proclaim the salvation that God was offering in and through Jesus. Christians should not forget that their faith is rooted in Judaism and in Israel's experience of God.

The Hebrew Scriptures are a complex set of documents comprised of many strands of tradition. They reflect nine centuries or more of written tradition and an even longer span of oral tradition. The understanding of salvation that is found in these texts manifests diverse perspectives and some significant developments. For example, belief in an afterlife is a late development that is expressed in only a few texts of the Old Testament. It is not possible to attend to all of the complexities of Hebrew thought about salvation in an overview such as this. I will simply highlight certain themes that were central to the faith and praxis of the people of Israel and reflected their experience of God's saving presence in their lives.

1

Salvation Terminology

In the introduction, I pointed out that language about salvation is drawn from ordinary human experience. This is certainly true of the terminology found in the Hebrew Scriptures, which reflects categories found in the legal, financial, and interpersonal spheres of life. While semantic considerations do not tell the whole story in understanding biblical soteriology, attention to terminology does offer insight into the ways in which God's saving action was experienced and expressed. I will explore just four terms that are found in the Hebrew Scriptures, noting all the while that this list is not exhaustive.

Words drawn from the Hebrew root *ys* (*yasa*, to save; *yeshua*, salvation) are found with great frequency. These terms have a wide-ranging sphere of meaning—to help in times of distress, to rescue, to deliver. They can signify being set free from many different forms of individual or communal distress—danger, injustice, sickness, war, famine, etc.[1] This Hebrew root is, of course, the basis of the name for "Jesus" (see Matt 1:21). In the ancient world, the king was envisioned as the king-savior, whose role was to protect his people from external enemies and to rule them with justice.[2] Israel will come to name God as the ultimate protector and source of justice. In the Song of the Sea, which extols God's act of liberating the Israelites from slavery in Egypt, the poet writes, "My strength and my courage is the LORD, and he has been my savior" (Exod 15:2). In the so-called enthronement psalms (Pss 47; 93; 96–99), God is praised as the king-savior who rules over Israel and over the whole world:

> Sing to the LORD a new song;
>   sing to the LORD, all the earth.
> Sing to the LORD, bless his name;
>   announce his salvation day after day. (Ps 96:1-2)

The Hebrew root *pdh* (*padah*) means to purchase or to ransom, and it originally had a commercial context. It can refer to the ransom of a person from slavery (e.g., Exod 21:7-11). It is also used to denote the redemption of one kind of firstborn animal with another. The firstborn male animal was to be sacrificed to God in commemoration of the tenth plague (see Exod 13:11-16; Lev 27:27). And at the age of one month, all firstborn boys were to be redeemed by the payment of five silver shekels (Num 18:16). This term is then employed to describe what God did to liberate Israel from oppression by the Egyptians. In the sermon about the covenant that Moses is depicted as giving in Deuteronomy, he enjoins the people to show justice to their servants, with the reminder that they, too, "were once slaves in the land of Egypt, and the LORD, your God, ransomed you" (Deut 15:15). God ransomed God's people from Egypt, making them God's special possession. There is, however, no mention of a purchase price; God is sovereign over all of creation and gives no recompense when he ransoms.[3]

Another Hebrew root for ransom is *kpr*. The recalcitrant owner of an ox that gores someone to death may spare his own life by paying a ransom (Exod 21:28-30). The verb *kipper* is used in the ritual of the Day of Atonement in Leviticus 16, and here it means "expiate" or "atone." The priest is instructed to take some of the blood of the goat that is sacrificed for sin and sprinkle it around the Holy of Holies: "Thus he shall make atonement for the sanctuary because of all the sinful defilements and faults of the Israelites" (16:16). This "making atonement" or "expiating" refers to the purging of the sanctuary, which has been polluted by human sin and impurity. The sacrificial blood is an effective cultic cleansing agent. Through this action, the Holy of Holies is made clean and holy; it is reconsecrated to God.[4] From the same root comes the noun *kapporet*, which designates the golden cover of the ark of the covenant, called the "Mercy Seat" (see Exod 37:6-7). On the Day of Atonement the priest applies the blood of a sacrificial bull to this golden cover in order to cleanse it (Lev 16:14). In all of these rituals, it is God who provides the means to remove the effects of the sins and impurities of the people. When we examine the passage from Paul's letter to the Romans, wherein Paul refers to Christ as having been "set forth as an expiation" (Rom 3:25), we will see that this ritual of the Day of Atonement forms the background for Paul's assertion about salvation in Christ.

The Hebrew root *gl* (*ga'al*, to redeem; *go'el*, redeemer) relates to family law. The *go'el* was the nearest adult male relative, who had a special responsibility to assist his kin in times of adversity or loss. The *go'el* was enjoined to redeem the property of a brother who had been forced to sell his ancestral property (Lev 25:25), to rescue kin who had sold themselves into indentured servitude (Lev 25:48), to marry the wife of a deceased brother in order to raise up the name of the deceased (Ruth 3:9, 12), and to avenge the murder or severe harm inflicted on a relative (the *go'el haddam*, blood redeemer; Num 35:19; Judg 8:18-21). This terminology, too, is applied to God to speak of God's redemptive activity on behalf of Israel. In Moses' encounter with God in Exodus 6, God instructs Moses to assure the enslaved people that he will redeem them with an outstretched arm and with mighty acts of judgment (6:6). God does this in order to take Israel as God's own people (v. 7). This term is also used in the Psalms to refer to God's saving action in the exodus (see Pss 78:35; 106:10). In the book of Job, in the midst of Job's fierce laments about his inexplicable suffering, he proclaims his trust in a divine *go'el*: "But as for me, I know that my Vindicator lives, and that he will at last stand forth upon the dust; Whom I myself shall see: my own eyes, not another's shall behold him, and from my flesh I shall see God" (Job 19:25-26). This term is also employed by Second Isaiah (Isa 40–55), the anonymous prophet who spoke a word of hope to those who had been exiled to Babylonia. In language that evoked the saving action of God in the exodus, the prophet assured these suffering people that God was about to act in a new way to liberate them and bring them home.[5] He promised them that God would be their *go'el*, their redeemer: "Break out together in song, O ruins of Jerusalem! For the LORD comforts his people, he redeems Jerusalem" (Isa 52:9). This naming of God as the *go'el* of Israel meant that God had established a relationship of closest kinship with the people. They were family to God and God had assumed responsibility for their well-being.

Eventually the terms *ga'al/go'el* and *padah* came to be employed interchangeably in the Hebrew Scriptures. For example, both words can be found in Psalm 78, which is a lengthy hymn of praise that celebrates God's saving deeds from the exodus up to the reign of King David.

The Experience and Tradition of the Exodus

Our brief consideration of Hebrew terminology for salvation shows that the memory of liberation from slavery in Egypt was central to Israel's conception of God and God's saving activity. The very existence of Israel—the covenant community—was dependent on God's gracious action of setting free a group of slaves living under grinding oppression. The Song of Miriam—appended to the Song of the Sea mentioned above—is one of the most ancient extant expressions of Hebrew poetry. In this refrain, Miriam (the sister of Moses) is depicted as dancing and proclaiming what God has done in liberating the people God has chosen:

> Sing to the LORD, for he is gloriously triumphant;
> horse and chariot he has cast into the sea. (Exod 15:21)

The memory of this foundational event became ingrained in the minds and hearts of the people of ancient Israel as it was commemorated each year in the celebration of Passover. K. A. Kitchen comments on the ways in which the memory of this event shaped the thinking of Israel: it provided the basic historical reason why Israel should accept and obey God's covenant, since God had acted as their deliverer from slavery in accord with the ancient promise; it was the motivating reason for Israel's proper treatment of one another and of strangers; it manifested the sovereignty of the God of Israel; and it was used as an initial dateline for the history of the people.[6] The exodus also revealed the corporate nature of salvation: it was the whole people of Israel who were saved by the liberating God.[7] Salvation is not an individualistic affair. "Within the biblical tradition, few other events enjoyed anything like the prominence accorded so pervasively in the work of so many writers, or were deemed of such basic importance for Israel's history."[8]

Scholars debate issues related to the historicity of the exodus event. There is an absence of extrabiblical sources documenting Israel's oppression in Egypt and its migration to Canaan. There is evidence, however, of Egypt exploiting the forced labor of foreign captives and of the presence of Semites at the Egyptian court.[9] There is also archaeological evidence of a rapid rise in the population of Palestine and the Transjordan between 1250 and 1150 BCE.[10] Some scholars argue that it is not so strange that Egypt would have failed to record this event. It would not have kept a chronicle of what would have been considered a minor military mishap.[11] Most scholars suggest that the escape of the slaves from Egypt was an event on a smaller scale than that which is depicted in book of Exodus. Though the historicity of the exodus event cannot be proved from historical records, the available external evidence and the enduring nature of the exodus tradition suggest an event that actually took place. Nahum Sarna asks why Israel would have preserved an embarrassing tradition about slavery if it did not have historical roots. He wonders how such a tradition would have left such an indelible mark on the national consciousness if it was pure fiction. And he asks what other cohesive force could have united heterogeneous groups into a nation.[12] Bernhard Anderson concludes, "Undoubtedly, the story of the Event at the Sea is not pure fiction; it rests upon something that actually happened, something that aroused ecstatic jubilation and became the undying memory of the people." Anderson adds, however, that it is not possible to penetrate beyond the faith language of the biblical account to ascertain the historical details of this event.[13]

The exodus tradition profoundly shaped Israel's perception of the character of God. In the extended speech of God in Exodus 6:2-8, there is a seminal self-disclosure in which God identifies God's self as the One who had entered into covenant with Abraham, Isaac, and Jacob. Witnessing the plight of the people, God remembers the covenant and promises to act on behalf of this oppressed people: "And now that I have heard the groaning of the Israelites, whom the Egyptians are treating as slaves, I am mindful of my covenant. Therefore, say to the Israelites: I am the LORD. I will free you from the forced labor of the Egyptians and will deliver you from their slavery. I will rescue you by my outstretched arm and with mighty acts of judgment. I will take you as my own people, and you will have me as your God" (Exod 6:5-6). Thus, to Moses is revealed the God of compassion, the One who is faithful to the divine promises. In commenting on this passage, Walter Brueggemann says, "As much as any text in the Exodus tradition, this one invites reflection upon the character of the God of Israel."[14] The character of God disclosed in this text, and in the primal event of the exodus, "is to make relationships, bring emancipation, and establish covenants."[15]

The memory of the exodus also formed the basis for the ethical life of ancient Israel. As God had acted toward the people, so were they to behave toward one another and toward the foreigners in their midst. The experience of salvation from God was not something to be merely received; it had to be actualized in human conduct in order to be effective. This is made clear in the code of laws that is part of the Sinai covenant tradition: "You shall not molest or oppress an alien, for you were once aliens yourselves in the land of Egypt. You shall not wrong any widow or orphan. If you ever wrong them and they cry out to me, I will surely hear their cry" (Exod 22:20-22). The liberating God who had restored the dignity of an enslaved people commanded these people to act in liberating ways in their relations with others. In particular, they were to demonstrate compassion toward the poor and vulnerable of society:

> If you lend money to one of your poor neighbors among my people, you shall not act like an extortioner toward him by demanding interest from him. If you take your neighbor's cloak as a pledge, you shall return it to him before sunset; for this cloak of his is the only covering he has for his body. What else has he to sleep in? If he cries out to me, I will hear him; for I am compassionate. (Exod 22:24-26)

Brueggemann observes that the commandments relating to treatment of one's neighbor in the book of Exodus "have their warrant, impetus, and urgency in the character of this particular God. . . . Thus it is important to 'get it right' about Yahweh, in order to 'get it right' about neighbor."[16] The Hebrew Scriptures teach us that a people's image of God indelibly marks their understanding of proper conduct in interpersonal and social relations. In the case of Israel, the living memory of the exodus served as an impetus to compassion and to a justice characterized by abiding concern for the weakest of society.

The enduring memory of God's saving action at the exodus also served as a catalyst for the hope of Israel at later times of crisis. To the exiles in Babylon, Second Isaiah speaks a word of hope that draws on this tradition. Through his instrument Cyrus, God will again act to set God's people free. In his portrayal of this new deed of God, the prophet draws freely on the exodus and wilderness traditions: the flight from Egypt, the deliverance at the sea, the march through the wilderness, and the journey toward the Promised Land.[17] He blends this exodus language with imagery drawn from creation myths, so that the "new exodus" represents a new creative act of God. God's redemption of the exiles is, in this prophet's mind, a new act of creation. The waters of the sea that Israel traversed represent the waters of chaos, over which God is victorious:[18]

Awake, awake, put on strength,
   O arm of the LORD!
Awake as in the days of old,
   in ages long ago!
Was it not you who crushed Rahab,
   you who pierced the dragon?
Was it not you who dried up the sea,
   the waters of the great deep,
Who made the depths of the sea into a way
   for the redeemed to pass over?
Those whom the LORD has ransomed will return
   and enter Zion signing,
crowned with everlasting joy. (Isa 51:9-11)

Anderson aptly summarizes the critical significance of the experience and tradition of the exodus for the faith of Israel: "The Exodus was regarded as the clue to who God is and how God acts to deliver the downtrodden and oppressed; more than that, it provided the model for how the people of God should seek justice in society as the appropriate response to the liberation they had experienced (Mic 6:1-8)."[19] The saving God who had liberated the slaves of Egypt was present in the midst of God's people, acting to liberate anew and calling the people to act in the same way toward one another. To live in communion with this redeeming God implied living in communion with one another.

Covenant

The tradition of God establishing a covenant (*berith*) with the people of Israel is interwoven with the narrative of the exodus. The biblical author tells us that when the Israelites arrived at the desert of Sinai, Moses ascended the mountain and encountered God. The text that follows pierces right to the heart of the faith of ancient Israel:

Moses went up the mountain to God. Then the LORD called to him and said, "Thus shall you say to the house of Jacob; tell the Israelites: You have seen for yourselves how I treated the Egyptians and how I bore you up on eagle wings and brought you here to myself. Therefore, if you hearken to my voice and keep my covenant, you shall be my special possession, dearer to me than all other people, though all the earth is mine. You shall be to me a kingdom of priests, a holy nation. That is what you must tell the Israelites."

So Moses went and summoned the elders of the people. When he set before them all that the LORD had ordered him to tell them, the people all answered together, "Everything the LORD has said, we will do." Then Moses brought back to the LORD the response of the people. (Exod 19:3-8)

The rhythmic quality of this passage suggests that it existed as an ancient poetic piece before it was incorporated into the narrative of the book of Exodus. It may have been used for catechesis in the fundamentals of the faith of Israel, particularly because of its message about Israel having been specially called (elected) by God.[20] The God who had liberated Israel from slavery in Egypt sought to enter into an enduring relationship with this people, making them God's very own. God is depicted here as an eagle, mighty in power and tender in care so as to bear an oppressed people on his wings. This compelling image of the eagle "holds together majestic power and protective nurturing."[21] The universal and the particular are brought together in this passage: though all the earth belongs to God, Israel has been particularly chosen to belong to God. Israel's "belongingness" to the holy God is the reason that it can be called a "holy nation." It is a holy nation because it is God's special possession.

There is, however, a resounding "if" in this proclamation about Israel's relation to God: this people must hearken to God's voice and keep the covenant. The future of Israel is conditioned upon its response to the God of liberation. The demands of this covenantal pact are spelled out beginning in chapter 20, with the Ten Commandments, or Ten "Words" (*debarim*), followed by a set of stipulations usually called the "Covenant Code." Before enumerating the Ten Commandments, there is another reminder of God's saving action in Exodus: "I, the LORD, am your God, who brought you out of the land of Egypt, that place of slavery" (20:2). Anderson observes that the gracious initiative of God evokes a response from the people; their liberation has placed them in a situation of decision, "summoned them to a task within the divine purpose."[22] They are to be faithful in their worship of the one God and just and compassionate in their relations with one another. As Brueggemann puts it, "While Yahweh's initial rescue is unconditional and without reservation, a sustained relation with Yahweh is one of rigorous demand for covenant. Indeed, the long Sinai text that follows is a statement of condition whereby this rescued people can be a community of ongoing covenant."[23]

The biblical concept of covenant was related to the establishment of political treaties in the ancient Near East. Fundamentally, a covenant is "an agreement between two parties in which one or both make promises under oath to perform or refrain from certain actions stipulated in advance."[24] Covenant agreements were integral to the social and political life of the ancient Near East. Parity covenants were bilateral agreements between equals characterized by reciprocity. Suzerainty, or vassal, covenants were pacts made between a superior and an inferior party. There is evidence of such agreements from Hittite sources of the late second millennium BCE. In these treaties, the superior ruler gives a covenant and within that agreement the vassal—the head of a subordinate state—finds protection and security.[25] These pacts usually highlight the benevolent deeds of the superior ruler on behalf of the vassal. The vassal is required to swear an oath of loyalty to the king and to assist him in a time of war. Witnesses to the covenant include the gods of both parties, though preference is given to those of the superior ruler.

The covenant between God and Israel was most definitely a pact between unequals. This is clear in the exodus narratives, where the covenant is given and ratified in the context of a theophany. The utter holiness of God is signified in thunder and lightning. Careful instructions about who can and cannot draw near to God are given. God freely and graciously initiates the covenant with the people God has liberated; the only fitting response is one of gratitude for God's benevolence toward them. Obviously, the witnesses to this pact are not other gods, since YHWH does not recognize any other deities. The people are the witnesses to the covenant, placing their future on the line in their response to it.

The people's response to the initiative of God expressed above (Exod 19:8) is further illustrated in the ratification ceremony narrated in Exodus 24. Biblical scholars conclude that two versions of this story have been woven together.[26] In the first, the ratification of the covenant is enacted by specially chosen representatives of the people—Moses, Aaron and his two eldest sons, and seventy elders. These leaders ratify the covenant through a sacred meal that is celebrated at the top of the mountain where they have been privileged to gaze upon God (24:1-2; 9-11). This account of the event does not set conditions for the covenant. In another version (24:3-8), the whole assembly of Israel takes part in the ceremony at the foot of the mountain. In this account, the conditions of the covenant are implied and the people again express their assent to its demands: "We will do everything that the LORD has told us" (23:3b). The covenant ratification culminates in the sacrifice of young bulls, given as peace offerings to God. Moses sprinkles half of the blood from these sacrificed bulls on the altar and the other half on the people, naming it "the blood of the covenant" (24:8). Some scholars assert that the symbolic act of sprinkling the blood on the people points to the expected fate of the people if they are unfaithful to the covenant.[27] Bernhard Anderson, on the other hand, suggests that this blood ritual reflects "the ancient belief that sacrificial blood has the sacramental power to bring together two parties in covenant."[28]

The two versions of the covenant ratification in Exodus 24 reflect two conceptions of the covenant relationship between God and Israel that stand in tension within the Hebrew Scriptures. The tradition that comes to be linked with Moses and Sinai includes conditions for the permanence of the relationship. In order for the covenant relationship to continue, the people must be faithful to the covenant demands given by God, who is always faithful. Infidelity leads to a breaking of the covenant. The other tradition speaks of an "everlasting covenant" (*berith olam*) that can never be broken. It is reflected in the covenants with Noah (Gen 9:1-17), Abraham (Gen 17:7-8), and David (2 Sam 7:8-17). In the story of God's promise to David, the prophet Nathan tells the king, "Your house and your kingdom shall endure forever before me; your throne shall stand firm forever." In fact, the Davidic dynasty was marked by tragedy, and it was not restored to rule after the exile in the sixth century BCE. Some later prophets will challenge the notion of an unconditional, everlasting covenant, drawing instead on the Mosaic tradition of a relationship conditioned by the response of the people. Leslie Hoppe comments on the coexistence of these two covenant traditions in the Scriptures of Israel: "The Scriptures preserve both the Mosaic and the Davidic covenants, and the two should be seen as complementary. The former emphasizes human responsibility and the latter divine constancy."[29]

At the time of the exile, the prophet Jeremiah promised the gift of a "new covenant" between God and Israel (Jer 31:31-34). Here the prophet acknowledges that the people broke the covenant that God had made with them after their deliverance from Egypt. The new covenant will fulfill the original intention of the covenant that was established at Sinai.[30] It will be different from the Mosaic covenant, however, because the law of God will be written on the hearts of the people. All of the people, from the most humble to the most sophisticated, will be blessed with an intimate knowledge of God. In a line that epitomizes covenant theology, God promises through Jeremiah: "I will be their God, and they shall be my people" (31:33). This covenant will be based on God's forgiveness of the past infidelities of the people: "for I will forgive their evildoing and remember their sin no more" (31:34). The early Christian community will draw on this theme of the new covenant in speaking of what God has done for all humanity in and through Jesus Christ.[31]

Covenant, a notion drawn from political and social relations in the ancient Near East, was the primary metaphor for expressing the relationship between Israel and God in the Hebrew Scriptures.[32] The liberation of a group of people from the oppression of slavery was not the totality of God's saving action; rather, this act of grace was only the beginning. God had formed a new people and called them to live in close relationship with him. The transcendent God, who could say "all the earth is mine," had drawn near to a particular people, giving of Self to them in faithful, steadfast love (*hesed*). Salvation for Israel meant living in communion with the living God. As the Jewish philosopher Abraham Heschel put it, the foundation of the community of Israel was "coexistence with God."[33] This entailed observance of Torah, a requirement that was envisioned not as an onerous burden but as a blessing, a privilege. In acting as their redeemer, God engaged the freedom of the people whom God had called. There was a sense of mutuality about this relationship that encompassed divine and human freedom. When individuals or the people as a whole rejected this relationship—forfeited communion with God—they were as good as dead. Anderson aptly summarizes the significance of covenant for the Hebrew understanding of salvation:

> Israel believed that the holy God who is "far off" (transcendent) is also "near" (immanent)—indeed, that God had taken

the initiative to enter into relationship with a people and thus to become, in a special sense, "the God of Israel." The tradition testifies that Israel's relation to Yahweh was not that of a slave who serves God by performing menial tasks, but that of a "first-born son" (Exod 4:22-23) who has been graciously redeemed and given an inheritance. Gratitude for divine liberation was the primary motive for Israel's response of faith. And that faith was expressed in obeying the laws of the covenant and in facing the future with confidence that Yahweh would be with, and go with, the people.[34]

Sacrifice

In the introductory chapter, I mentioned that the concept of sacrifice has been embedded in Christian soteriology through the centuries. In particular, the meaning of Jesus' death on the cross has often been interpreted through sacrificial images and concepts. The Eucharist, as the memorial of Jesus' death and resurrection, has also been understood as a sacrifice. Some contemporary thinkers, however, argue that this sacrificial imagery and terminology are no longer serviceable for Christian soteriology. We will see that feminist theologians are often critical of the language of sacrifice, especially because of the ways in which exhortations to imitate the self-sacrifice of Jesus have exacerbated the suffering of women living in oppressive situations. The well-known work of the literary critic and social anthropologist René Girard also includes a critique of the use of sacrificial imagery within Christian soteriology.[35] Such an interpretation, Girard thinks, extols the mechanism of violence, particularly the dynamic of scapegoating, which he thinks lies at the foundation of culture and society. By taking out their aggression on social outsiders, human beings have found relief from the inherent conflict that arises from "mimetic desire"—the tendency to imitate others out of envy and rivalry. Human beings have a tendency to desire what they see other people desiring, and this leads to conflict. Girard thinks that the Hebrew and Christian Scriptures, especially the gospels, unmask this destructive dynamic in human society.[36] They point to alternative, nonviolent ways of relating. Interpreting Jesus' atoning work in the categories of sacrifice, then, is misleading.[37]

In order to address such critiques, it is important to examine the meaning of sacrifice in the Bible. Sacrifice was an essential dimension of the religious practice of ancient Israel, as it was a feature of the religious practice of Israel's neighbors in the Near East. It was a foundational expression of worship of God that became part of Israel's covenant tradition. Sacrifice was a multivalent reality. There were a number of different kinds of sacrifice, and various explanations of its function existed.[38] The first seven chapters of the book of Leviticus—part of the Priestly tradition of the Pentateuch—provide a description of the different forms of sacrifice believed to be prescribed by God.[39] The holocaust (*hola*) was a whole burnt offering to God made as an expression of worship or as an atonement for the sins of the one offering the sacrifice. The cereal offering (*minha*) involved the gift of vegetal substances, a small part of which was burnt (with the addition of frankincense) and the rest given to the priest. This type of sacrifice was often made as an expression of thanksgiving to God and included a festive component. Very importantly, this was a sacrifice that did not involve the killing of any animal. The peace offering (sacrifice of well-being; *zebah selamim*) was the offering of an animal that was not completely burnt up but largely saved and eaten by those making the offering. This sacrifice was also marked by a spirit of celebration. The sin offering (*hattat*) was the offering of an animal made to atone for the violation of something sacred. Often such transgressions were inadvertent rather than intentional. Since the violation entailed the pollution of the sanctuary, purification needed to take place. This was done through the sprinkling of the animal's blood around the sanctuary. Blood, understood as the life-force of a living being, was viewed as having purifying effects (Lev 17:11). The guilt offering (reparation offering; *asam*) was the sacrifice of an animal made to atone for a failure in something that should have been given or done. God or the covenant community had been cheated in some way, and so something "extra" had to be given by the offerer. This act involved a combination of sacrifice and a monetary payment.

Related to this system of sacrifices was the ritual of the annual Day of Atonement, carefully spelled out in Leviticus 16. This rite blended sacrifice and an "elimination ritual."[40] It was intended to purify the people and the land for unintentional and intentional sins and transgressions.[41] This elaborate ritual included the sacrifice of a bull and a goat as a sin offering to atone for the sins of the priest and the entire Israelite community. Entering the sacred Holy of Holies on this day alone, the priest sprinkled some of the blood from the bull on the golden cover (*kapporet*) of the ark of the covenant. Blood was also sprinkled on the altar of sacrifice and the other parts of the sanctuary for the purpose of purification and reconsecration: "Thus he [the priest] shall render it clean and holy, purged of the defilements of the Israelites" (Lev 16:19). After the sacrificial offerings, the priest placed his hands on another goat, confessed "the sinful faults and transgressions of the Israelites" (16:21), and sent the goat into the desert "to carry off their iniquities to an isolated region" (16:22). This "scapegoat" was not killed but "escaped" into an uninhabited region, taking the sins of Israel with him.

Christian Eberhart has carefully analyzed the practice and theology of sacrifice in ancient Israel and has offered some illuminating insights. Eberhart draws on the comprehensive Hebrew term for sacrifice, *korban*, derived from the Hebrew root "to bring near, to make approach."[42] Sacrifices help to bridge the gap between God and humanity, between the sacred and the profane, allowing human beings to enter into the presence of God. The dynamics of the sacrificial process entail "a gradual movement toward and through sacred space and an approach to God."[43] Eberhart emphasizes that, as we have seen, not all sacrificial rituals entail killing. Thus, he disputes the claim that sacrifice is essentially an act of violence. He observes, "This means that *ritualized killing is not the purpose of cultic sacrifices* in the Hebrew Bible, and killing alone does not qualify a given set of activities as a sacrifice."[44] Sacrifices that make atonement for sins and transgressions are means given by God for the removing of the pollution of sin (expiation). They are not a human means of appeasing an angry God.[45] Eberhart argues against the view that sacrifices involve existential substitution—the punishment of the animal instead of the guilty person making the offering. He concludes that ritual sacrifices are ways of honoring God and establishing a lasting relationship between humans and God.[46] Bernhard Anderson draws similar conclusions in his discussion of sacrifice in the Hebrew Scriptures; he thinks that sacrifice is all about restoring communion with God:

> In Priestly tradition, sacrifice was not understood as a means of appeasing the divine wrath or of cajoling God to show favors. Rather, the sacrifices described in Leviticus 1–7 are

means of atonement, that is, of healing the breach of the covenant relationship and reuniting the people in communion
with God. It was believed that sacrifice was efficacious in restoring broken relationship, not because there was something
magical in the power of blood which contains the potency
of life, but because God had provided the means of grace by
which guilt was pardoned and the people could live in the
presence of the holy God (see the key text in Lev 17:11).[47]

Visions of Salvation

The main focus of Hebrew thinking with regard to the nature of
salvation is centered on this-worldly flourishing. God's saving action
on behalf of Israel is closely linked with possession of the land. The
land is perceived as a special divine gift to God's elect people. Salvation means living a long life in the land and bequeathing prosperity to
one's children and grandchildren. The laws regulating social relations
in the Torah are meant to create the conditions for the flourishing of
the community in the land. We have already seen the way in which
the demand to protect the widow and orphan—symbolizing the most
vulnerable members of society—was rooted in the memory of what
God had done for the people in the exodus. The land itself was also
the object of protection through the institution of Sabbath rest, where
the land was left fallow every seventh year (Lev 25:1-7).[48] John Collins
points out that in the Hebrew Scriptures we find "a clear insistence
that the welfare of society is of the essence of salvation."[49] Even after
the exile, the vision of "the new heavens and the new earth" given in
Third Isaiah is one that focuses on fullness of life in this world where
there is freedom from oppression and all people are able to flourish:

> I will rejoice in Jerusalem
>   and exult in my people.
> No longer shall the sound of weeping be heard there,
>   or the sound of crying.
> No longer shall there be in it
>   an infant who lives but a few days,
>   or an old man who does not round out
>   his full lifetime;
> He dies a mere youth who reaches but a
>   hundred years,

and he who fails of a hundred shall be
    thought accursed.
They shall live in the houses they build,
    and eat the fruit of the vineyards they
        plant;
They shall not build houses for others to
    live in,
        or plant for others to eat. (Isa 65:19-22)

At the same time, the Hebrew Scriptures also attest to spiritual dimensions of salvation.[50] Salvation also refers to deliverance from guilt and sin. This is found especially in the literature of the prophets, for whom earthly prosperity means nothing if built on a foundation of social injustice and oppression. Amos, prophesying just before the northern kingdom of Israel was destroyed by Assyria (eighth century BCE), denounces the powerful of his day because "they trample the heads of the weak into the dust of the earth, and force the lowly out of the way" (2:7).[51] Social justice is an essential condition for experiencing God's salvation. We saw above that Jeremiah speaks of a new covenant, where God's law will be written on the hearts of the people and they will be renewed in their relationship with God. Ezekiel proclaims that the renewed Israel will be saved from uncleanness and apostasy: "I will deliver them from all their sins of apostasy, and cleanse them so that they may be my people and I may be their God" (37:23). These prophetic visions of salvation imply God's creation of a people who have been spiritually renewed in their covenant relationship with God and one another.

There are countless references to God's saving action in the psalms. In these individual and communal prayers, salvation is no abstract theological notion; rather God's saving presence is acknowledged and desperately sought in very concrete ways. "Communal and individual laments, psalms of confidence, and psalms of thanksgiving are replete with cries for help, reminders of past deliverance and divine promises for the future, and gratitude for rescue realized."[52] The psalms of lament are especially compelling expressions of pleading for God's saving presence in times of hardship or crisis. Starkly honest in their expression of pain and sorrow, these prayers are also imbued with a stubborn confidence that God will listen and act to save. In a time of illness, the psalmist cries out, "How long, LORD? Will you utterly forget me? How long will you hide your face from me?" For ancient Israel, the hiding of God's face—God's turning away from the people—meant utter disaster. Further along in this same prayer, however, the psalmist confesses his deep trust in God's fidelity: "I trust in your faithfulness. Grant my heart joy in your help" (Ps 13:2, 6). God was so utterly real to the Hebrew people—so much a vital part of their lives—they knew they could, and even should, bring everything to God in prayer. And that was precisely the way that God remained such a vital force in their lives. Trust in the God of salvation was a belief that was eminently personal for ancient Israel.

The memory of God's saving, liberating actions in the past eventually led to the formulation of visions of future salvation. These passages envision God acting in a definitive way to fulfill the deepest hopes of God's people. Sometimes, this salvation has a universal scope that extends beyond the salvation of Israel alone.[53] For Second Isaiah (Isa 40–55), Israel is an instrument through which God's salvation will reach out to all the nations. God will reveal God's self to all people through Israel, and they will respond in obedience (e.g., Isa 45:18-25). The eschatological age of redemption would be characterized by: the return of exiles to the land of Israel, bountiful harvests, secure dwelling in the land, the rule of a just and pious leader, the reconstitution of worship and priesthood in a restored temple, and faithful adherence to the Torah by all.

In some later books of the Old Testament, there is articulated the hope that God will save the individual in death. The experience of suffering and even martyrdom for the faith, as attested in the Second Book of Maccabees, Daniel, and Wisdom, led to reflection on hope beyond death (see 2 Macc 7; Dan 12:1-3; Wis 3:1-3).[54] In the story of the mother and her seven sons who are tortured and executed during the rule of Antiochus IV Epiphanes, the second son defiantly exclaims to his torturer: "You accursed fiend, you are depriving us of this present life, but the King of the world will raise us up to live again forever. It is for his laws that we are dying" (2 Macc 7:9). The question had to arise: Is God's creative and saving power limited to life in this world? Does death negate this divine power? There are passages that attest to the hope that it is not so limited, that one's relationship with God is not severed with death. Collins observes that "the apocalyptic hope for life beyond death radically changed the spirituality of the Jewish tradition, and formulated the premises for Christianity."[55]

Agents of Salvation

Though for Israel it is always God who is the ultimate savior, certain figures do emerge who serve as agents, or instruments, of God's salvific activity. The most famous of these is the messiah, or "anointed one" (*mashiach*).[56] In the broad sense of the term, "messiah" could be used to refer to any expected agent of God's definitive salvation. In its more precise meaning, however, the term "messiah" designated the anointed king of the Davidic dynasty who would establish the enduring reign of YHWH in the world.[57] We have already taken note of the Davidic covenant theology reflected in 2 Samuel 7 and in other passages like Psalm 89. Messianic expectation underwent a lengthy development in ancient Israel, beginning with the hope for a king who, in the near future, would rule the nation in the way that David had governed. The ideal reign of this Davidic ruler is hymned in the so-called royal psalms (e.g., Pss 2; 18; 20; 21; 72; 89; 101; 110; 132; 144). In Psalm 72, the psalmist prays that God will endow the king with wise judgment so that he may govern with justice. In particular, this ruler is envisioned as one who will "defend the oppressed among the people, save the poor and crush the oppressor" (Ps 72:4). As disillusionment with the actual experience of kingship grew, some of the prophets held on to the promise of a future ruler who would be worthy of the Davidic name. Near the end of the eighth century BCE, Isaiah promises the gift of an heir who will be a sign that God is still with God's people in the person of the Davidic king (Isa 7:14).[58] At the time of the Babylonian invasion, Jeremiah excoriates the corrupt leaders who "mislead and scatter the flock of [God's] pasture" (Jer 23:1). He promises that God will "raise up a righteous shoot to David" who will "reign and govern wisely" (Jer 23:5). During the rule of this ideal leader, "Judah shall be saved and Israel shall dwell in security" (Jer 23:6). After the return from exile, this messianic hope is expressed in less definite terms. Since there were no successors in the line of David, the hope for a leader who would establish the definitive reign of God became a more idealized, messianic hope. This messianic hope is articulated in some passages in Jewish intertestamental literature (texts authored between 200 BCE and 200 CE).[59] For example, the Psalms of Solomon (written in the middle of the first century BCE) express an ardent desire for a Davidic king: "Behold, O Lord, and raise up unto them their king, the son of David, at the time you have (fore)seen, O God, to rule over Israel your servant" (17:21).[60] During the just rule of this pious king, Israel will be freed from its enemies and wickedness will be banished from the country. By the time of Jesus, the hope for a Davidic messiah represented one of the eschatological trajectories in the tradition of Israel, though it was not the only one and it was not prominent in the minds of all of the contemporaries of Jesus.[61]

The mysterious figure of the servant of YHWH was also part of the eschatological imagination of Israel (Isa 42:1-9; 49:1-6; 50:4-11; 52:13–53:12).[62] As the time of the exile was drawing to a close, Second Isaiah envisioned a specially chosen representative whose experience and destiny were to be emblematic of Israel. Whether this servant represents the nation of Israel as a whole, an individual within the nation, or both, is a matter of scholarly debate. This servant will not only lead the people to return to their God (Isa 49:5) but also be a "light to the nations," enabling God's salvation to reach to the ends of the earth (49:6). In the Fourth Servant Song (Isa 52:13–53:12), the servant is depicted as one who suffers on behalf of the people. The prophet extols the vicarious and expiatory nature of the servant's sufferings:

> Yet it was our infirmities that he bore,
>   our sufferings that he endured,
> While we thought of him as stricken,
>   as one smitten by God and afflicted.
> But he was pierced for our offenses,
>   crushed for our sins,
> Upon him was the chastisement that
>   makes us whole,
>   by his stripes we were healed. (53:4-5)

Daniel Harrington observes that in the background of this theology is the logic of sacrifice as a means of atoning for sin and renewing the relationship with God.[63] At a time in which the Jerusalem temple had been destroyed and the temple sacrifices were no more, Second Isaiah conceived of the suffering of God's servant as making possible the restoration of right relationship with God. The servant performs a singular service on behalf of the people and is given "his portion among the great" (53:12). The Fourth Servant Song influenced early Christian reflection on the person and saving work of Jesus. The important saying of Jesus in Mark 10:45 draws from it: "For the Son of Man did not come to be served but to serve and to give his life as a ransom for many." In the story of Philip and the Ethiopian eunuch found in Acts 8, Philip proclaims the fulfillment of this text in the person of Jesus, leading to the eunuch's request for baptism. Commenting on this passage, Richard Clifford says, "One can infer from the eunuch's request for baptism that the text was very important in early Christian instruction, providing a way of understanding the death and resurrection of Jesus."[64]

There were other figures that were part of Israel's hope for definitive salvation from God. The book of Deuteronomy preserves the promise that God will raise up from among the people a prophet who will be like Moses. This prophet will receive the word of God and instruct the people in all that God commands (Deut 18:15-18). The scrolls of the priestly, sectarian community at Qumran appear to reflect the hope for two, or even three, agents of divine salvation.[65] These writings express the hope for a future prophet who may embody the qualities of the prophet-like-Moses of Deuteronomy 18 (1QS 9:11). Reference is also made to "the anointed one of Aaron" (a priestly figure) and "the anointed one of Israel" (a royal figure named in one text as "the Branch of David") (4QFlor). The scrolls make it clear that the priestly messiah is the most important figure in the Qumran community's eschatology.[66] This community "looked forward to the times when the meaning of the Law would be fully clear and when God's will would be obeyed completely."[67] While the Davidic messiah would take the lead in the cosmic battle against the forces of evil, the future high priest would be the prominent agent in the establishment of God's rule.[68]

Biblical scholars stress that Christians need to be careful in the way they interpret these Jewish texts about future salvation, particularly those that refer to a messiah.[69] Christians sometimes assume that the Jews of the first century had corrupted the true meaning of messianic salvation, turning the promise of a spiritual savior into hope for a secular, nationalistic messiah. They think that Jesus and the disciples who handed on the story of Jesus revived the authentic understanding of the messiah. In mainline Jewish thought, however, the salvation mediated by the Davidic messiah was envisioned as occurring within human history, where the ideal rule of God would be established. And while the portrait of the servant of YHWH depicted in Second Isaiah is one of a suffering servant, "none of the messianic expectations of early Judaism inherited by the Church envisioned a messiah who would suffer and die a humiliating death."[70] McKenzie observes that "nationalistic coloring was never absent from any stage of pre-Christian development of messianic thought" and that the Christian conception of a spiritual messiah "represented a change rather than a restoration."[71] While Christians believe that their confession of Jesus as the Messiah is an authentic interpretation of the eschatology of the Hebrew Scriptures, this confession does entail a transformation of Jewish messianic hopes.

Conclusion

Psalm 136 is known as the "Great Hallel" and is sung on the morning of the Sabbath and for the feast of Passover.[72] It is a postexilic psalm that is composed in the style of a litany, designed perhaps for antiphonal singing by a cantor and chorus. This prayer enumerates the creative and saving deeds of God, with each recitation followed by the refrain, "God's love endures forever." God's creation of the heavens and the earth, God's liberation of Israel from slavery, God's leading of the people through the wilderness and into the land are all expressions of God's *hesed*—steadfast love. Carroll Stuhlmueller points out that *hesed* is generally understood in the Hebrew Scriptures in terms of blood relationship, or at the very least, treaty alliance. The message of Psalm 136 is that "the history of the universe and of the people of Israel develops from a bond of 'blood' or kinship between Yahweh and his chosen nation."[73] The rhythmic repetition of the refrain reflects a conviction that lies at the heart of the faith of Israel: it is the faithful, enduring love of God that is the source of life and freedom. In a variety of historical contexts and through an array of literary expressions, the Hebrew Scriptures give witness to Israel's belief that "God's love endures forever." The people of Israel experienced God as One who acts in history to give freedom and new life to people living under oppression. As the psalmist expressed it, "The LORD remembered us in our misery" (Ps 136:23). Though all the earth belongs to this Creator God (Exod 19:5), God called a people to live in covenant relationship, to live as God's "kin." The God of steadfast love summoned the people of Israel to be steadfast in their fidelity to the covenant and to reflect the compassion they had experienced from God in their relations with one another. It was the God of gracious, liberating love who brought this people into existence and called them to live in communion with him and with one another.

CHAPTER 2

Salvation in the New Testament

Introduction

The Hebrew Scriptures provided a rich vocabulary and colorful palette of images for Christians who confessed God's saving work in Jesus. They were the Scriptures used by the first Christians, and it was in light of these texts that believers in Jesus interpreted what had taken place in and through his ministry, death, and resurrection. Jesus' followers came to realize that no single image or category could exhaust the meaning of Jesus' person and redemptive work. Thus, they employed a variety of concepts and images in their efforts to proclaim the way in which God had accomplished salvation in Jesus and the benefits that this salvation had brought to them.

When examining the New Testament, it is important to keep in mind that we are confronted with a diversity of types of literature written for different groups of Christians who lived in particular contexts. The books of the New Testament were composed over a period of about seventy years, beginning with the letters of Paul (ca. 50 CE) and ending with texts written after the turn of the first century. New Testament authors crafted their accounts of salvation in Jesus to speak to the different audiences to which they were writing. For example, audiences composed of mostly Jewish Christians would have greater familiarity with the soteriological images and concepts of the Hebrew Scriptures such as exodus, sacrifice, and covenant. For mainly Gentile Christian groups, concepts such as reconciliation—taken from Greco-Roman life and society—had greater intelligibility. The soteriological statements in the New Testament need to be situated within their particular contexts.

When thinking about the articulation of the saving work of Christ in the New Testament, it is important to keep in mind the three stages of development in New Testament Christology: (1) the encounter between Jesus and his disciples during the period of his public ministry; (2) the post-Easter apostolic preaching and oral tradition about Jesus; (3) the written expression of the apostolic testimony that is found in the New Testament. The experience of people discovering salvation from God in Jesus happened at all three stages. First, people who encountered Jesus during his public ministry discovered mercy, healing, freedom, and a fresh start in his presence. They found a "new lease on life." As Edward Schillebeeckx liked to say, it all began in an encounter.[1] This happened especially through Jesus' proclamation of the reign of God, which we will explore below. Jesus did not just talk about the coming of God's reign; he made the rule of a loving God present, and this experience transformed people's lives. Second, the experience of God's saving action in and through Jesus was confirmed and intensified as a result of the disciples' encounter with the risen Christ. They came to confess Jesus as the One who had been raised from the dead and the One through whom the Spirit of God had been poured out anew. The Christian community began to proclaim that salvation for all people comes through Jesus (see Acts 4:12). During this period of apostolic preaching and oral tradition, the letters of Paul were written. In his letters, Paul quotes from oral tradition expressed in hymns and creedal statements in talking about what God has accomplished in and through Jesus (e.g., 1 Cor 15:3-8). Third, this apostolic proclamation was given literary expression in the gospels (beginning with Mark about 70 CE) and other books of the New Testament. In these texts, there is a rich variety of ways of talking about what God's saving action in Christ consisted of and what it has brought to believers, humankind, and the whole of creation.

The Public Ministry of Jesus

One must examine the entire Jesus story in order to understand the ways in which the New Testament portrays the saving work of

God in Jesus. In the development of Christian thought through the centuries, some soteriological accounts have focused exclusively on Jesus' death and resurrection as *the* saving work of God in him. Though we will see that Jesus' death and resurrection do have a central place in early Christian confession about salvation, an exclusive focus on these events can lead to a limited understanding of the meaning of salvation and a distorted notion of the character of God. Eberhart observes that "according to the New Testament, Christ's entire mission and life have salvific value."[2] In our exploration of the soteriology of the New Testament, then, we need to begin with the public ministry of Jesus, particularly his proclamation of the reign (kingdom) of God.

Luke places the scene of Jesus' presence at the Nazareth synagogue at the beginning of his account of Jesus' public ministry (Luke 4:16-30). The evangelist highlights this moment in the Jesus story by taking an incident that in Mark occurs after an extended period of ministry and setting it as the inaugural event in his ministry (see Mark 6:1-6). Jesus comes to his hometown synagogue and reads a passage from Second Isaiah (Isa 61:1-2a; 58:6). He proceeds to proclaim that this passage "is fulfilled in your hearing" (Luke 4:21):

> The Spirit of the Lord is upon me,
>> because he has anointed me
>>> to bring glad tidings to the poor.
> He has sent me to proclaim liberty to captives
>> and recovery of sight to the blind,
>>> to let the oppressed go free,
> and to proclaim a year acceptable to the Lord. (Luke 4:18-19)

This is a programmatic text in the Gospel of Luke, a kind of gospel-in-miniature that augurs what will happen in the course of Jesus' ministry.[3] The quotation from Isaiah omits a saying that can be translated as speaking of divine vengeance (Isa 61:2b).[4] Jesus' ministry will not be one of vengeance but of reconciliation and healing. The citation from the book of Isaiah provides insight into the character of Jesus' ministry. His "messianic program" is to announce good news to those who are poor, blind, imprisoned, and oppressed.[5] Commenting on this gospel passage, Luke Timothy Johnson says, "The radical character of this mission is specified above all by its being offered to and accepted by those who were the outcasts of the people."[6] The double-sided reaction of the people gathered at the Nazareth synagogue prefigures what will take place during the course of Jesus' ministry. He receives an initially favorable response: "And all spoke highly of him and were amazed at the gracious words that came from his mouth" (4:22). But when Jesus recalls incidents associated with the prophets Elijah and Elisha, in which God's visitation was extended to Gentiles outside the boundaries of Israel, the tide quickly turns. The crowd tries to drive him out of town, leading him to "the brow of the hill" (4:29)—a hill that becomes symbolic of the hill of Calvary.[7] There will be no favoritism in the mission of Jesus. One of the reasons that Jesus will not be accepted in his native country is that the Spirit will impel him to extend his mission beyond his own people.

Immediately after this scene at the Nazareth synagogue, Luke follows the narrative in Mark by chronicling a series of acts of healing and exorcism by Jesus: the cure of a demoniac in the Capernaum synagogue, the healing of Simon Peter's mother-in-law, and a whole host of other healings. Luke tells us that "at sunset, all who had people sick with various diseases brought them to him. He laid hands on each of them and cured them" (4:40). In deciding to move on from Capernaum, Jesus tells his disciples, "To the other towns also I must proclaim the good news of the kingdom of God, because for this purpose I have been sent" (4:43). The opening scenes of Jesus' public ministry recounted by Luke are like "snapshots" of the reign of God. The evangelist is beginning to describe what it was like when Jesus made the reign of God present in the lives of the people who encountered him.[8]

Jesus never gave his disciples a concise definition of the reign of God. Rather, his descriptions of the reign of God are allusive; they are conveyed through his provocative parables, his table fellowship with all kinds of people, and the healings and exorcisms that he effects for those in need. N. T. Wright observes that by using the language of the reign of God, Jesus evoked an entire story line for the people of his day. His proclamation of God's reign evoked the longing of Israel for God to come in power and rule the world in the way that God had always intended.[9] The primary meaning of the kingdom, then, is dynamic rather than spatial. It refers to an activity: God drawing near to God's beloved creation to establish God's loving rule over it.

The reign of God comes—or happens—when God's love is the ruling force in people's lives and relationships, indeed within creation itself.

Jesus' proclamation of the reign of God, then, implies that something has gone awry in human history—that people are in (desperate) need of salvation. It assumes that there are powers active in creation that are distinct from God and opposed to the divine purposes.[10] These death-dealing powers co-opt and oppress people. Gerald O'Collins observes, "On Jesus' lips 'the kingdom' was tantamount to talking of God as Lord of the world, whose decisive intervention would liberate sinful men and women from the grip of evil and give them a new, final, and lasting age of salvation."[11] The evangelists do not offer a theological explanation of the source or extent of this evil, though they assume the existence and hostility of Satan and demonic forces. They presuppose, however, that all is not right in God's beloved creation and that through Jesus, "God is now beginning to assert his rightful claim over his rebellious creatures."[12]

Jesus' message about the reign of God is inextricably bound up with his person. In a famous saying in Mark's gospel, Jesus links fidelity to his teaching with fidelity to his person: "Whoever is ashamed of me and of my words in this faithless and sinful generation, the Son of Man will be ashamed of when he comes in his Father's glory with the holy angels" (Mark 8:38; cf. Matt 10:32-33; Luke 12:8-9). Other gospel sayings of Jesus depict him as having the power to assign to his disciples roles in heaven: "Amen I say to you that you who have followed me, in the new age, when the Son of Man is seated on his throne of glory, will yourselves sit on twelve thrones, judging the twelve tribes of Israel" (Matt 19:28; cf. Luke 22:28-30). Jesus associates response to him with response to his proclamation of the kingdom, and he assumes a unique role in that kingdom. As O'Collins points out, "To accept the coming rule of God was to become a follower of Jesus."[13]

The allusions to the "new age" and the coming of the Son of Man in the gospel passages quoted above point to the future dimension of Jesus' proclamation of God's reign. Jesus' message "was focused on a future coming of God to rule as king, a time when he would manifest himself in all his transcendent glory and power to regather and save his sinful but repentant people Israel."[14] This future dimension is elicited in the petition found in the prayer that Jesus taught his disciples, "Your kingdom come." At the same time, there is also a present dimension to his message about the reign of God and to the experiences of salvation that accompanied it. Jesus could also speak of the reign of God as already present in his ministry, as when he responds to opponents who suspect that his power to expel demons derives from Beelzebul, the prince of demons. Jesus says, "But if it is by the finger of God that I drive out demons, then the kingdom of God has come upon you" (Luke 11:20). Jesus insists that his actions of freeing people from demonic power disclose the presence of God's rule. "Effectively, Jesus declares his exorcisms to be both manifestations and at least partial realizations of God's coming in power to rule his people in the end time."[15] There is an inescapable tension between the "already" and the "not yet" of the reign of God in the New Testament that should not be dissolved. Raymond Brown observes, "The kingly rule of God was already making itself present in Jesus' person, proclamation, and actions, but the complete and visible manifestation of the kingdom lay in the future and would also be brought about through Jesus, the Son of Man."[16] This tension is intrinsic to the Christian understanding of God's saving work in Jesus.

The Death and Resurrection of Jesus

Luke's account of the inaugural scene of Jesus' public ministry portrays the hostile response of the gathered assembly, a reaction that becomes ever more intense as the gospel narrative proceeds. It implies that opposition to Jesus' preaching and conduct arose relatively early in his ministry. Mark situates the negative reaction of the religious leaders early in his ministry in Galilee, when they react to the cure of a man on the Sabbath by conspiring to get rid of Jesus (Mark 3:6). The accusation by some leaders that Jesus acted by diabolical power is recounted in all three of the Synoptic Gospels (Matt 12:22-30; Mark 3:20-27; Luke 11:14-23). Though it is difficult to specify the precise charges that were brought against Jesus at his trial or to list the exact sequence of events that led to his crucifixion, it is clear that Jesus' words and deeds provoked a negative reaction from some devout Jews and that he posed a threat to the religious establishment.[17] O'Collins observes, "His mission for the kingdom had provoked various charges of violating the Sabbath, working miracles through diabolical power, rejecting purity regulations, showing

contempt for the divine law, acting as a false prophet, and expressing blasphemous pretensions."[18] His entry into Jerusalem and act of
protest in the temple, even if less dramatic in nature than presented
in the gospels, would have provoked further hostility at the time of
the Passover. Toward the end of his life, the possibility of a violent
death must have become ever clearer to Jesus and, perhaps, to his
closest followers.[19]

Did Jesus speak of his impending death as having salvific significance? Scholarly opinion on this issue varies widely. It is evident
that some gospel passages in which Jesus tells of his coming death
and resurrection reflect later interpretation by the Christian community. For example, many scholars conclude that the famous saying
in Mark 10:45 evinces the Christian community's later reflection on
the meaning of Jesus' death: "For the Son of Man did not come to
be served but to serve and to give his life as a ransom for many."[20]
Similarly, the accounts of the institution of the Eucharist found in
Paul (1 Cor 11:23-26) and the Synoptic Gospels (Matt 26:26-30; Mark
14:22-26; Luke 22:14-20) have been influenced by the varying liturgical traditions of the Christian communities.

Nevertheless, there is solid evidence in the gospels that Jesus
did not approach his death blindly or as a meaningless fate that he
passively endured. The Markan account of the ambition of James
and John, in which Jesus gives a vague reference to the cup that he
must drink and the baptism that he must undergo may well be an
authentic saying of Jesus (Mark 10:35-45).[21] Many scholars also judge
as genuine the saying at the Last Supper in Mark 14:25: "Amen, I say
to you, I shall not drink again the fruit of the vine until the day when
I drink it new in the kingdom of God." This saying of Jesus "both
predicts and expresses certitude that his death will prevent neither
the coming of God's kingdom nor Jesus' own participation in it."[22]
The tradition behind the prayer of Jesus in Gethsemane suggests
Jesus' agonizing struggle in facing his impending death but also his
eventual acceptance of it and the entrusting of his life to the God he
addressed as "Abba" (Matt 26:36-45; Mark 14:32-42; Luke 22:39-46).

In a study of the Last Supper narratives, John Meier finds evidence
of Jesus' approach to his death.[23] Though Meier concludes that the
actual words of Jesus were probably simpler than those found in Paul
or the Synoptic Gospels, he argues that Jesus' words over the bread

indicated that he was going to his death giving his whole self for the restoration of Israel in the end time. His words over the cup signified a renewed covenant that Jesus would bring to consummation with his own blood. Meier says, "Jesus celebrates this unique ritual at his farewell meal to proclaim his own faith that God his Father would not let Jesus' work be destroyed, that somehow God would integrate even Jesus' death into his life's work, yes, that God would vindicate Jesus beyond death and bring him to the eschatological banquet."[24]

Gerald O'Collins argues vigorously for a line of continuity between the way in which Jesus consciously approached his death and early Christian interpretations of the meaning of his death.[25] First, he emphasizes that Jesus' ministry was imbued with a radical commitment to service, including an outreach to the lost and marginalized that scandalized some religious people. This characteristic way of living informed the way he died: he approached his death as one final act of service. "In death, as in life, he served and sacrificed himself for others."[26] Second, O'Collins points out that there were contemporary ways of thinking about the death of a righteous person that may well have influenced Jesus and his followers. In particular, the memory of the Maccabean martyrs of the second century BCE included the notion that the martyrdom of a faithful Jew could atone for the sins of the people (2 Macc 7:37-38). It is also possible that the Servant Songs of Isaiah, especially the Fourth Song (Isa 52:13–53:12), influenced the thinking of Jesus and his followers about the role of vicarious suffering in the divine plan. Third, O'Collins argues that the early Christian tradition confessing Jesus' death as a death "for us" or "for our sins" (see 1 Thess 5:10; Rom 4:25; 1 Cor 15:3) must have been grounded in the attitude and words of Jesus.

The idea of a suffering messiah—especially a messiah who had been crucified—was so foreign to Jewish thinking of the time that it could only have arisen if Jesus had interpreted his suffering and death as intrinsic to his saving mission. Referring to Mark 14:25, O'Collins asserts,

> The argument is this: since Jesus interpreted his death in terms of the coming kingdom, he saw that death as a saving event; for he had consistently presented the equation: the kingdom = human salvation. He integrated his death not only into his surrender to his Father's will but also into his offer of salvation to human beings.[27]

Some scholars would contest O'Collins's suggestion that the earthly Jesus indicated that his coming death would have atoning value. They would attribute such explicit claims to the early church.[28] Others take a mediating position, focusing more on the manner of Jesus' living and dying than on his explicit words about his impending death. John Galvin, for example, argues that "the validity of theological interpretations of the crucifixion depends on their corresponding to the way Jesus lived and died, not on their explicit origin with Jesus."[29] Still, the points that O'Collins makes are worthy of consideration in any discussion of the connection between later Christian understanding of Jesus' death and the intentions and words of Jesus himself.

The experience of certain of his followers that Jesus had been raised up and was present in their midst gave them a new "set of eyeglasses" through which to look back at Jesus' ministry and death.[30] Paul cites a very early tradition of appearances of the risen Jesus, appending his own experience of the risen Lord at the end (1 Cor 15:3-8). Though there is significant divergence in the accounts of the empty tomb and resurrection appearances, it is clear that his disciples came to acknowledge that Jesus himself had been raised up by the Father and lived on in a transformed state. They came to believe that Jesus' death as an act of loving service had been accepted by the Father. This experience also disclosed to them that God had ultimately been revealed in Jesus.[31] Through this experience they came to confess that the reign of God that Jesus had proclaimed had been inaugurated, though its fullness was still to come. The raising of Jesus from the dead in anticipation of the universal resurrection also disclosed the universal significance of Jesus' person, message, and saving work. This experience quickly led to the mission to the Gentiles.[32]

Finally, as O'Collins observes, the vindication of Jesus in the resurrection disclosed that God can be found in the suffering one, even in a person who undergoes a shameful and horrific death by crucifixion: "But with the resurrection the disclosive power of the cross comes into play, and shows that the weak, the despised, and the suffering—those who become fools for God's sake—can serve as special mediators of revelation (and salvation)."[33]

It is evident that a soteriological interpretation of Jesus' death and resurrection arose very early in the community's tradition. The ancient tradition quoted by Paul in 1 Corinthians includes the confession "that Christ died for our sins in accordance with the scriptures" (1 Cor 15:3b). Here Jesus is already being designated as "Christ"—the Anointed One, or Messiah. His death is envisioned not just as a historical event but as "for our sins"—thus as having salvific significance. And it is understood as "according to the scriptures," that is, as integral to the revelation of God's saving will. This confessional statement also claims that Jesus "was raised on the third day according to the scriptures" (1 Cor 15:4). The resurrection of Jesus is perceived as intrinsic to the revelation of God's salvific design. In his discussion of justification through faith in Romans, Paul affirms the salvific significance of Jesus' death and resurrection by describing Christians as those "who believe in the one who raised Jesus our Lord from the dead, who was handed over for our transgressions and raised for our justification" (4:24-25). Both his handing over (death) and his being raised up (resurrection) are integral to his saving work. Joseph Fitzmyer notes that these verses are usually regarded as a Pauline quotation of an early Christian kerygmatic formula.[34] Arland Hultgren's study of the soteriology of the New Testament leads him to conclude that from the outset the cross and resurrection, understood as a unity, were viewed as the event in which redemption is achieved.[35] Followers of Jesus came to believe that "a new world is made possible for humanity through Christ who has been crucified and raised, now reigns, and is present through the Spirit in the communities of those who acclaim him as Lord."[36]

A Typology of New Testament Soteriologies

In a survey of Christian soteriology there is not space to examine the way in which each New Testament author treats the saving work of Christ. Instead, I will draw from the studies of Arland Hultgren and Edward Schillebeeckx, each of whom presents general categories derived from detailed study of the New Testament. Hultgren identifies four "types" of "redemptive Christologies" found among the various New Testament authors. His work is particularly helpful for thinking about the ways in which early Christians portrayed Christ in his redemptive role.[37] Schillebeeckx explores the various theologies of salvation found in the diverse books of the New Testament, and from that study he develops a list of key concepts pertaining to the experience of God's saving work in Jesus. His discussion illumines the different ways in which early Christians conceived of the "benefits" of salvation in Christ.

Hultgren distinguishes between "theopractic" and "christoprac-tic" conceptions of God's saving work in Christ. By "theopractic," Hultgren means that, "although Christ is the agent of redemption, the major actor in redemption is God; God is the one who sends the Son or reconciles the world to himself."[38] "Christopractic" signifies that, "although God is still the one who wills redemption and exerts his saving purpose in Christ, the major actor in redemption is Christ; Christ is the one who comes from above to rescue humanity and to bring humanity into a reconciled relationship to God."[39] The designations "theopractic" and "christopractic" are instructive, though they denote matters of emphasis and not hard-and-fast divisions. Hultgren admits this point, though he may at times downplay some of the nuances among the New Testament authors. Nevertheless, his discussion does shed light on the soteriologies found within the New Testament.

Hultgren calls the first of his two theopractic types "redemption accomplished in Christ."[40] He thinks that this description fits the soteriologies of Paul (in his authentic letters) and the Gospel of Mark. In this type, the God of Israel is the One who performs the redemptive act in Christ. The crucified and risen Christ is the agent or instrument of God's saving action. There is a consistent focus on Jesus' death and resurrection in this soteriology. Jesus dies on behalf of humanity, assuming onto himself the divine judgment on sin. Hultgren highlights the use of the preposition *hyper* ("on behalf of" or "for the sake of") in Paul's letters.[41] This term is used in formulas that antedate Paul, though the apostle makes them his own. It is found in a number of passages, for example, when Paul writes that "while we were still sinners Christ died for us" (Rom 5:8), and in the creedal formula cited above, which states that "Christ died for our sins in accordance with the scriptures" (1 Cor 15:3). The same idea is found in Mark's gospel, in the famous passage where the Markan Jesus instructs his disciples that the Son of Man has come "to give his life as a ransom for the many" (Mark 10:45) and in Jesus' words over the cup: "This is my blood of the covenant, which will be shed for many" (Mark 14:24). This soteriological type is theopractic because, while Jesus is front and center in the drama of redemption, the One who initiates and brings the drama to conclusion is the God of Israel. This is evident in the "sending" formulas found in Paul's letters, in which God is always the subject, for example, "When the fullness of time had come, God sent his Son . . . to ransom those under the law, so that we might have adoption" (Gal 4:4-5). These authors portray Jesus as the suffering Messiah, the lowly one who, by divine appointment, bears the consequences of sin for the benefit of humanity. His death has atoning significance. The resurrection of Jesus is the action of God raising him from the dead, in and through which God vindicates Jesus.

There is a strong sense of objectivity and universality in this soteriology. God has accomplished something definitive through Jesus' death and resurrection, and what has been accomplished has universal significance. Thus, the good news of God's saving action in Jesus must be proclaimed to the whole world. Hultgren concludes that both Paul and Mark "portray Christ as having given his life for the redemption of the world, the one for the many, and the 'many' is humanity as a whole."[42]

Hultgren labels the second of his two theopractic types of redemptive Christology "redemption confirmed through Christ."[43] He finds this soteriology in the Gospels of Matthew and Luke and in Luke's Acts of the Apostles. These authors emphasize the divine initiative in redemption and the continuity of Jesus with the story of Israel. They want to show that God is faithful to God's promises, bringing these promises to fulfillment in Jesus. This idea is evident in the fulfillment quotations in Matthew's gospel (e.g., Matt 1:22-23) and in the Lukan Nazareth synagogue scene discussed above. Both authors depict salvation as the forgiveness of sins extended to believers by the risen Lord. While Paul speaks of "sin" in the singular as a power at work in creation (see Rom 7:13-25), Matthew and Luke speak of "sins" in the plural. Though salvation in its fullest sense is envisioned as a future reality, believers experience the effects of Jesus' saving work because the risen, exalted Lord is present in the midst of the community granting forgiveness of sins. The church is the earthly instrument for the mediation of salvation.

In addition to forgiveness of sins, Matthew and Luke also lay emphasis on the guidance for life that Jesus offers to his disciples through his teaching, particularly in Matthew's Sermon on the Mount (Matt 5:1–7:29) and Luke's Sermon on the Plain (Luke 6:20-49). The cross is much less of a focal point in this soteriological type than in the first. Hultgren concludes that in Matthew and Luke "virtually no thought is given concerning the saving benefits of Christ for the rest of humanity, for those who have not heard the gospel."[44] The beneficiaries of the saving work of Christ are the members of the believing community, who receive forgiveness of sins in his name and formation in a way of life through the teaching of Jesus.

The third type enumerated by Hultgren is found in a diverse collection of New Testament texts—the Deutero-Pauline Letters to the Colossians and the Ephesians, the Pastoral Letters to Timothy and Titus, the First Letter of Peter, the Letter to the Hebrews, and the apocalyptic book of Revelation. Hultgren names this type "redemption won by Christ," and he counts it as the first of two christopractic types found in the New Testament.[45] According to Hultgren, it is christopractic because in these texts Jesus emerges more forthrightly as the redeemer figure. While redemption is in accord with the will of God, Christ is the main actor in the drama who has won redemption through his cross and resurrection. These writings do not speak of God "sending" the Son or "giving up" the Son for the benefit of humanity. Rather, Christ the preexistent One has come into the world for the purpose of salvation, representing God and winning redemption for all of humanity.[46] While the divine status of Jesus is acknowledged in the previous two soteriological types, it is affirmed in a more explicit way among these authors. As the one who manifests God, or as the image of the invisible God, Christ performs his saving work.[47] As in the first type, Christ bears the sins of others through his death. Hultgren points out that this redemptive Christology is the foundation for a view of Christ that we will see in the early church, that is, Christ the Victor (*Christus Victor*). Through his cross and resurrection, Christ is the victor over sin, death, and all of the cosmic powers that are hostile to humanity. Among these authors, there is an emphasis on the saving work of Jesus as universal; he gave himself for all of humanity, and the salvation that he won is at least potentially effective for all humanity.[48]

The fourth soteriological type catalogued by Hultgren—the second of the christopractic categories—is "redemption mediated by Christ."

Hultgren gives this name to the soteriologies found in John's gospel and the letters of John.[49] There is a distinctive focus on *revelation* in the Johannine literature: Jesus is the Son who comes into the world from above to reveal the Father and to mediate salvation to humanity. He is the One who has been "sent" by the Father. "Jesus' saving work is that of revealing the Father and at the same time revealing himself to be the Revealer of the Father."[50] Though Jesus, the Good Shepherd, lays down his life for his sheep (John 10:11), the cross is envisioned less as an act of atonement and more as the means by which the Son completes his earthly work and returns to the Father. As risen and glorified, Christ gives life to those who believe in him; eternal life is a gift that believers enjoy now, in the present (John 5:24). There is a polemical tone in this Johannine literature, reflecting conflicts with Jews and with other Christians. While the Gospel of John emphasizes against unbelievers the divine status of Jesus, the letters of John stress against secessionist Christians his genuine humanity and the need to put his teaching into practice. Johannine soteriology tends to be exclusivistic, reserving the benefits of salvation for those who accept the true revelation of God given by Jesus and abide by it.

Having proposed this typology, does Hultgren find any under-lying unity between these diverse soteriological perspectives? He suggests four points of commonality among them.[51] First, redemption is always grounded in the purposes of God. Christ neither replaces the God of Israel nor becomes a second God. As Christian thought develops, however, the church will be forced to reflect on how the divine in Christ relates to the divine in the Father. This issue will entail reflection on the meaning of the Christian confession of the incarnation, and it will come to a head in the fourth century with the Arian crisis. Hultgren simply observes that within the New Testament, redemption in and through Christ is always willed and initiated by the God of Israel. Second, New Testament accounts of the saving work of Christ do *not* depict Christ performing an action on behalf of humanity *over against* God. This point follows from the first and will be very important to keep in mind as we explore later Christian accounts of salvation. Hultgren argues that the New Testament does not portray Christ appeasing the wrath or justice of God. Christ does not intervene to avert the wrath of an angry God. Some texts do speak of Christ bearing our sins and dying on our behalf, but this is viewed as the work of God "in him, through him, or by him."[52] Third, each of the four soteriological types presupposes the cross and resurrection of Jesus. Though in each perspective the cross and resurrection fit into the drama of salvation in a different way, the cross and resurrection— taken as a unity—"are seen to be the event in which redemption is achieved (as in types one and three) or made possible (as in types two and four)."[53] Whether or not an atoning significance is ascribed specifically and solely to Jesus' death, a redemptive effect is ascribed to the death and resurrection taken as a unity. Fourth, throughout the New Testament there is a conviction that "a decisive turn of the ages" has taken place in the death and resurrection of Jesus.[54] The tension between the "already" and the "not yet" of salvation is treated differently by the various New Testament authors. But all four of the soteriological types envision the inauguration of a new age and the possibility of participation in this new age through fellowship with the risen Christ and with one another.

Hultgren's analysis of the soteriological perspectives within the New Testament bears the limitations associated with any such typology. The distinctive emphases and nuances of individual authors and texts can be minimized, and they can be forced to fit into "prefabricated" categories. This may be true in some instances with Hultgren, though he does make an effort to acknowledge the particular emphases of the New Testament authors and to point out where the "fit" with a particular category is less than perfect. Conversely, at times the distinctions between the four types can appear to involve "splitting hairs," as with the distinction between "redemption accomplished in Christ" and "redemption confirmed through Christ." All in all, however, Hultgren's analysis does offer key insights into the different ways early Christians experienced and articulated God's saving work in and through Jesus. His typology is instructive and worth keeping in mind as we progress in our exploration of the Christian tradition on this topic.

Schillebeeckx on New Testament Elaborations of Salvation

In his work *Christ: The Experience of Jesus as Lord*, Edward Schillebeeckx engages in an in-depth study of the various theologies of salvation found in the New Testament. As a result of that study, he delineates a number of concepts that "give us a good idea of the New

Testament understanding of what redemption through Christ Jesus is from and what it is for."[55] As I mentioned in the introduction, salvation in the Christian sense is usually envisioned as salvation *from* something (a negative condition or reality) and salvation *for* something (a positive way of being and of living). The experience of God's saving action in Jesus initiates believers into something new in their lives. Schillebeeckx's discussion of these soteriological concepts illumines the richness of the early Christian perspective on salvation. I will briefly summarize his discussion of these concepts, supplementing his observations with the insights of other commentators.

Salvation and Redemption

The Greek noun *sotēria* and the verb *sozein* are terms that apply in a general way to help in or deliverance from distress. In the New Testament, they can refer to: the forgiveness of sins, victory over Satan, victory over death and eternal life.[56] Since rulers were often acclaimed as the saviors and benefactors of their people, calling God or Christ "Savior" may have been a way for Christian writers to affirm that it is God in Christ who is the true author of salvation, the true benefactor, and not the emperor. In Luke's infancy narrative, the angel informs the shepherds, "For today in the city of David a savior has been born for you who is Messiah and Lord" (Luke 2:11; see also Acts 5:31; Titus 1:4; 2:13).

Being Freed from Forms of Servitude and Slavery

New Testament authors sometimes interpret salvation in Christ in terms of "rescue"—a clear echo of the exodus tradition of the Hebrew Scriptures. Through Jesus, believers experience rescue from various forms of oppression. They are freed from: eternal judgment, the hands of the devil, death itself, the constraint of the demands of the Torah, the evil of the present times, and so forth. Paul tells the Galatians that Jesus "gave himself for our sins that he might rescue us from the present evil age in accord with the will of our God and Father" (Gal 1:4).

Redemption as Liberation through Purchase or for a Ransom

We discussed the Hebrew terms *padah* and *go'el* in the first chapter. The practice of ransoming a slave or a prisoner of war, or of redeeming the property of a close relative, formed the background for interpreting God's saving action in terms of being ransomed. This was especially true, of course, with regard to Israel's understanding of what took place at the exodus. New Testament authors also employed this metaphor to speak of what God had done in and through Jesus. The author of 1 Peter uses it to remind his community of the inestimable worth of the gift of redemption:

> conduct yourself with reverence during the time of your sojourning, realizing that you were ransomed from your futile conduct, handed on by your ancestors, not with perishable things like silver or gold but with the precious blood of Christ as of a spotless unblemished lamb. (1 Pet 1:17-19)

As is clear from this passage, the act of ransoming a people is closely associated with the death of Jesus on the cross.

Reconciliation after Dispute

In the Second Letter of Paul to the Corinthians, Paul writes: "And all this is from God, who has reconciled us to himself in Christ and given us the ministry of reconciliation, namely, God was reconciling the world to himself in Christ, not counting their trespasses against them and entrusting to us the message of reconciliation" (2 Cor 5:18-19; cf. Rom 5:8-10). Paul envisions God's work of reconciliation (*katallagē*) in Christ as cosmic in scope and as the defining act of God.[57] In his letter to the Romans, Paul emphasizes that the motive for God's reconciling action is the divine love for humanity: "But God proves his love for us in that while we were still sinners Christ died for us" (Rom 5:8). This soteriological concept implies that there was hostility between God and humanity because of sin. But through God's gracious action in Christ, human beings become friends rather than enemies of God.[58] It is important to note that in these texts, it is not God who is reconciled to humanity but humanity that is reconciled to God. God is the subject, not the object, of reconciliation in and through Christ. The author of Ephesians understands God's reconciling action in Christ as having the effect of breaking down the barriers between Jew and Gentile (Eph 2:14-18).

Redemption as Satisfaction: Peace

Schillebeeckx relates the New Testament concept of peace (*eirēnē*) to the Hebrew notion of *shalom*. He notes that in the Hebrew Scriptures *shalom* connotes recompense, or the making good of damages.[59] It entails the making good of a situation that was not right, for example, through a treaty after a war. Schillebeeckx finds in this terminology the roots of the notion of satisfaction, a concept that Anselm of Canterbury will develop into a full-blown soteriological theory. Schillebeeckx argues that early Christians applied Jewish concepts of recompense to the making good of our sins through the death of Jesus.

Redemption as Expiation for Sins through a Sin Offering

We explored the Hebrew practice of sacrifice and the related notion of expiation in the first chapter. Expiation means the removal of sin; it is distinct from propitiation, which denotes the removal or soothing of wrath. Schillebeeckx points out that in certain places in the New Testament, the death of Jesus is understood as a sacrifice in terms of the Hebrew theology of sacrifice. This is especially true in the Letter to the Hebrews, which portrays Jesus as both priest and victim offering the one true and enduring sacrifice to God on behalf of others. The most notable New Testament passage about expiation is found in Romans, where Paul speaks of "the redemption in Christ Jesus, whom God set forth as an expiation" (Rom 3:25).[60] The Greek term for "expiation" (*hilastērion*) is used in the Septuagint to translate *kapporet*, the Hebrew word for the golden covering of the ark of the covenant, the "mercy seat." Joseph Fitzmyer asserts that in Romans Paul is depicting Christ as the new mercy seat, "presented or displayed by the Father as a means of expiating or wiping away the sins of humanity, indeed, as the place of the presence of God, of his revelation, and of his expiating power."[61]

Redemption as the Forgiveness of Sins

As we saw above, Hultgren's second soteriological type highlights Matthew and Luke, each of whom features salvation as forgiveness of sins. Schillebeeckx argues that this same theme is prominent in the letters of Paul and the Johannine literature.[62] The Gospel of John identifies Jesus as "the Lamb of God, who takes away the sin of the world" (John 1:29). The gift of forgiveness is made possible through the death and resurrection of Jesus. Through Christ and because of him, sinners are accepted by God. Schillebeeckx notes that the acceptance of the sinner by God is the heart of New Testament redemption as the forgiveness of sins: "Jesus Christ is God's forgiveness, he is 'life;' in him life is made possible for us; we may *be*."[63]

Justification and Sanctification

The interpretation of God's saving work in Christ as justifying and sanctifying sinful people is at the heart of the Gospel preached by Paul. Through the death and resurrection of Jesus, sinners, who had been unjust in the sight of God, have become just by the gracious action of God. Those who had been estranged from God are brought into right relationship with God. Paul associates this justifying action of God especially with the death of Jesus.[64] As Fitzmyer puts it, "The process of justification begins in God who is 'upright' and who 'justifies' the godless sinner as a result of what Christ has done for humanity. The sinner becomes *dikaios* and stands before God as 'upright,' 'acquitted.'"[65] The free gift of justification is received in baptism, through which sinners are liberated from the death-dealing power of sin and brought into the life-giving realm of grace (Rom 6:1-11). Paul tends to distinguish between justification and sanctification—being made holy—though this distinction is not always upheld in the Deutero-Pauline literature (Colossians and Ephesians). He reminds the Christians to whom he writes that they are "called to be holy" (Rom 1:7; 1 Cor 1:2). Christians are called "holy" (*hagios*) because they belong to Jesus Christ (Rom 1:6). Having died to sin in baptism they are now "living for God in Christ Jesus" (Rom 6:11).

Salvation in Jesus as Legal Aid

The New Testament also speaks of Jesus' saving work in terms of advocacy on behalf of humanity. When in John 14:16, Jesus promises to give his disciples *another* Advocate (*Paraklētos*) who will be with them always (the Holy Spirit), this suggests that during his earthly life Jesus himself acted as their advocate. Raymond Brown points out that the First Letter of John portrays Jesus also as a *heavenly* intercessor with the Father after the resurrection: "But if anyone does sin, we have an Advocate with the Father, Jesus Christ the righteous one" (1 John 2:1).[66] This idea of heavenly intercession is also found in the Letter to the Hebrews, in which the author asserts that Jesus has a priesthood that does not pass away; in his role as Eternal Priest, he intercedes for believers: "Therefore, he is always able to save those who approach God through him, since he lives forever to make intercession for them" (Heb 7:24-25). The risen Christ is the defender and advocate of the human cause with God. This soteriological concept has its roots in the Hebrew Scriptures with personages like Abraham and Moses who intercede for a wayward people (Gen 18:23-33; Exod 32:11-14). Schillebeeckx observes that according to this notion of salvation as legal aid, "to be redeemed means to go through life in the encouraging awareness that the Christian is always assured of a powerful legal defense."[67]

Being Redeemed for Community

In 1 Corinthians Paul speaks about the implications of celebrating the Eucharist for life in community: "The cup of blessing that we bless, is it not a participation in the blood of Christ? The bread that we break, is it not a participation in the body of Christ? Because the loaf of bread is one we, though many, are one body, for we all partake of the one loaf" (1 Cor 10:16-17). The Greek term translated as "participation" is *koinōnia*, which means a sharing in something. It can also be translated as "communion." In the New Testament, there is the consistent understanding that communion with Christ also entails communion with other believers. The salvation that comes through Jesus is never just an individual affair; it always involves commitment to community.

Being Freed for Brotherly Love

In the Gospel of Matthew, within the context of Jesus' criticism of the scribes and Pharisees, he instructs his disciples, "As for you, do not be called 'Rabbi.' You have but one teacher, and you are all brothers" (Matt 23:8). Jesus is referred to as the "firstborn among many brothers" in a number of places in the New Testament (e.g., Rom 8:29; see also Heb 2:11, 17). The injunction to love one's brothers and sisters is particularly prominent in Johannine theology. The author of the First Letter of John writes, "We know that we have passed from death to life because we love our brothers" (1 John 3:14). Schillebeeckx observes,

> We may say that at the heart of the New Testament lies the recognition that we are redeemed for brotherly love. . . . Redemption is freedom for self-surrender in love for fellow men; that is abiding in God. Ethics, and above all love of one's neighbor, is the public manifestation of the state of being redeemed.[68]

Being Freed for Freedom

Paul writes to the Christians in Galatia: "For freedom Christ has set us free; so stand firm and do not submit again to the yoke of slavery" (Gal 5:1). In this context, he is admonishing them not to make the observance of the Torah their criterion for salvation. Paul is convinced that such a return to the "yoke" of the Law would negate the freedom that Christ gives. There is in the New Testament the sense that salvation from God in Christ entails freedom from all forms of fear and alienation. This includes fear of demons and other powers that might be thought to control human destiny. With this freedom, too, the distinctions between slave and free, Jew and non-Jew, male and female are overcome (Gal 3:28). At the same time, New Testament authors warn believers not to use their freedom as license. The Letter of James speaks of "the perfect law of freedom" (James 1:25), and Paul exhorts the Galatians, "For you were called for freedom, brothers. But do not use this freedom as an opportunity for the flesh; rather, serve one another through love" (Gal 5:13).

Renewal of Humanity and the World

The concept of "newness" is closely associated with the experience of salvation in Christ. Paul tells the Christians in Rome that they were baptized into Christ's death in order that they "might live in newness of life" (Rom 6:4). In the seer's vision of the New Jerusalem in the book of Revelation, the One who sits on the throne (God) says, "Behold, I make all things new" (Rev 21:5). We saw above that Hultgren counts as one of the common soteriological themes in the New Testament the conviction that a new age has been inaugurated in Christ. Fitzmyer associates this theme with Paul's idea that Christ is the New, or Last, Adam—the head of a new humanity (1 Cor 15:45). There is a sense that in Christ, humanity and human history have been given a "fresh start." In the next chapter, we will see this biblical theme developed in the soteriology of Irenaeus of Lyons.

Life in Fullness

The term *zōē* is found throughout the New Testament. Perhaps the most well-known passage in which salvation is portrayed in terms of "life" is found in the Good Shepherd discourse in the Gospel of John: "I came so that they might have life and have it more abundantly" (John 10:10). Believers in Jesus were convinced that because of him life was meaningful and death would not have the last word. Even amid the struggles and pain of life, one can find consolation and hope in Christ, since "nether death nor life, nor angels, nor principalities, nor present things, nor future things, nor powers, nor height, nor depth, nor any other creatures will be able to separate us from the love of God in Christ Jesus our Lord" (Rom 8:38-39). This theme of life in fullness is also related to that of "joy." The theme of joy is particularly prominent in Luke, who speaks of joy in the announcement of Christ's birth (Luke 2:10), the repentance of a sinner (Luke 15:7), and the appearance of the risen Lord (Luke 24:41). Paul exhorted the community at Philippi to give witness to their faith in Christ through a spirit of joy: "Rejoice in the Lord always. I shall say it again: 'rejoice'" (Phil 4:4).

Victory over Alienating Powers

Hultgren identified the theme of Christ the Victor in his third soteriological type. This concept of "victory" (*nikē*) over hostile powers is present throughout the New Testament. Belief in Satan and demons was widespread in the first century, influenced by extrabiblical literature that originated after about 150 BCE.[69] The presence and activity of the demonic are assumed among the New Testament authors. The Synoptic Gospels depict Jesus as tempted by Satan in the desert; they portray his ministry as a kind of mortal combat against all the forces of evil that drain the life out of people. This includes his exorcisms, which liberate those who are oppressed by demonic powers. In the Gospel of Luke, after the return of the seventy who were commissioned by Jesus to proclaim the nearness of the reign of God, Jesus exclaims, "I have observed Satan fall like lightning from the sky" (Luke 10:18). In a particular way, the resurrection and exaltation of Jesus are envisioned as the victory over all heavenly beings.[70] The author of Ephesians lauds the power of God in raising Christ from the dead and seating him "far above every principality, authority, power, and dominion, and every name that is named not only in this age but also in the one to come" (Eph 1:20-21). At the same time, the victory of Christ over the powers of evil will not be fully realized until the end of history. In his lengthy discussion of the resurrection, Paul speaks of Christ as the "firstfruits" of those who have been raised from the dead. At the end he will hand over the kingdom to the Father, "when he has destroyed every sovereignty and every authority and power" (1 Cor 15:24).

In sum, Schillebeeckx observes that the New Testament moves beyond generalities in its descriptions of salvation from God in Jesus.[71] It offers concrete specifications of this experience, describing what believers feel themselves to be freed from and freed for. He emphasizes that in the New Testament redemption is always both grace and requirement. It is the free gift by a gracious God but also a task to be taken up, for the benefit not only of believers themselves but also others as well. "Despite the objective foundation of this hope, namely what has already been achieved in the life, death and resurrection of Jesus, liberation remains a task which is to be realized in the dimension of our history."[72]

Schillebeeckx's detailed study of New Testament theologies of salvation leads him to enumerate four "structural elements" found within them. First, salvation is made possible by the initiative of God, whose honor is the salvation and happiness of humankind. The experience of salvation has to do with human wholeness and happiness. This is found in solidarity with the living God, who has made the well-being of the human family his own deepest concern. Second, the nucleus of God's saving action on behalf of humankind is found in the person and life of Jesus. "Jesus is God's countenance turned towards man, the countenance of God who is concerned for all men, especially and concernedly for the humble of the earth, all those who are crucified."[73] Third, salvation is experienced through the following of Jesus within a community of faith. As we saw above, the New Testament vision of salvation is not individualistic. God's gift of salvation in and through Jesus entails a call to discipleship lived out within community. Fourth, the final consummation of salvation comes from God beyond human history. At the same time, fragmentary experiences of salvation within history point toward this fullness of the end time. Schillebeeckx emphasizes that there must be these fragmentary experiences of salvation for the Christian message about it to be credible. In other words, faith in Christ must make a real difference in people's lives, and Christians must endeavor to make the world more whole. Schillebeeckx's four structural elements indicate that any soteriology grounded in the New Testament must integrate the dimensions of God (the Creator), Jesus Christ, church, and eschatology.

Conclusion

This brief survey of New Testament soteriology does not do justice to the wealth of testimony about salvation found in the Christian Scriptures. It does make it clear that followers of Jesus experienced the presence and power of God in a unique way in and through his ministry, death, and resurrection. This began with his public ministry, in which he not only announced but also made present the reign of God in the lives of the people who encountered him. Schillebeeckx rightly says that it all began with an encounter. Through this encounter, people discovered life in new ways. This discovery of new life was confirmed and intensified in those who mysteriously experienced the risen Jesus present in their midst. These Easter witnesses began to proclaim that God had enacted salvation in a definitive way in and through the crucified-and-risen One. Christians believe that this proclamation was empowered and made effective by the Spirit of God. Through this proclamation new communities of faith were formed, comprised of people who believed that their lives had also been transformed through the presence of the risen Christ.

We have seen that the interpretation of this experience of salvation was expressed in diverse ways in the New Testament. The relationship between experience and interpretation is a complex one that has given rise to much scholarly debate among philosophers and

theologians in recent times. It is not easy to give a precise account
of the interplay between experience and interpretation. But it does
appear that there is a dialectical interplay between the two: the way in
which we experience reality is always influenced by the interpretive
categories that we bring to it; at the same time, reality confronts us
as it is and compels us to interpret it anew. Followers of Jesus brought
their own categories to their experience of him in his earthly ministry
and as risen Lord. His Jewish disciples brought with them their own
tradition of belief in a saving God (surveyed in our first chapter). Categories like exodus, covenant, sacrifice, prophecy, messiah, suffering
servant, martyrdom, and so forth influenced both their experience of
Jesus and their interpretation of that experience. For Gentiles from the
Greco-Roman world, categories like reconciliation and benefaction
were part of their background. It is also clear, however, that what
Jesus did and said, especially in his death and resurrection, exploded
the categories that were at the disposal of both Jews and Gentiles.
Jesus' followers, both Jew and Gentile, came to realize that no single
category was adequate to describe the salvation from God brought to
humanity by Jesus. No single metaphor or image could adequately
depict the "how" or the "what" of salvation—exactly *how* God had
acted in Jesus to save humanity and *what* the benefits of that saving
action are. So the first believers had to search their traditions for the
most compelling ways of speaking about what God had accomplished
in Jesus. And they needed to employ many metaphors and images
in their interpretation. The studies of Hultgren and Schillebeeckx
make that clear. It is important for contemporary believers to attend
to this soteriological diversity in order to gain deeper insight into the
mystery of salvation in Christ.

As we now move forward to explore the soteriology of the early
church, I believe that it is important to keep in mind a salient point
expounded above by Schillebeeckx, Hultgren, and Fitzmyer. The
salvation that is effected and made available in and through Jesus is
initiated by the Creator God—the God of the covenant. As Paul says
in his letter to the Romans, salvation in Christ originates from the
love of God. In Jesus, God was acting to reconcile the world to God's
self. Though New Testament authors do suggest that sin produces
a state of alienation between humanity and God, and that sin is the
object of God's wrath (see Rom 1:18-3:20), it is not the case that God

has to be reconciled to humanity or to the world. The saving act of Jesus is not accomplished *over against* God but is *from* God, the God who has made (and continues to make) the well-being of humanity God's own deepest concern. The words of Schillebeeckx quoted above bear repeating: "Jesus is God's countenance turned towards man, the countenance of God who is concerned for all men, especially and concernedly for the humble of the earth, all those who are crucified." For the New Testament, the entire Jesus story—his kingdom ministry, his laying down his life, and God's overcoming of his unjust execution in the resurrection—is the ultimate expression of God's saving love, the love of the God who created the world and established a covenant relationship with the people of Israel.

CHAPTER 3

Perspectives on Salvation in Early Christian Thought

n the last chapter, we saw that there is a diversity of expressions of soteriology within the New Testament. Early Christian communities drew on images and metaphors taken from the Hebrew Scriptures and from Greco-Roman thought to describe what God had accomplished in the life, death, and resurrection of Jesus and to express the difference it was making in their lives. They employed a multiplicity of images and metaphors because no single line of thought could capture the fullness of God's saving action in Jesus.

Among theologians of the early church, we find expressed the shared Christian belief that Jesus Christ was the One who had been sent by God to save humanity. "The one object of belief is therefore, Jesus the Christ, human being, God, and savior."[1] The ways of describing God's saving work in Christ, however, were multiple. In his classic study of the patristic understanding of redemption, H. E. W. Turner points out that the church's experience of redemption through Christ was far richer than its attempted formulation of that experience. Expression in prayer and worship (first-order language) was prior to theological articulation (second-order language).[2] Gerard Ettlinger observes, "One of the most striking characteristics of early Christian teaching about Christ and salvation is, therefore, its diversity."[3] While the church gradually moved to craft dogmatic statements concerning the person of Jesus Christ, the spectrum of orthodoxy with regard to soteriology was a broad one, giving rise to a wealth of descriptions.

In this chapter I will simply delineate a number of salient soteriological themes that emerge from the writings of leading Christian theologians of the early church. I will cite select passages from these authors as expressions of these themes. While individual authors sometimes place emphasis on one or more of these motifs, they generally incorporate a number of them into their reflection on the saving work of God in Christ. Each of them offers a glimpse of insight into the mystery of redemption in Christ. Michael Slusser calls these themes "primitive soteriological ideas which took root in the imagination of the first Christians and grew into the more elaborate constructions of patristic theology."[4] As he puts it, "the metaphors are complementary rather than mutually exclusive, and the 'mix' varies from one community, one set of personal and historical circumstances to another."[5]

Opposition to Dualism

Opposition to dualism within early Christian theology is not an explicitly soteriological image or metaphor in itself. It is, however, a foundational conviction of Christian theologians who will come to be considered orthodox, and it must be kept in mind in exploring ways of talking about Jesus and salvation in the early church.[6]

Various forms of philosophical and religious dualism were influential both outside of Christianity and among certain groups of Christians. These strains of thought usually posited two absolute metaphysical principles—one that was the source of goodness/light and the other that was the origin of evil/darkness. These metaphysical principles were viewed as hostile to each other. Dualistic thinking usually envisions the created world as the result of a flaw or a fall in a premundane heavenly realm. Something negative happened in the heavenly sphere, and as a result the world was formed. Thus, creation—the material world—is seen in a negative light.

This dualistic thinking is evident in Gnosticism, a complex blend of religious and philosophical thought that arose about the same time as the birth of Christianity and flourished in the second century. Certain Christians came to adopt aspects of Gnostic teaching. Gnostic thinking emerged from the experience of perceived disorder in the world and the human need to discover the reasons for this disorder. Gnostics viewed the created world as the product of the Demiurge, or Craftsman, a lower-level heavenly being who was cast out of the heavenly abode (the "Pleroma"). Some Gnostics identified the Demiurge with the God of the Old Testament, whom they contrasted with the God of the New Testament. The existence of the material world is thus the result of something that went wrong in the heavenly realm. For Gnostic Christians, Jesus was the Revealer who came down from the heavenly abode to disclose to a select group of people true knowledge about their origin, identity, and destiny. This conception of redemption leads to a soteriological dualism because in this system, the great majority of people will be lost. God does not will the salvation of all. Valentinian Gnosticism, for example, divided the human race into three distinct groups. The "gnostics" will be saved because of the knowledge revealed to them by the redeemer figure; their ultimate destination is the heavenly pleroma. A middle group—the "psychics"—can achieve a minimal level of salvation through diligent work. The "materialists"—the majority of the human race—have no share in salvation. Gnosticism envisioned salvation as salvation *from* the world rather than as the salvation *of* the world. Salvation, for the Gnostic, entailed escaping the world and the disordered, mundane existence that marked life in the world.

Dualistic thinking envisioned the created, material world as a dark place, a kind of prison. It could not accept a doctrine of incarnation, since the material world is not the proper domain in which the divine should dwell. Many Gnostic Christians espoused a docetic view of Christ, that is, they held that the humanity of Jesus (and especially his suffering) was only an appearance; it was not real. The resurrection of the body was also a problem, since salvation involved only the "spiritual" dimension of human existence. Gnostics also ran into difficulty with the practice of the sacraments, especially the Eucharist, because the sacraments involve the use of material objects. While for Gnostics matter can serve as a pointer to deeper spiritual realities, it can never be an efficacious sign of divine grace.

Orthodox Christian thinkers, among them Irenaeus of Lyons (early second century—ca. 202) and Augustine of Hippo (354–430), vigorously opposed this dualistic thinking. They insisted that there is only one God and that the God of redemption is also the God of creation. Creation is not the result of some premundane fall in the heavenly sphere; it is the good gift of a good God, even if it has been wounded by sin. In Christ, the Word of God truly became flesh (John 1:14), and thus the material world was the place where God's saving purposes were accomplished. The world of flesh and spirit is the fitting realm for the Son of God to embrace in the incarnation.[7] This belief in the incarnation leads to the sacramental practice of the church, since the presence of God can be authentically mediated through created things.

Near the end of the second century, Irenaeus, the chief opponent of the Gnostics, emphasized that there is only one God, who is the Creator of all that is. He envisioned the Word and Wisdom of God (the Son and the Spirit) as God's "hands" through which God freely and spontaneously created all things. Thus, the created world comes directly from the "hands" of the one God and is intrinsically good.[8] Irenaeus is insistent on the reality of the incarnation, the mystery of God becoming truly human in Jesus. He poses a rhetorical question to his Gnostic opponents: "And how again, supposing that he was not flesh, but was a man merely in appearance, could he have been crucified, and could blood and water have issued from his pierced side?"[9] He also defends Christian belief in the Eucharist, which, he affirms, is grounded in what Jesus did at the Last Supper with real bread and real wine. Through the reception of these elements, Christians experience communion with Christ and a foretaste of the redemption of their whole selves. Irenaeus asserts, "But vain in every respect are they who despise the entire dispensation of God, and disallow the salvation of the flesh, and treat with contempt its regeneration, maintaining that it is not capable of incorruption. But if this indeed do not attain salvation, then neither did the Lord redeem us with his blood, nor is the cup of the Eucharist the communion of his blood, nor the bread which we break the communion of his body."[10]

Augustine of Hippo confronted the dualism inherent in Manichaeism, a sect in which he had been an auditor in his early years. Augustine grappled with the mystery of evil and suffering throughout his life, and Manichaeism provided a straightforward solution to this dilemma. It posited two absolute principles, a source of goodness and a source of evil. The created world is essentially a dark place. Augustine came to reject this dualism, arguing that the presence of evil in creation arises not from some metaphysical principle but from the misuse of human freedom at the very origins of human existence. In his *Confessions*, he affirms that all created things are essentially good: "Hence I saw and it was made clear to me that you made all things good, and there are absolutely no substances which you did not make."[11] Evil, for Augustine, is a privation of the good, a corruption of something that is essentially good. This conviction about the essential goodness of the created world led to Augustine's defense of the doctrine of the incarnation, a teaching that he had not found in his earlier study of Neoplatonic thinkers. The incarnation is the ultimate expression of the "humility of God"—God stooping low to enter the world in a personal way. The humanity of Jesus is real and complete, lacking nothing that is intrinsic to human nature:

> nor do we say that he is a human being in such a way as to lack something which clearly belongs to human nature, as for example, a soul, or a rational mind in that very soul, or flesh . . . But we say that Christ is true God, born of the Father with no beginning in time; we also say that the same person is a true human being, born of a human mother at the fixed fullness of time; we do not say that his humanity, because of which he is inferior to the Father, in any way diminishes his divinity, because of which he is equal to the Father.[12]

In the next section, we will see that theologians of the early church took very seriously the presence of evil in the world; they often envisioned the saving work of Christ as a struggle with, and ultimate victory over, the powers of evil. They do so, however, with the underlying conviction that creation itself is intrinsically good, since it is the gift of a good Creator. In defeating the powers of evil, God is redeeming a good creation. This means that a Christian vision of salvation means the salvation *of* the world, not salvation *from* the world. Material creation—the human body and even the cosmos itself—is the object of God's saving action in Jesus Christ.

Victory

In chapter 2, we saw that Hultgren identifies the theme of Christ's victory over powers hostile to humanity as part of his third "type" of New Testament redemptive Christology. We also noted that Schillebeeckx includes the concept of "victory over alienating powers" as one of the soteriological categories found within the New Testament. Michael Slusser observes that in both New Testament and patristic times "it seemed obvious to people that this world is an arena of conflict between God and that which prevents the divine plan from being realized."[13] Christian theologians, then, envisioned Christ as God's champion who does battle against the enemies of the human race and wins the palm of victory. The enemies over which Christ triumphs are variously designated; they include sin, death, ignorance, and the devil. The triumphant work of Christ encompasses all of the aspects of his existence, including his victory over the devil when he is tempted in the desert and his ministry of healing and exorcism. The moment of most intense conflict is found in the crucifixion, when Jesus meets these opponents head-on in order to engage in battle with them. His triumph is revealed in the resurrection. "Resurrection is the trophy of victory in this theme, an integral part of the defeat of death."[14] From this perspective, the death and resurrection of Jesus are usually envisioned as forming a unity; they constitute one unified act of conflict and triumph.

The second-century writer Melito of Sardis (d. ca. 180) says of Christ that "through the Spirit which could not die he killed death, the killer of human beings."[15] Writing against the Gnostics, Irenaeus employs "battle" language in describing the saving work of Christ:

> For he fought and conquered; for he was man contending for the fathers, and through obedience doing away with disobedience completely: for he bound the strong man and set free the weak, and endowed his own handiwork with salvation, by destroying sin. For he is a most holy and merciful Lord, and loves the human race.[16]

In the early third century, Clement of Alexandria (ca. 150–ca. 215) says that Christ "conquered the serpent, enslaved the tyrant death, and most unexpectedly showed that this human being, who had wandered off to pleasure and been tied down by corruption, was free, with hands untied."[17] Reflecting on the christological hymn found in the second chapter of Philippians, Gregory of Nazianzus (329–389/90) says that Christ "bears in himself all of me, along with all that is mine, so that in himself he might destroy evil, as fire does wax, or as the sun does the mist of the earth, and so that, through this mingling,

I might share in what is his."[18] Reflecting on the crucifixion of Jesus, Ambrose of Milan (ca. 340–397) exclaims, "O divine mystery of that cross on which weakness hangs, power is free, vices are nailed, and victory trophies are raised up."[19]

In the early twentieth century, Gustaf Aulén famously characterized this theme of Christ the Victor as the "classic" theory of the atonement. He emphasized its dramatic quality and its depiction of the work of salvation as from first to last a movement of God to humanity.[20] It is true that this theme depicts God as the origin of the entire Christ event, and it images God as one who fights against the enemies that hold human beings in thrall. There is a kind of "relative dualism" in this conception insofar as there are forces at work in the cosmos that oppose the designs of God. But these forces will ultimately be vanquished by the saving power of the Creator God. The benefits of salvation in Christ according to this conception consist especially of an interior freedom that comes through incorporation into Christ. If Christ has defeated death itself, he has also freed his followers from fear of all other types of suffering.[21] The Christians for whom these authors wrote could live free from the fears that dominated the lives of so many of their contemporaries. And because of the victory won by Christ, they could be people of enduring hope.

Recapitulation

Hultgren lists as one of the common soteriological themes of the New Testament the conviction that a new age has been inaugurated in Christ. And Schillebeeckx identifies "renewal of humanity and the world" as one of the central soteriological concepts in the New Testament. The first Christians were convinced that in Christ, humanity and human history had been given a fresh start. Near the beginning of the Letter to the Ephesians, the Pauline author includes a blessing (in the form of a Jewish *berakah*) that lauds the saving plan of God accomplished in Christ. This blessing proclaims that God "has made known to us the mystery of his will in accord with his favor that he has set forth in him as a plan for the fullness of times, to sum up (*anakephalaiōsasthai*) all things in Christ, in heaven and on earth" (Eph 1:9-10). Probably drawing on an early Christian hymn, this biblical author celebrates God's plan to bring all of creation under the definitive rule of Christ.

This notion of the "summing up" or "recapitulation" (*anakeph-alaiōsis*) of all things in Christ became another way that early Christian theologians spoke about his saving work and the new beginning that it had inaugurated. Related to the theme of victory,[22] this idea was developed most fully by Irenaeus. It is biblically grounded in Paul's doctrine of Christ as the New, or Second, Adam whose act of redemption has an effect that is as universal as that of the sin of the first Adam (see Rom 5:12-21; 1 Cor 15:20-28, 45-49). Irenaeus takes up this biblical image and asserts that, as the New Adam, Christ the Word made flesh united in himself all of humanity and all of human history. He lived through all the stages of human life and human history in gracious obedience to the Father. Christ sanctified each of these stages, thereby inaugurating a redeemed race of people. In *Against Heresies*, Irenaeus says that when the Son of God became incarnate "he commenced afresh the long line of human beings, and furnished us, in a brief, comprehensive manner with salvation; so that what we had lost in Adam—namely, to be according to the image and likeness of God—that we might recover in Christ Jesus."[23] The perfect obedience of Christ undid the damage done by Adam's disobedience. Now creation and human history are oriented to Christ, who is the head of the church and of all creation. All things are summed up in Christ and find their meaning in him. Because the Word of God entered into communion with humanity, he was able to restore the communion between humanity and God that had been forfeited through sin: "Wherefore also he passed through every stage of life, restoring to all communion with God."[24]

Turner enumerates three components of Irenaeus's doctrine of recapitulation: restoration, summation, and iteration.[25] First, by his obedience Christ restores to humanity that which primal humanity lost by its disobedience, especially our likeness to God. The saving action of God in Christ reveals a unity of mind and purpose behind creation and redemption. Recapitulation serves as a kind of bridge between creation and redemption. This was an important affirmation to make in the struggle against Gnostic thought, which tended to separate creation and redemption. Second, as we have seen from the passages cited above, Christ sums up, or embodies in himself, the long course of human history that was prepared by God in God's original creation. Christ's single act of obedience has the same universal range as Adam's act of disobedience. Christ is the focal point and summation of all human history. Third, Christ reiterates, or goes over, the whole human process again. He shares in all of the experiences of humanity except sin. Whereas Adam suffered defeat, Christ wins victory.

The theme of recapitulation clearly affirms the importance of the humanity of Jesus in redeeming the human race. And it portrays all of the aspects of his existence as integral to his saving work, from the incarnation to the resurrection. J. N. D. Kelly underlines this point in his discussion of Irenaeus.[26] It is the obedience of Christ throughout all of the stages of his life that is the key to his redemptive work. Thus, Irenaeus's treatment of the redemptive death of Christ is integrated into his doctrine of recapitulation, since "the Lord's passion and sacrificial death were the supreme and necessary expression of his obedience."[27] And it is through his resurrection that Christ becomes the "firstborn of the dead" (Col 1:18) and thus the new head of the human race.[28] The soteriology of Irenaeus highlights the profound mercy of God revealed in Christ. He describes the Son of God as "truly good and patient" and as one who "is a most holy and merciful Lord" who "loves the human race."[29] God's saving action in Christ is a work of divine love.

Education/Illumination

Christ can also be conceived of as the One who imparts the truth about God and human living; he is the teacher par excellence. Christ instructs a human race that has become mired in ignorance because of sin. He teaches us about God and about ourselves, and he does this not simply through his instruction but also by means of the example of his life. As such he is both revealer and exemplar.[30] Theologians of the early church sometimes use the language of "illumination" in this regard—Christ came to bring light to a people walking in darkness (Isa 9:1). The sacrament of baptism was often understood as the sacrament of enlightenment.

The Apostolic Fathers, writing in the late first and early second century, describe Christ as the bestower of knowledge and giver of a new law.[31] The author of the First Letter of Clement (ca. 96 CE) says that through Christ God has called us from darkness to light, from ignorance to recognition of his glorious name.[32] This theme is also found in the work of the Apologists. In their defense of Christianity against the criticisms of leading thinkers, they present Christianity as the new philosophy. As such, it is not just a body of thought but a guide for a way of life. In his *First Apology*, Justin Martyr (c. 100–c. 165) describes Jesus as "our teacher" who was crucified, died, rose, and returned to heaven. Jesus is the One who incarnates the wisdom of God.[33] Irenaeus highlights what has been revealed of God through the incarnation: "For in no other way could we have learned the things of God, unless our Master, existing as the Word, had become man. For no other being had the power of revealing to us the things of the Father, except his own proper Word." Irenaeus proceeds to argue that the correct way of life for Christians is one of emulating their teacher: "Again, we could have learned in no other way than by seeing our Teacher, and hearing his voice with our own ears, that, having become imitators of his words as well as doers of his words, we may have communion with him, receiving increase from the perfect One, and from him who is prior to all creation."[34] Clement of Alexandria developed this soteriological theme in his *Paidagōgos*, "The Instructor." There he attributes this educative function to the Logos: "Therefore, the Word who leads us his children to salvation is unquestionably an educator of little ones. . . . The material he educates us in is fear of God, for this fear instructs us in the service of God, educates to the knowledge of truth, and guides us by a path leading straight up to heaven."[35] Theologians of the early church viewed the passion of Christ as having a particular educational value for believers. Reflection on the passion teaches believers about the God who in Christ was present in the very depths of human suffering, and it schools them in the selflessness that is necessary for faithful discipleship.

This conception of salvation is based, at least in part, on the Greek notion of *paideia*, a pattern of education that forms people in the image of the good through participation in it. This is a Platonic notion that has a mystical component. Slusser observes that Christians viewed the knowledge of God revealed by Jesus to entail "a real meeting of minds and hearts, with mutual recognition." In this kind of knowledge, "there results a certain connaturality, a participation in wisdom and an ability to discern the divine power and plan in the midst of all reality."[36] In contemporary parlance, the term "formation" may be an apt word to signify this kind of personal knowing that draws one into intimate friendship with God and constitutes a new life.

This theme of Christ's saving work as education/illumination never seems to have stood alone in the soteriology of patristic authors. It was one facet of soteriology but not sufficient by itself. As reflection on Christ and redemption developed in the early church, theologians realized that something more had to have taken place in Christ's saving work than simply a new teaching and example. Something more transformative was necessary. In the early fifth century, Augustine collided with Pelagius (ca. 354–ca. 420) and his followers over the doctrine of grace. One dimension of that protracted controversy was that Augustine understood the Pelagians to be saying that Christ saves us through his teaching and example. Augustine argues that Christ's teaching and example are important as far as they go, but they are not enough. We need the saving grace of Christ to undo the power of sin in the world and in our lives. We need Christ's grace to reach in and touch our desires and will in order to make it possible for us to live by the teaching of Jesus. Thus, the theme of Christ the Teacher was one soteriological conception that needed to be supplemented by others.

Divinization

Theologians of the early church also employed the language of "divinization" (deification; *theopoiēsis*) to describe God's saving work in Christ. This theme is pervasive in the thought of Eastern (Greek) theologians, though it is also present among Western (Latin) thinkers. Salvation as divinization means that salvation in Christ is more than just the forgiveness of sins or justification in the sight of God. In its most profound sense, it entails a sharing in the very life of God—communion with God. The grace of God in Christ has a profoundly transformative effect in the lives of believers. The notion of divinization is usually linked with the New Testament language of "adoption" (*huiothesia*; see Rom 8:14-17). In Christ, and through the action of the Spirit, believers have been adopted as daughters and sons of God. The salvific action associated with divinization/adoption is often called the "marvelous exchange" (*commercium admirabile*): in the incarnation God humbled God's self to share in the life of human beings in order that human beings might share in the life of God.[37] A passage from the Second Letter of Peter is typically cited as the biblical foundation for this theme:

> His divine power has bestowed on us everything that makes for life and devotion, through the knowledge of him who called us by his own glory and power. Through these, he has bestowed on us the precious and very great promises, so that through them you may come to *share in the divine nature*, after escaping from the corruption that is in the world because of evil desire. (2 Pet 1:3-4)

This theme is articulated in the brief prayer still said (quietly) by the priest at the celebration of the Eucharist: "By the mystery of this water and wine, may we come to share in the divinity of Christ who humbled himself to share in our humanity."[38]

The theme of divinization is present as early as the writings of Irenaeus. In *Against Heresies*, he speaks of the Word of God, our Lord Jesus Christ, "who did, through his transcendent love, become what we are, that he might bring us to be even what he is in himself."[39] Irenaeus associates this transforming work of Christ with a sharing in divine incorruptibility: "For by no other means could we have attained to incorruptibility and immortality, unless we had been united to incorruptibility and immortality."[40] A century and a half later, Athanasius of Alexandria (ca. 296–373) speaks in language similar to that of Irenaeus: "For he [the Son] became human in order to make us gods through himself; he came into being through a woman and was born of a virgin, in order to change our sinful form of birth into himself, so that we might become a holy people and 'share in the divine nature,' as blessed Peter wrote."[41] Gregory of Nazianzus asserts that the incarnation occurred "so that I could become God to the extent that God became human."[42] For these writers, divinization does not mean that believers cease to be creatures or that they become divine by nature. It means that through the grace of Christ they share in the life and love of the triune God in a way that is transformative. They receive transforming communion with God.

Gerald Bonner has expounded the theme of divinization in the writings of Augustine.[43] He shows that, though Augustine does not always employ the terminology of deification/divinization, the idea is significant for his theology.[44] Drawing on the Platonic notion of participation, Augustine holds that we participate in the life of God through the humanity of Christ.[45] It is because of the humility of God in the incarnation that human beings can be elevated to share in God's life by becoming united with God through Christ's humanity. In his *City of God*, Augustine, referring to Romans 8:14, says, "For there is but one Son of God by nature, who in his compassion became Son of man for our sakes, that we, by nature sons of men, might by grace through him become sons of God."[46] He proceeds to say that Christ shared in our infirmity in order that we might participate in his righteousness and immortality.[47] Augustine insists that divinization is possible not because of some natural human endowment (as in Neoplatonic thought) but solely because of divine grace. Nor is it a state that is attained instantaneously; rather, it is the outcome of a lengthy process, the completion of which is experienced only in eternal life. Augustine likens this process to the regaining of health after suffering fevers. Baptism, which gives renewal through the remission of sins, is analogous to the relieving of fevers. The regaining of full health (deification), however, is a process that embraces a lifetime.[48] The process of deification is also an ecclesial one for Augustine; it takes place within the communion of the church and is nourished through participation in the sacraments, especially the Eucharist. Finally, Augustine's doctrine of predestination means that in his mind, this gift of sharing in the life of God is "the privilege of the elect, a small minority, while the great majority of the human race pertains to the *massa damnata*."[49]

Sacrifice

When we explored the concept of sacrifice in the Hebrew Scriptures, we saw that sacrifices were ways of honoring and drawing near to God. Expiatory sacrifices were means given by God for the removal of the pollution of sin. For the people of ancient Israel, sacrifice was not envisioned as a means of appeasing a wrathful God. We also saw that in the New Testament, the death of Jesus is sometimes portrayed as a sacrificial act that results in atonement. This is particularly true in the Letter to the Hebrews, where Christ is depicted as both the priest and victim who offers the one true sacrifice to God on behalf of others. Among theologians of the early church the interpretation of the saving work of Jesus in sacrificial imagery is pervasive. Reference is often made to the Fourth Servant Song in Isaiah (Isa 52:13–53:12) in depicting the death of Jesus as a vicarious sacrifice for the remission of sins. This theme is especially prominent among Western theologians, but it is also present in Eastern theology. Her study of the theme of sacrifice leads Frances Young to observe, "For the early church, sacrifice was an image which could focus with peculiar intensity the full significance of the life and death of Christ for the salvation of the world; it played a vital part in the belief and worship of Christians of that period."[50]

Clement of Rome appeals to the Corinthian Christians, "Let us fix our eyes on the blood of Christ and let us realize how precious it is to the Father, since it was poured out for our salvation and brought the grace of repentance to the whole world."[51] Athanasius links the sacrificial death of Jesus with the destruction of death itself: "It was by surrendering to death the body which he had taken, as an offering and sacrifice free from every stain, that he forthwith abolished death for his human brethren by the offering of the equivalent."[52] Athanasius speaks of a "debt" that was paid by Christ "surrendering his own temple to death in place of all, to settle man's account with death and free him from the primal transgression."[53] Ambrose asserts that Christ "offered a sacrifice from our reality." Through his self-offering, the flesh, which was the subject of sin, was redeemed.[54]

There are some places in these patristic texts where the sacrifice of Christ is depicted as propitiating God. Young argues that the early church became disconnected from its Jewish roots in interpreting Jesus' death as sacrificial. As we saw in our exploration of the Hebrew Scriptures, for the people of Israel sacrifice was not a human means of appeasing an angry God. It was a way given by God of honoring God and restoring communion with God. Young observes, however, that in the early centuries of Christianity, ideas of propitiation and aversion were introduced to explain how Christ's sacrifice dealt with sin.[55] Young points especially to the sermons of John Chrysostom (ca. 347–407) on the Letter to the Hebrews. While Chrysostom sometimes refers (like the Hebrew Scriptures) to the purifying effects of blood, he can also speak of Christ's sacrifice as "buying off" God's anger. Christ "went up with a sacrifice which had the power to propitiate the Father."[56] Young points out that Chrysostom is ambiguous on this matter, since he also wants to argue that God's love is the ground of our salvation. Augustine, on the other hand, opposes this propitiatory interpretation in his *De Trinitate*. He insists that the sacrifice of Christ was not a matter of appeasing an angry God through the shedding of blood. Citing Paul's hymn to the love of God in Romans 8:28-39, Augustine asserts that God loved us not only before Christ died for us but also before God created the world. He insists that "the Father, the Son, and the Spirit of both of them, therefore, do all things together in an equal and harmonious way."[57] At the same time, he adds that "we are nevertheless justified by the blood of Christ and reconciled to the Father through the death of his Son."[58]

Augustine defined sacrifice as "every work which is done that we may be united with God in holy fellowship, and which has a reference to that supreme good and end in which alone we can be truly blessed."[59] Such an act represents true worship (*latreia*). He interprets the death of Jesus, the mediator between God and humanity, as the perfection and fulfillment of all sacrifice. Augustine argues that Christians are called to remember and participate in the sacrifice of Jesus. Citing Paul's statement that Christ was made sin for our sake (2 Cor 5:21), he says that "God made him a sacrifice for our sins, by which we might be reconciled to God."[60] John Cavadini argues that Augustine develops a spirituality of the cross centered on the sacrificial death of Christ.[61] It begins with the humility of God in the incarnation, whereby God stretches out a hand to fallen humanity.[62] In Christ, God chooses to be in solidarity with a lost, wounded humanity. This solidarity is most intense at the cross, where out of love the Word made flesh becomes "our companion in death."[63] Cavadini says that for Augustine, "Christ's sacrifice on the cross is God descending into shame and death; it is the cross that reveals the specific character of the incarnation as God's 'stretching out of a hand to the helpless.'"[64] In the Eucharist the entire Christian community "is offered to God as our sacrifice through the great high priest, who offered himself to God in his passion for us, that we might be members of his glorious head, according to the form of a servant."[65] Believers who become so conformed to Christ's self-offering are impelled to deeds of compassion, which for Augustine represent true sacrifices offered to God.

Ransom

In our exploration of the "victory" motif in patristic soteriology, we saw that the devil is one of the enemies of humanity over which Christ triumphs through his life, death, and resurrection. Some authors expound on this idea and express it in terms of the ransoming of captive humanity from the power of the devil. They appeal to the "ransom" language found in the Scriptures, especially the passage in Mark 10:45: "For the Son of Man did not come to be served but to serve and to give his life as a ransom for the many." Gregory of Nyssa (ca. 330–ca. 395) and Augustine are two prominent writers who include the notion of ransoming humanity from the devil in their reflections on God's saving work in Christ.

Gregory of Nyssa asserts that humanity had voluntarily sold itself into slavery through sin. Because of the fall, the devil had become the "overlord" of humanity.[66] The devil obtained rightful ownership over us. Thus, it becomes a question of justice as to how God is going to free human beings from the stranglehold of the devil—how God is going to purchase humanity back from its overlord. For Gregory, it was important that God's method of restoring humanity to its original condition before the fall be an act of justice rather than an arbitrary exercise of divine power. In order to save us, then, God must "give the master the chance to take whatever he wants to as the price of the slave."[67] The devil saw in Christ—the One who was born of a virgin and who accomplished all the miracles and wonders recounted in the gospels—someone who was more valuable than the rest of the human race. Thus, he exchanged captive humanity for the person of Christ. The devil was deceived, however, because he failed to recognize the divinity of Christ that was hidden within his humanity. "Hence it was that God, in order to make himself easily accessible to him who sought the ransom for us, veiled himself in our nature. In that way, as it is with greedy fish, he might swallow the Godhead like a fishhook along with the flesh, which was the bait."[68] The devil did not realize the power of the One whom he was taking as a ransom payment. When Christ rose from the dead, he overpowered the devil, making captive our captivity. Integrating the notion of physical redemption, Gregory argues that because human nature constitutes a single living organism, the resurrection of one part of it extends to the whole. Gregory can justify the deception involved in this ransoming scheme because he argues that the devil himself will ultimately benefit from it.[69] Gregory claims, at least in certain places in his writings, that the devil and fallen angels will be included in the final restoration of all things.[70] Through his death and resurrection, therefore, Christ ransomed the human race from the power of the devil, and he did this in a manner that was entirely just and ultimately beneficial for all.

Augustine also incorporates this ransom theme into his soteriology. He, too, is concerned about the justice of God in saving humanity. For Augustine, the devil acquired rights over humanity when Adam and Eve sinned and God permitted them (and all of humanity contained in them) to be delivered into the devil's power. "For when God abandoned the sinner, the originator of sin marched in there."[71] In response to this catastrophe, God chose to free the human race by an act, not of divine power, but of divine justice. Once again, Augustine highlights the humility of God in the incarnation. Christ emptied himself not only by becoming one with humanity but also by freely undergoing suffering, even though he was innocent. Because the devil killed an innocent man, he lost his power over humanity. Augustine argues that it was only right for the devil "to free these people through the one who was guilty of no sin, but whom he undeservedly afflicted with the punishment of death."[72] The power of Christ was revealed in his rising from the dead, through which he conquered death.

This notion of ransom from the devil was never universally accepted. Gregory of Nazianzus criticized it severely at the end of the fourth century. In his second oration on Easter, he posed the question, "To whom was it shed on our behalf, and why—the blood, mighty and famous, of God, the high priest and offering?"[73] Gregory of Nazianzus did not believe that the devil had any justice on his side. He argued that if the blood was paid to the devil—who is a thief and a tyrant—such a transaction would be a "shocking outrage."[74] Moreover, he questioned the idea of the blood of Christ being paid to God, who did not accept Isaac as a sacrifice to be offered by Abraham. It seems that he encountered a conundrum here. He concludes simply that the Father took the offering of Christ's blood, not because he demanded it, but because in the economy of salvation "the human had to be sanctified by the humanity of God, so that he could free us by forcefully conquering the tyrant, and could lead us to himself through the mediation of the Son."[75] Christ's self-offering was, therefore, part of the eternal divine plan of redemption.

It wasn't just Gregory of Nazianzus who found the notion of God acting to save humanity by paying a ransom to the devil somewhat bizarre—many modern readers respond to the idea this way as well. It is actually closely related to the victory theme, though it delves into greater detail about the way in which God through Christ conquered the power of evil. Frances Young argues that, by means of this idea, patristic writers wanted to underline the depths of God's redemptive love. God went to the greatest lengths in order to free a captive humanity.[76] John Cavadini makes a similar point in his exploration of Augustine's spirituality of the cross. Cavadini observes that Augustine's emphasis is on the love of God as revealed in the incarnation and in the death and resurrection of Christ. God renounces the use of power in favor of humility, choosing to reveal God's greatness not through domination but through love.[77] Ultimately it is divine love—a love willing to undergo humiliation—that saves. Cavadini argues that according to Augustine, "in Christ's perfectly loving and obviously lovable human choice, we find the actual solidarity of God with us through which the spell of the devil over the human heart is broken."[78]

Salvation: Universal or Particular?

J. Patout Burns points out that there are two different accounts of the economy of creation and salvation present in the theology of the early church.[79] Greek thought, as found particularly in the theology of Origen and Gregory of Nyssa, stresses the general availability of the means of salvation and a developmental continuity in holiness from birth to beatitude. This line of thinking envisions a universal operation of Christ, and it sees the church as the fullness of Christ's effective presence in the world. These thinkers chart a lengthy path of spiritual growth leading to union with God. Latin theology, as represented by Tertullian (ca. 160–ca. 220), Cyprian of Carthage (d. 258), and Augustine tends to view salvation as available only through the church and to think of it in terms of a definitive divine intervention that raises the believer from death to new life. According to this Western perspective, "one must believe the teaching of Christ, receive baptism, and belong to the communion of the proper church in order to be freed from sin and raised to the glory of Christ."[80] Augustine gives the fullest expression of this account of the economy of salvation.

The Greek viewpoint inspired some theologians to argue for universal salvation, or the universal restoration (*apocatastasis*) of all things. Clement of Alexandria speaks of a fire of divine punishment for sin, but he envisions this fire as having a pedagogical, purifying, and healing function that will ultimately sanctify sinful souls.[81] Origen of Alexandria (185–253/4) focuses on the saving power of the divine Logos, "who is stronger than every sin and whose divine power will heal all, so that the final end of all things will include the destruction of evil."[82] Origen's reading of 1 Corinthians 15:23-28 leads him to conclude that the subjection of all things to Christ will mean the victory of God's saving love for all. He, too, generally views the punishing fire spoken of in the Scriptures as having a pedagogical and purifying effect. For Origen, "God's judgment is at once an act of purifying, saving mercy, for God only punishes sinners in order to save them from their death-dealing entanglement with sin and to prepare them for the eternal happiness which God has prepared for them."[83] Influenced by Origen, the views of salvation in Gregory of Nazianzus and Gregory of Nyssa tend in the same direction. Gregory of Nyssa envisions a process of purification from sin and of spiritual growth extending throughout earthly life and beyond, through which human beings are restored to their original state as the image and likeness of God. He emphasizes the communal nature of salvation, arguing that the image of God will come to its full realization only in the human race as a whole.[84] As noted above, his discussion of humanity's ransom from the devil includes the idea that even the devil may benefit from having been deceived by the humanity of Christ. In this same text, he speaks of the purifying action of God on behalf of humanity, removing the evil that is mingled with human nature: "When, over long periods of time, it [evil] has been removed and those now lying in sin have been restored to their original state, all creation will join in united thanksgiving, both those whose purification has involved punishment and those who never needed purification at all."[85]

For Augustine, on the other hand, the idea of universal salvation represents a misguided sense of compassion.[86] He taught that in order to receive the forgiveness of sins one must be baptized into the death and resurrection of Christ and remain in communion with the Catholic Church. In the *City of God*, Augustine explicitly opposes the position of Origen on universal salvation, as well as the more modest views of "tender-hearted Christians" who think that condemned sinners "shall be delivered after a fixed term of punishment, longer or shorter according to the amount of each man's sin."[87] Appealing especially to the Matthean parable of the sheep and the goats (Matt 25:31-46), Augustine teaches that those who are condemned will be punished eternally, though the suffering of some will be mitigated, with that of unbaptized infants being the mildest. For Augustine the sin of Adam, in which all humanity shares, is such a heinous crime that if no one had been saved God's justice could not be questioned. The fact that any are saved—however few they may be—is a miracle of divine grace.[88] He has to wrestle with the text from the First Letter to Timothy (2:3-4), which speaks of God willing that everyone be saved and come to knowledge of the truth. Since Augustine asserts the sovereignty of God's will, he argues that the passage must mean either that no one is saved unless God wills his or her salvation, or that "everyone" in this text signifies that all varieties of human beings will be represented among those who are saved. It does not mean that God wills to save every human being.[89]

In the sixth century, the church condemned certain theses associated with Origen that were espoused by Palestinian monks, including the notion that "the punishment of the demons and of impious human beings is temporary."[90] Randall Sachs argues that the ideas condemned at this time represented exaggerations of Origen's thought.[91] Sachs also points out that the church did not condemn the ideas about *apocatastasis* taught by Clement and the two Gregorys, even though they argued in the same direction as Origen. Sachs observes that at the heart of this question about the scope of salvation is the issue of the relationship between human freedom and divine grace. In the end, is human freedom powerful enough to defeat the saving grace of God in a definitive way?

Conclusion

The diversity of soteriological expressions found in the New Testament is echoed among early Christian theologians. No single theme or motif was viewed as the exclusive way to depict God's saving grace in Christ. As John Galvin observes, "the fathers developed instead a wide variety of themes and images, each of which contributed something to the overall picture."[92] Michael Slusser attributes this diversity to the polyvalence of the biblical testimony to salvation as well as the polyvalence in descriptions of what it is that human beings need to be saved *from*. He calls early Christian soteriology "polyphonic" rather than "eclectic," with "each line having its own integrity but all of the lines together forming a complex whole which is greater than the sum of its parts."[93]

Traditional accounts of early Christian soteriology have contrasted Western and Eastern perspectives. We have seen that Burns makes such a distinction in his treatment of the economy of salvation in patristic thought. Western soteriology is usually described as highlighting juridical and sacrificial images, with a focus on Christ's payment of the debt of sin—an act that wins forgiveness for humanity. The influence of Roman legal categories is a factor here. Eastern soteriology is replete with mystical, transformational models of salvation, and it is usually seen as more optimistic about grace than Western soteriology.[94] While this categorization is illuminating to some extent, it does not do justice to the richness and complexity of patristic thought. Athanasius can expound Christ's saving work in terms of sacrifice, and Augustine can employ the notion of divinization. The "polyphonic" character of soteriology in the early church defies simple categorization.

CHAPTER 4

Medieval
and Reformation Soteriologies

n the introduction to this study, I referred to the distinction between images and theories used in soteriology. Gerald O'Collins
suggests that images and metaphors (first-order language) "show"
God's redeeming action, while theories (second-order language) attempt to "explain" God's redeeming action.[1] O'Collins emphasizes
that theories that try to explain salvation in Christ cannot take the
place of images and metaphors that show Christ's saving work. I
noted that with Anselm of Canterbury (1033–1109), we see a definite
move from the use of a variety of soteriological images—as found in
biblical and patristic treatments of salvation—to the development
of a coherent theory of salvation. Anselm constructs his account of
salvation in the most famous soteriological work in the history of
Christianity, *Cur Deus Homo* (*Why God Became Human*).[2] In this
chapter, we will discuss the soteriologies of Anselm of Canterbury,
Peter Abelard, Thomas Aquinas, Martin Luther, and John Calvin.
We will also take a brief look at the Council of Trent, specifically its
decree on the Mass as a sacrifice. We will notice a move from image
to theory—from first-order language to second-order language.

Two factors that influenced the development of Christian theology in the Middle Ages were the rise of universities and the translation of the thought of Aristotle. The soteriology of the early church
was, for the most part, worked out in pastoral settings. Many of the
leading theologians of the early church were bishops whose primary
concern was the pastoral care of their people. With the emergence of

monasticism in the Latin West, the main locus of theology became the monastery. Theology was a contemplative endeavor that consisted mainly of the interpretation of the Scriptures in light of the teaching of the fathers. Around the time of Anselm, theology began to be done in secular schools and universities. Theologians had to grapple with differences in viewpoint among the fathers of the church, made evident in compilations of their opinions on various theological questions. Extended argument and the use of dialectic began to play a more prominent role in the doing of theology.

Accessibility to the thought of Aristotle also made a significant impact on Christian theology. While Boethius (480–524/5) had made some of Aristotle's philosophy available in Latin, his thought began to be disseminated more widely after the Islamic invasion of southern Europe in the eighth century. The Aristotelian corpus arrived in Europe in three waves: first, his grammar; then his logic (rules of argumentation); and finally his substantive concepts (metaphysics). Increasing familiarity with Aristotle's method of arguing and metaphysical concepts profoundly affected the ways in which many Christian theologians expressed the content of the faith.

Anselm of Canterbury

The Context of Cur Deus Homo

Anselm was a kind of bridge figure in these theological developments. He has sometimes been called "the last of the fathers and the first of the scholastics." He joined the recently founded Benedictine monastery of Bec in central Normandy in 1059 as a young man. He was attracted to Bec by its prior, the influential theologian Lanfranc. Anselm eventually replaced Lanfranc as prior and later became the abbot of Bec. In 1093, he was named archbishop of Canterbury. Anselm was convinced that there is a fundamental harmony between faith and reason. He thought that, once one accepted the mysteries of revelation in faith, one could move to a deeper understanding of these truths through the employment of rational thinking. He can even speak of "necessary reasons" for revealed truths. Though human logic does not produce the truths of revelation, their intelligibility can be made clear through rational reflection and systematization.

As one commentator puts it, what characterizes Anselmian theology is *ratio*—the full use of reason in the elucidation of the mysteries of faith.[3]

In *Cur Deus Homo*, Anselm investigates the reasons for the incarnation. He explores these same questions in a briefer and more contemplative manner in his *Meditation on Human Redemption*, composed about the same time as *Cur Deus Homo*.[4] He wants to explore the "logic" of the incarnation. In the commendation of *Cur Deus Homo* that Anselm addressed to Pope Urban II, he says that he is attempting, insofar as grace allows, "to arise to contemplate the logic of our beliefs."[5] And in his preface to the work, he explains to the reader that his investigation "proves, by unavoidable logical steps, that, supposing Christ were left out of the case, as if there had never existed anything to do with him, it is impossible that, without him, any member of the human race could be saved."[6] Anselm undertakes this investigation in the form of a dialogue with Boso, a monk who had come to Bec in 1085 and whom Anselm had summoned to Canterbury in 1094 to help him in writing this work.[7] Boso plays a significant role in the development of Anselm's argument.

R. W. Southern points out that Anselm's effort to elucidate the logic of the incarnation was much more than a theological exercise; it had apologetic purposes. It was undertaken in light of challenges to Christian belief, particularly critiques of Christianity raised by Jewish thinkers in western Europe.[8] When Anselm came to London, he conversed with Gilbert Crispin, the abbot of Westminster, who was engaged in debates with Jewish thinkers in London. Crispin told Anselm that for these Jews, the notion of the incarnation was derogatory to the dignity and impassibility of God. At a time when Christian art and piety were placing new emphasis on the sufferings of Jesus in his passion, these critics found it unacceptable to associate the divine with such indignities. Belief in the incarnation could even be viewed as idolatrous.[9] As Southern observes, in this context, "Christian apologists felt more embattled than the self-sufficiency and completeness of the Christian system of life and thought might suggest. The sense of being ill-prepared for repelling intellectual attacks was widespread."[10] It is in this atmosphere of debate and challenge that Anselm writes *Cur Deus Homo* for his fellow believers and also for non-Christians who do not understand Christian belief in the incarnation. Convinced of the inviolable dignity of God, Anselm had to show that the incarnation was compatible with that divine dignity.

The Argument

In order to understand Anselm's argument, one must be cognizant of the contextual elements and foundational premises that helped to shape it. The first contextual element is the organization of feudal society in northern Europe. Anselmian scholars differ in their assessment of the influence that social and cultural factors had on Anselm's argument, but it is clear that they made some impact on his thinking.[11] Feudal society was based on a system of protection of the masses by the nobility in exchange for services and goods. The interpersonal bond between the lord and the vassal guaranteed the order of society. The vassal obtained from the lord protection and a fief. The lord received the promise of the vassal's allegiance and service. In this world, *honor* was at the heart of life in society. The preservation of social order depended on respect for and maintenance of this honor. If the honor of a superior was impugned in some way, there was the threat of social chaos. The restoration of honor occurred either through the punishment of the guilty or by the guilty making satisfaction to the one who had been offended. The degree of injustice and thus the requisite level of satisfaction were measured according to relative honor (social status) of the injured party. This restoration needed to exceed what had been taken away. For Anselm, the former monastic prior and abbot, the interpersonal bond between a monk and his superior was a reflection of this societal hierarchy. Submission to the will of the person in authority was essential for the maintenance of order in society and in the monastery.

Another dimension of the background for Anselm's argument was the penitential practice of the church.[12] In the early church, there was a period of public penance (and an order of penitents) for serious sins such as murder, apostasy, and adultery. As private confession became the order of the day, set penitential practices were established, for example, those developed by Irish missionaries. Penitential books with prescribed penances for specific sins became part of the practice of the sacrament. The notion of "satisfaction" had become part of the standard penitential lexicon to speak of the reparation made for sins committed after baptism. The satisfaction offered by the penitent became a natural analogy to use when thinking about what Christ offered to redeem the human race.

Anselm's soteriological argument is also based on two key prem-ises.[13] The first is that without the incarnation the salvation of the human race would be impossible. The second premise is that salva-tion is God's intention. It is especially important to remember the second of these premises when examining Anselm's analysis of what Christ offers to God on behalf of humanity. The redemptive work of Christ is grounded in the divine intention to effect salvation for humanity. All that Christ does to accomplish salvation flows from God's gracious love for the human race.

In the last chapter, we saw that some theologians of the early church conceived of Christ's saving work in terms of a ransom paid to the devil. In these theologians' understanding, the devil had gained legitimate authority over human beings because of Adam's sin. The devil had rights that had to be respected by God. Even though this idea was controversial among patristic theologians, it remained popular in the early Middle Ages. For example, theologians of the school of Laon argued that the incarnation happened because Adam's sin had delivered humankind into the dominion of the devil; the devil had to be trapped into overstepping his rights by subjecting a sinless man to death.[14]

Anselm vigorously opposed the idea of the devil's rights. In *Cur Deus Homo*, he allows Boso to refute this idea when he says, "I do not see what validity there is in that argument."[15] For Boso and Anselm, the devil belongs to God just as much as human beings do; thus God needed only to punish "this bond-slave of his who had persuaded his fellow-bondslave to desert his master and come over to join him, and had treacherously taken in the fugitive."[16] The devil is nothing other than a thief who has no justice on his side. In his *Meditation on Human Redemption*, Anselm makes the argument directly: "But clearly God owes nothing to the devil except punishment, nor does man owe him anything except to reverse the defeat which in some way he allowed himself to suffer by sinning."[17] Southern points out that Anselm's notion of sin meant that it could not create or convey any rights whatsoever; the devil's sin "made him irretrievably lower than the least created thing in the universe."[18]

Anselm's rational argument assumes the Christian belief that humanity is ordered to communion with God and that all human beings are sinners.[19] God's intention in creating humanity was our eternal blessedness, which requires complete submission of the human will to the will of God. By sinning, human beings refused this submission. Anselm conceives of sin as a failure to render to God what is God's due. By sinning, human beings robbed God of God's honor. He admits that no one can take away God's personal honor, which is "inherently incorruptible and in no way capable of change."[20] In sinning, however, a human being "dishonors God, with regard to himself, since he is not willingly subordinating himself to God's governance, and is disturbing, as far as he is able, the order and beauty of the universe."[21] Southern summarizes Anselm's understanding of divine honor in these words: "God's honor is the complex of service and worship which the whole creation, animate and inanimate, in heaven and earth, owes to the Creator, and which preserves everything in its place. Regarded in this way, God's honor is simply another word for the ordering of the universe in its due relationship to God."[22] The overcoming of sin, then, involves reestablishing the order of the universe.

By offending against the honor of God, humanity has put itself in the position either of incurring divine punishment or making satisfaction to God. God's punishment of the human race would prevent human beings from attaining the blessedness for which they were created. Thus, God's intention in creating humankind would be frustrated—an intolerable notion. At the same time, the satisfaction that is owed is measured by the dignity of the One who was offended, namely, God. Since God's dignity is infinite, the offense against God is infinite. In order to make satisfaction for its offense, then, humanity must offer to God something that is greater than everything that is not God. And the person who makes this satisfaction "must himself be superior to everything that exists apart from God."[23] Anselm concludes that no mere human being can make such an offering. First of all, the only one who is superior to all that exists apart from God is God himself. Second, human beings owe everything to God anyway. We owe God complete obedience. So humanity finds itself trapped in a pit, though it is a pit into which we have leaped despite being warned by our Master.[24] On its own, humanity is incapable of making the satisfaction for sin that is due to God.

In the course of this dialogue, Boso asks Anselm why God cannot just forgive sin and forego satisfaction. Anselm responds by asserting that it is not fitting for God to do anything unjustly or without due order. He says, "Consider it, then, an absolute certainty, that God cannot remit a sin unpunished, without recompense, that is, without the voluntary paying off of a debt, and that a sinner cannot, without this, attain to a state of blessedness, not even the state which was his before he sinned."[25] If God simply remitted sin without punishment or requisite satisfaction, it would mean that there would be no difference between the guilty and the nonguilty. It is important to Anselm that God's saving work integrate the demands of justice as well as mercy. It is the order of creation, disrupted by sin, that must be restored. Southern observes, "Within the created order, therefore, there are two intertwined strands, justice and mercy, both deriving from God's rational plan of creation. In being merciful, God is also just, not in the sense of rendering to each his due, for God owes nothing to anyone, but in the sense of achieving that perfect rectitude which displays the supreme goodness of God."[26] Indeed, near the end of *Cur Deus Homo*, Anselm says to Boso, "Now, the mercy of God which, when we were considering the justice of God and the sin of mankind, seemed to you to be dead, we have found to be so great, and so consonant with justice, that a greater and juster mercy cannot be imagined."[27]

Humanity, then, owes a debt to God that it is unable to pay. Only God is capable of making an offering that is greater than everything that is not God. This means that God's intention in creating the human family is in jeopardy. Anselm contends that "it is not fitting for God to fail to bring to completion a good beginning."[28] He acknowledges that "it was no secret to God what man was going to do, when he created him, and yet, by his own goodness in creating him, he put himself under an obligation to bring his good beginning to fulfillment."[29] Despite this "obligation," however, the whole work of salvation is a gift of grace. It can only be called a necessity because of the "unchangeability of God's honor, which he possesses of himself, and from no one apart from himself."[30] It is actually "an act of grace, because it is under no one's compulsion that he undertakes it and carries it out, but freely."[31] Here Anselm employs for Boso the image of someone who promises to give a gift to another and is faithful to his or her promise. The recipient of the gift "is no less indebted to you than if you had not made the promise, because you did not hesitate to make yourself his debtor before presenting the gift."[32]

Anselm proceeds to argue that only the God-man can make the necessary satisfaction for sin. The debt must be paid by someone who is perfect God and perfect human. Since it must be paid "from our side," the one who pays it must be taken from the race of Adam. But in order to make an offering of value befitting the infinite status of the One whose honor was offended, it must be paid by someone who is divine. Therefore, there is the necessity of the incarnation, of the "coming" of the God-man to render satisfaction to God. Anselm follows very closely the teaching of the Council of Chalcedon about Christ being one person in two natures.

Anselm follows the tradition that death is a consequence of sin. If the first human beings had not sinned, he asserts, they would not have been subject to death. As one who was truly human, Jesus owed perfect obedience to God. As one who was sinless, he was not obliged to die. Nonetheless, in order to make satisfaction to God on behalf of the human race, Jesus freely underwent death. Anselm claims that "it makes no difference, so far as his power is concerned, whether he lays his soul aside without involvement of any other person in the action, or whether it is another person who will bring it about that he lays it aside, having given his own consent."[33] The historical circumstances and causes of Jesus' death, which are of such interest to biblical scholars and theologians today, do not factor into Anselm's argument. What is essential is that Jesus underwent death of his own accord, even though he could have avoided it. The Son "prefers to suffer rather than to allow the human race not to be saved."[34]

In the course of this argument, Boso challenges Anselm about the cause of Jesus' death, adducing New Testament passages that imply that the death of the Son was according to the will of the Father or that the Father "handed over" the Son to death (e.g., John 6:38; Rom 8:32; Matt 26:39). Did God require the death of an innocent person as the payment for sin? Anselm responds by arguing that Christ died not by any compulsion but by his own free choice. He was killed because he "maintained truth and righteousness unflinchingly in his way of life and in what he said."[35] The Father was not pleased by the suffering of the Son, but he was pleased that the Son would willingly offer his life for sinful humanity. Anselm asserts, "God, therefore, did not force Christ to die, there being no sin in him. Rather he underwent death of his own accord, not out of an obedience consisting in the abandonment of his life, but out of an obedience consisting in the upholding of righteousness so bravely and pertinaciously that as a result he incurred death."[36] At the same time, Anselm admits that it can be said that the Father wished the death of the Son "because the Father was unwilling for the restoration of the human race to be brought about by other means than that a man should perform an action of the magnitude of his death."[37]

For such a great deed, Christ deserves a reward. But, as the Son of God who shares everything with the Father, he is in need of nothing. So he assigns this reward to humanity. The self-gift of Jesus in his death is of infinite value. It outweighs the evil of all sins. Anselm says to Boso: "You see, therefore, how, if this life is given for all sins, it outweighs them all."[38] The death of Christ has such power that its redemptive effect reaches backward and forward in history. It is an appropriate satisfaction to God and brings about the redemption of the human race. We should note that, according to Anselm's theory, the soteriological focus is on the incarnation and the death of Christ. Little is said about his public life and ministry or the resurrection.

Modern Responses to Anselm

The soteriology of Anselm has been very influential in Christian theology, spirituality, and preaching. While it did not make an immediate impact in the twelfth century, it did influence thirteenth-century theologians who constructed *summas*, including Alexander of Hales and Thomas Aquinas. Anselm's theory also influenced Christian preaching on the redemptive death of Christ, though it was sometimes distorted in such a way as to depict a sacrificial victim whose death appeased an angry God. Contemporary theologians read Anselm's soteriology critically, and their responses to it vary widely.

Gustaf Aulén criticized Anselm's theory—which he viewed as paradigmatic of the "Latin type" of soteriology—for its emphasis on the saving work done by Christ as a human being before God.[39] Aulén argues that, in contrast to the *Christus Victor* soteriology (the "classic" type that he preferred), Anselm's soteriology fails to present the work of Christ as from start to finish the work of God. Moreover, Anselm's focus on the death of Jesus as the great act of satisfaction is an impoverishment of the classic type, which viewed Jesus' death as the climax of his lifelong conflict with the powers of evil. Hans Küng argues that Anselm's theory, with its formal clarity, juridical consistency, and systematic compactness was fascinating for its time. It attempted, however, to fit everything into a juridical scheme of objective equivalence: guilt and atonement, injury and reparation. Anselm's theory did not uphold either God's incomprehensibility or God's freedom. The divine grace and mercy that are proclaimed in so much of the New Testament are subordinated to a theory of justice; the theory is dominated by a legalistic logic.[40] Gerald O'Collins offers a mixed review of Anselm's soteriology. On the negative side, he faults Anselm for failing to give attention to Jesus' public life and ministry or his resurrection from the dead. He also judges Anselm's soteriology to be vulnerable because of its nonbiblical view of justice and sin. Instead of the biblical vision of divine justice as God's fidelity to creation, Anselm's commutative notion of justice "seemed to picture God as so bound to an abstract order of things that it would be 'unthinkable' simply to grant forgiveness without requiring reparation."[41] O'Collins concludes that Anselm's view of sin as a dishonoring of God that upsets the order of things is different from the biblical view of sin as infidelity leading to a break in personal relationship with a loving God.[42]

Other modern theologians are more positive in their evaluation of Anselm's soteriology. While they do not think that his theory can simply be repeated for contemporary believers, they discern important values and critical insights in Anselm that should be preserved. Gisbert Greshake counters those who argue that the theory of satisfaction obscures the mercy of God. He contends that Anselm does in fact uphold God's mercy, though he thinks that God's mercy is not something that is arbitrary. God's mercy is attached to the divinely established order of justice. Greshake thinks that Anselm's account of satisfaction presents it as a positive act on the part of God through which God reconciles the world to God's self. He argues that Anselm's soteriology preserves the importance of human freedom in the order of salvation.[43] Walter Kasper echoes much of Greshake's positive assessment. He thinks that Anselm's satisfaction theory accords well with the biblical covenant theology. God's righteousness in the covenant opens up a living space for humanity where human beings can be not only recipients of divine goodness but also God's free partners. Jesus is such a covenant partner in his saving work. He is a representative (not a substitute) in the biblical sense of one person representing a group. By his representation, he does not replace our action but makes it possible, liberating us for the obedience of faith and the service of love. Kasper also thinks that Anselm's soteriology is valuable because it fosters a sense of human solidarity in disaster and in salvation, something that is missing in the individualism that is prevalent in post-Enlightenment thought.[44] O'Collins also affirms Anselm for laying "a fresh stress on the humanity and human freedom of Christ, who spontaneously acts as our representative and in no way is to be construed as a penal substitute who passively endured suffering to appease the anger of a 'vindictive' God."[45] And while he is critical of Anselm's conception of sin as dishonoring God, O'Collins applauds him for illuminating the real effects of sin in the world, the way that sin, "in all its various manifestations, disrupts the life and fabric of the universe."[46] As O'Collins puts it, "God cannot treat an evil past and the lasting damage done by sin as if they were not there."[47] He thinks, then, that Anselm was right in rejecting a view of divine mercy that ignored the real effects of sin and the demands of justice. Writing from a feminist perspective, Lisa Sowle Cahill makes a similar point. Though she acknowledges the difficulty that many feminist thinkers have with cross-centered atonement theories (a topic that will be explored in chapter 6), she explains that for Anselm the incarnation and death of Christ "must be understood in terms of God's mercy as undeterred love for creation, and in terms of God's justice as the will and power to make creation right." In Anselm's soteriology, "God's mercy and God's justice meet in God's determination to restore to the entire creation the beauty, harmony, and rectitude for which it has been created, and which participates in God's own supreme goodness."[48]

Peter Abelard

Peter Abelard (1079–1142) taught theology a generation after Anselm of Canterbury. Like Anselm, he was strongly influenced by

Augustine's theology—for example, Augustine's thought on charity and on predestination. Like Anselm, too, Abelard repudiates the theory of the devil's rights, a stance that provoked opposition from other leading theologians of his day.[49] Abelard was also similar to Anselm in his eagerness to employ *ratio* in theology, gaining fame as an accomplished debater and dialectician in the years before he took up theology. He analyzed contradictory opinions in the tradition and made frequent appeal to non-Christian philosophical authorities in his theological argumentation.[50] Despite these similarities, Abelard is critical of Anselm's account of the saving work of Christ. Their soteriologies have often been viewed as representing contrasting approaches in the tradition.

Abelard's soteriology is built on what Richard Weingart has called "the logic of divine love."[51] It receives its most famous articulation in his *Commentary on the Epistle to the Romans*, though that is not the only text in which Abelard treats the saving work of Christ.[52] Scholars conclude that this work was written between 1134 and 1138 during one of Abelard's periods of teaching in Paris.[53] In his commentary on Romans 3:26—a passage in which Paul proclaims the righteousness of God in justifying human beings through grace—Abelard introduces a *quaestio* and offers a response to his own question. He asks, "What is that redemption of ours through the death of Christ? or, how does the Apostle say that we are justified in his blood, we who seem worthy of a greater punishment, because we, unjust servants, committed that deed on account of which the innocent Lord was murdered?"[54] He immediately proceeds to criticize the theory of the devil's rights.

For Abelard, the devil was merely a seducer who possessed no *de iure* authority over humanity: "What right, even, could the devil have to possess a man, unless perhaps because, with the Lord allowing it or even handing him over, he had received him for the purpose of tormenting him?"[55] Abelard is also critical of what he appears to take as Anselm's argument in *Cur Deus Homo*.[56] Interpreting the work of satisfaction as the offering of a ransom, Abelard asks: "How very cruel and unjust it seems that someone should require the blood of an innocent person as a ransom, or that in any way it might please him that an innocent person be slain, still less that God should have so accepted the death of his Son that through it he was reconciled to the world."[57] Here he assumes that in Anselm's theory of satisfaction it is God who is reconciled to the world, rather than God reconciling the world to God's self. Abelard thought that both the devil's rights/ ransom theory and the theory of satisfaction had the effect of subjecting God to external necessity in redeeming humanity. For Abelard, God was under no external necessity in salvation. God could have redeemed humanity simply by granting forgiveness for sin or in any other way God might have chosen.[58]

Abelard's response to the *quaestio* accentuates the depths of divine love manifested in Christ. Christ, who taught us by word and example, "persevered to the death and bound us to himself even more through love, so that when we have been kindled by so great a benefit of divine grace, true charity might fear to endure nothing for his sake."[59] He describes "our redemption" as "that supreme love in us through the Passion of Christ, which not only frees us from slavery to sin, but gains for us the true liberty of the sons of God, so that we may complete all things by his love."[60] Abelard equates the righteousness of God (*iustitia Dei*) with divine charity; human beings are justified when charity is infused into their souls. Commenting on the fifth chapter of Romans (especially Rom 5:5), Abelard says that this charity of God demonstrated in Christ is "spread abroad in us."[61] He asserts that "Christ died for the wicked so that charity might be poured out in our hearts."[62]

Abelard's soteriology is often characterized as "subjective" or "exemplarist" and contrasted with the "objective" theory of Anselm. Some of Abelard's opponents, including Bernard of Clairvaux and William of Saint Thierry, interpreted him as espousing such an exemplarist view. They thought that Abelard restricted the saving work of Christ to the revelation of divine love through his teaching, example, and willingness to suffer. They understood Abelard to be saying that God's love is *revealed* in Christ, but it is not *communicated* to believers. Because of this interpretation, Abelard's opponents accused him of Pelagianism: teaching that human beings save themselves through their own free response to the manifestation of divine love in Christ. Scholars of Abelard point out, however, that there are passages in his commentary on Romans and in other of his works in which he affirms more traditional, "objective," interpretations of Christ's saving work.[63] For example, in his commentary on Romans 4:25, he blends the language of "demonstration" with that of "price" (*pretium*;

echoing ransom language), asserting that Christ "swept away the penalty for sins by the price of his death, leading us into paradise, and through the demonstration of so much grace—by which, as he says, 'No one has greater love'—he drew back our souls from the will to sin and kindled the highest love of himself."[64] Further along, Abelard describes Christ's death as a sacrifice that leads to the remission of sins.[65] Commenting on Romans 8:32, he affirms the expiatory value of Christ's death, saying that the Son was handed over for us "that he might cleanse the stains of our sins in his blood."[66] And he employs traditional biblical and liturgical language when he says that Christ died "for us and on account of our sins."[67]

Abelard's soteriology, then, is difficult to assess. Focusing on the question and response in his commentary on Romans 3:26, many interpreters—both in his own day and in modern times—have viewed him as espousing an exemplarist view of redemption.[68] William of Saint Thierry accused him of teaching that Christ died for nothing and that his coming into the world was unnecessary.[69] In the twentieth century, the distinguished Protestant theologian Paul Tillich concluded that Abelard's soteriology was not sufficient to remove human anxiety about guilt and the feeling of having to undergo punishment. Tillich asserted that divine justice cannot be reestablished by the message of divine love alone.[70] Steven Cartwright concludes that there are contradictory statements about Christ's saving work in Abelard's writings. Cartwright argues that such contradictions were common to the theological writers of Abelard's day and were "the result of trying to explain complex questions rationally."[71] Cartwright thinks that, as a well-known and vigorous debater, Abelard "could forcefully reject concepts and language that he might later return to use."[72]

Weingart offers a balanced assessment of Abelard's soteriology. He observes that the oft-quoted passage from his commentary on Romans 3:26 presents a summary and fragmentary outline of Abelard's soteriological view, but it does not offer a complete account of his thought on redemption. He admits that Abelard's interpretation of *Cur Deus Homo* is a misreading of Anselm's theory of satisfaction. Abelard read Anselm to say that God needed to be reconciled to the world rather than the world reconciled to God.[73] He did not recognize that "for Anselm, the God who demands satisfaction is the same who himself makes the satisfaction in the person of Jesus Christ."[74] More positively, Weingart stresses that Abelard's vision of God's redeeming work in Christ is that of a God whose essence is love and who is willing to go the greatest lengths to reconcile humanity to God's self. "God, who is absolutely free from all alien necessity, acts in the self-determination of his own essence as love to reconcile sinners to himself. The divine love is the only motive for the incarnation."[75] For Weingart, Abelard is not a Pelagian, nor is he merely an exemplarist, in his view of redemption. Abelard accentuates the primacy of grace in the life of the believer—redemptive grace, which is the transforming love of God that is poured into the hearts of men and women. The saving love of God is revealed, or demonstrated, in Christ, but it is also communicated to believers in a way that effects real transformation. "Nowhere does Abelard suggest that the drama of Christ's advent, ministry, death, and resurrection is an empty declaration; instead it is the mighty act of God in removing the obstacle, lodged in the heart of the sinner, to man's fellowship with the divine Father."[76] Weingart argues that, though Abelard gives primary attention to Christ as the revealer of divine love, he never dissociates this revelation from the redemptive efficacy of God's love.[77]

Gerald O'Collins acknowledges that Abelard "is regularly criticized and found wanting for proposing only a 'subjective' view of redemption."[78] He thinks, however, that such criticism fails to recognize "the power and presence of love."[79] O'Collins then proceeds to develop his own reflections on redemption as transforming love. The brief observations on Abelard's soteriology offered by O'Collins are, I believe, instructive. When talking about the love of God, a hard-and-fast distinction between disclosure and effective presence is impossible to make. Abelard certainly does not make such a distinction in his reflections on the saving love of God at work in and through Christ. For him, the love of God that is "shown" in Christ is also "communicated" to us in and through Christ. It is an efficacious love through which God reconciles humanity and the world to God's self. The revelation of divine love is not without real effect.

Thomas Aquinas

Thomas Aquinas (1225–1274) wrote at a time in which the "question" (*quaestio*) had become integral to the method of Christian theology. Questions arose from different interpretations of the Scriptures offered by patristic theologians and other authorities. As a master of theology, it was Aquinas's task to know the various theological opinions about these questions and offer well-reasoned opinions of his own. His famous *Summa Theologiae* is divided into questions and further subdivided into articles, each of which is another question. While Aquinas bases his theological exploration on the doctrines of faith, he is confident that the use of reason within faith will enable him to arrive at a deeper comprehension of what is believed. This process will lead to the resolution of at least some of the disputed questions. Yves Congar describes Aquinas's understanding of the work of theology (what Aquinas calls *sacra doctrina*) as "a rational and scientific consideration of the revealed datum, striving to procure for the believing human spirit a certain understanding of the datum."[80] Aquinas makes use of the philosophy of Aristotle in order to articulate the intelligibility of Christian belief. In his soteriology, for example, Aquinas draws on Aristotelian categories of causality to portray the way in which God saves humanity in Christ.[81]

The Christology of Aquinas is distinct from that of Anselm in that Aquinas addresses the life and ministry of Jesus, not just his incarnation and death. For example, in the *Summa Theologiae* Aquinas discusses Jesus' baptism, temptations, preaching, miracles, and transfiguration. O'Collins observes that "Aquinas showed an appreciation for the concrete historical christology—the identity of Christ's person and his redemptive work—mediated through the story of his ministry."[82]

It is clear, however, that Aquinas was influenced by Anselm's *Cur Deus Homo.* He accepts the heart of Anselm's argument as a convincing account of Christ's saving work. Like Anselm, he employs the concept of satisfaction in his soteriology, and he sometimes sounds like Anselm in his explanation of satisfaction. For example, he says, "A man effectively atones for an offense when he offers to the one who has been offended something which he accepts as matching or outweighing the former offense. Christ, suffering in a loving and obedient spirit, offered more to God than was demanded in recompense for all the sins of mankind . . . Christ's passion, then, was not only sufficient but superabundant atonement (*superabundans satisfactio*) for the sins of mankind."[83] Aquinas frequently uses the image of

Christ paying a debt on our behalf. He thinks of sin as deserving of punishment, since it transgresses the order of divine justice. He maintains that "by sin man was held to the debt of punishment according to divine justice."[84] Some restitution is needed to restore the balance of justice. As O'Collins observes, Aquinas, more than Anselm, conceives of Christ's making satisfaction for sin in penitential terms, as a great act of penance for the sins of humanity.[85]

Aquinas also introduces subtle changes into Anselm's account of Christ's saving work. First of all, he does not want to speak of "necessity" in the same way that Anselm does. Aquinas denies that the incarnation was necessary for the restoration of humanity, if "necessary" means that people could not have been saved without it.[86] Aquinas is convinced that by his infinite power God had many other ways to accomplish his goal of redeeming humankind. On this point, he appeals to the opinion of Augustine in the latter's *On the Trinity*.[87] Aquinas conceives of the incarnation as the most fitting (*conveniens*) way for God to save us. It is especially fitting because: it reveals the goodness of God; it helps people believe the content of faith more easily, since it is God speaking to us in person; and it is the best way for God to evoke faith, build up hope, and enkindle charity in us.

Aquinas also avoids ascribing necessity to the passion and death of Jesus.[88] He thinks that if God had wanted to free humanity from sin without any satisfaction, God would not have been acting against justice. This is true because God has no one above him; God himself is "the supreme and common good of the entire universe."[89] Thus, even though there is a divine order of justice, if God had chosen to forgive sin without any satisfaction having been made, no one's rights would have been violated. Nevertheless, Aquinas endeavors to show that there was no more fitting way for God to save us than by means of the passion and death of Christ.[90] Like Anselm, Aquinas argues that in the passion of Christ God was acting out of both mercy and justice. It was consonant with justice because through his passion and death Christ made satisfaction for sin. It was consonant with mercy because, since human beings were unable to offer satisfaction, God gave God's Son in order to do so. Aquinas thinks this way of effecting salvation was a greater mercy than if God had simply forgiven sins without requiring satisfaction.[91] The passion of Jesus was the most excellent way to liberate humankind from sin because it showed us how much God loves us, provided an example of humility and obedience, and restored human dignity.[92]

These are subtle but significant changes in Anselm's argumentation. Where Anselm will speak of necessity, Aquinas will appeal to fittingness, or suitability. Aquinas is quite modest about the human capacity to perceive the mind of God and the ways in which God works. A further example of this intellectual humility is found in his answer to the question of whether God would have become incarnate if human beings had not sinned.[93] This question about the motive of the incarnation had been raised by Rupert of Deutz (1075–1129/30) in the twelfth century.[94] Aquinas answers that, though God could have become incarnate if there had been no sin, and though the incarnation falls under the eternal predestination of God, we only know about God's will from the Scriptures. Aquinas argues that the Scriptures tell us that the reason for the incarnation was the remedy for sin. We do not have sufficient knowledge of God's will to say with any confidence that the incarnation would have happened if there had been no sin. Further along in this study, we will see that Karl Rahner reasons differently about this question, appealing to the opinion of Duns Scotus (1265–1308). Nevertheless, while maintaining the position that the incarnation is the cure for sin, Aquinas does suggest that it is also the perfection of creation. He says that the union of divinity and humanity in Christ represents the consummation of human perfection: "Accordingly, for the finished perfection of man (*consummatam hominis perfectionem*) it was appropriate that the Word be joined in personal union with human nature."[95] Thus, the position of Aquinas on this question is not entirely contradictory to that of Scotus and Rahner.

In his exploration of Christ's saving work, Aquinas expands the range of metaphors beyond that of satisfaction. He "does not think that we rightly express the truth about Christ by focusing on only one concept or image."[96] Thus, in treating the efficacy of Christ's passion in his *Summa Theologiae*, he employs the metaphors of merit, satisfaction, sacrifice, and redemption/ransom. We have already examined his approach to satisfaction. About merit, Aquinas states that because the sinless Christ suffered for the sake of justice, he merited salvation for himself. But Christ is also the head of the church, not only as divine but also as human.[97] As head of the church, the saving grace of Christ is poured out on those who are members of his body. "Therefore, Christ by his passion merited salvation not only for himself, but for all who are his members, as well."[98] Citing Augustine's definition of sacrifice as a work performed for the purpose of being united to God in holy fellowship,[99] Aquinas emphasizes that Christ offered his very self to God as a sacrifice. This self-offering was most pleasing to God, "motivated as it was by the greatest of love."[100] With regard to redemption/ransom (*redemptio*), Aquinas asserts that, by sinning, humanity contracted a twofold obligation: to the devil and to the debt of punishment. He employs the language of "price" (*pretium*) in arguing that through his passion and death Christ redeemed us from these obligations: "As therefore Christ's passion provided adequate, and more than adequate satisfaction for man's sin and debt, his passion was as it were the price of punishment by which we are freed from both obligations."[101] Like Anselm and Abelard, Aquinas argues that the devil had no justice on his side and that the ransom price was paid to God, not to the devil.

Throughout his soteriology, Aquinas continues to stress that it was the obedience and charity of Christ that was the ultimate source of salvation. Humanity is offered salvation because of Christ's loving obedience to the Father and his steadfast love for us. In his earlier *summa*, the *Summa Contra Gentiles*, Aquinas says that the death of Christ "had its satisfying power from his charity in which he bore death voluntarily, and not from the iniquity of his killers who sinned in killing him."[102] In the *Summa Theologiae*, he asks whether God the Father gave Christ over to his passion. He concedes that the Father did not shield the Son from suffering. What is most significant, however, is that the Father filled Christ with charity, inspiring him to will to suffer for us: "It was from love that the Father delivered Christ, and that Christ gave himself up to death."[103] Aquinas adds, "To show the love which led him to suffer, Christ on the cross sought pardon for his persecutors," and "Christ's passion was the offering of a sacrifice inasmuch as Christ, by his own will, suffered death out of love."[104] Aquinas also asserts that "the love of the suffering Christ outweighed the wickedness of those who slew him."[105]

Thus, for Aquinas it is the divine and human charity in Christ expressed in and through his suffering that saves—not his suffering as such. Mary Ann Fatula observes, "Thomas saw that Jesus' death saves us not because it was full of pain, but because it was full of love."[106] Commenting on Aquinas's treatment of the passion of Jesus, Thomas O'Meara says, "In the last analysis it is God's countering moves of love which save humanity, for Calvary is an example and climax of divine activity struggling with evil in history."[107]

Aquinas also incorporates the resurrection of Jesus into his soteriology. His thought on the resurrection underwent development during the course of his career as a theologian, from his earlier *Sentences* to his later *Summa Theologiae*. In the latter work, he says that the resurrection of Jesus is a true instrumental cause of both our spiritual and corporeal resurrections.[108] Borrowing from John Damascene (ca. 675–ca. 749), Aquinas employs the category of instrumental causality to describe the way the humanity of Christ and his human actions have real effects. An instrumental cause is one that brings about an effect superior to itself precisely as it is moved and applied by a higher, or principal, cause. As a living, active instrument of the Word/Son, Christ's humanity has a real salvific function. Thus, Jesus' resurrection from the dead is an instrumental cause of our bodily resurrection (at the end of time) and our spiritual resurrection in the here and now, that is, the justification and newness of life that is given in Christ. Aquinas proceeds to argue that the presence of the risen humanity of Jesus in heaven has enduring salvific significance. About the risen Christ Aquinas says, "The presence of his human nature in heaven is itself an intercession for us, for God, who exalted the human nature in Christ, will also show mercy towards those for whose sake this nature was assumed."[109]

For Aquinas, human beings receive the saving grace of Christ by being incorporated into him, by becoming members of his body. And this incorporation takes place through participation in the sacraments, beginning with baptism. Aquinas argues that the reasons for the incarnation are the reasons for sacraments: "just as in the mystery of the incarnation the Word of God is united to the flesh which we can perceive with our senses, so too in the sacraments words are applied to sensible materials."[110] In his discussion of the grace of the sacraments, Aquinas asserts that "Christ delivered us from our sins chiefly (*praecipue*) through his passion."[111] He then states "that in a special way the sacraments of the church derive their power from the passion of Christ, and that it is through reception of the sacraments that the power flowing from this becomes, in a certain way, conjoined to us."[112] Aquinas finds the biblical foundation for this teaching in the Johannine account of the water and blood flowing from the side of the crucified Jesus, which signify baptism and Eucharist, the two greatest sacraments (John 19:34).

Contemporary scholars highlight the richness of the soteriology of Aquinas, particularly his focus on charity, though they also make note of problematic tendencies. Gerald O'Collins is a good example of a theologian who offers such a mixed assessment of Aquinas. While elucidating many positive aspects of Aquinas's soteriology, O'Collins also includes a point of criticism relating to two passages in the *Summa Theologiae* in which Aquinas treats the effects of Christ's passion. In his discussion of the passion as sacrifice, Aquinas says that sacrifice "designates what men offer to God in token of the special honor due to him, and in order to appease (*placendum*) him."[113] And in addressing the question of whether Christ's passion reconciled humanity with God, Aquinas maintains that "the fact that Christ suffered voluntarily was so great a good that, on account of seeing this good accomplished in human nature, God was appeased (*placatus est*) in regard to all the offenses of the human race."[114] In the same article, however, Aquinas denies that God began to love humanity anew because of Christ's passion. He cites Jeremiah 31:3 on the everlasting love of God, arguing that through the passion of Jesus sin is washed away. O'Collins argues that, though this notion of appeasement is not representative of Aquinas's soteriology as a whole, its presence in the *Summa Theologiae* did open the way to "a monstrous view of redemption: Christ as the penal substitute propitiating the divine anger."[115] While this observation by O'Collins is worth noting, he and other students of Aquinas would agree that Aquinas's overall depiction of the work of redemption in Christ is that of the gracious outpouring of God's love for humanity. In Christ, God acts to remove the obstacles that separate human beings from God and thus to reconcile humanity to God's self. The whole work is one of divine love. As O'Meara puts it, for Aquinas Christ is "a servant of graced history" who "restores what was injured in human existence, recreates the image and likeness of God, and initiates a new human race into future life."[116]

Martin Luther and John Calvin

Luther

Soteriology was a major focal point in the theology of the Protestant Reformers Martin Luther (1483–1546) and John Calvin (1509–1564). Luther and Calvin accepted the teaching of the early church councils about the humanity and divinity of Christ, but they were critical of the way in which scholastic theologians approached the mystery of Christ. They found scholastic Christology to be excessively abstract and speculative, preoccupied with esoteric discussion of the relation between the humanity and divinity of Christ. For Luther and Calvin, what is truly important to know about Christ is who he is *for me* and *for us*. Luther loved the passage in Paul's Letter to the Galatians where Paul says, "I live by faith in the Son of God who has loved me and given himself up for me" (Gal 2:20). In his 1535 *Lectures on Galatians*, Luther comments on this passage by emphasizing that believers need to speak this "me" in faith and apply it to themselves.[117] He says that he hears in this Pauline profession "that there is so much evil in my nature that the world and all creation would not suffice to placate God, but that the Son of God himself had to be given up for it."[118] In his *Small Catechism*, Luther makes a statement that reflects his emphasis on the personal experience of Christ as savior:

> I believe that Jesus Christ, true God, begotten of the Father from eternity, and also true man, born of the Virgin Mary, is my Lord, who has redeemed me, a lost and condemned creature, delivered me and freed me from all my sins, from death, and from the power of the devil, not with silver and gold but with his holy and precious blood and with his innocent sufferings and death, in order that I may be his, live under him in his kingdom and serve him in everlasting righteousness, innocence and blessedness, even as he is risen from the dead and lives and reigns to all eternity.[119]

Luther's great concern, shared by other leaders of the Protestant Reformation, was how to find a gracious God. A devout and somewhat scrupulous Augustinian monk, Luther felt that he was not able to encounter a God of mercy and salvation in the theology and religious practice in which he had been trained. Catholic spirituality and sacramental practice had come to place great emphasis on what each person should do in approaching God. For example, in the practice of confession special emphasis had been placed on the requirement that the penitent confess every sin, have true contrition for sin, and be firmly resolved to avoid sin in the future. If one did all that was in his or her power, God would respond with the gift of grace. Luther, who sometimes went to confession every day, found this approach to be burdensome and guilt-producing. He became convinced that no human effort can satisfy the demands of God's transcendent justice. He says, "If I lived and worked to all eternity, my conscience would never reach comfortable certainty as to how much it must do to satisfy God. Whatever work I had done, there would still be nagging doubt as to whether it pleased God, or whether he required something more."[120]

Between the years 1513 and 1519, Luther lectured on the Psalms and the letters of Paul, giving special attention to Galatians and Romans. At some point during that time, he had his "Tower experience," named after the tower of the Augustinian monastery at Wittenberg where Luther prepared his lectures. This experience involved insight into the meaning of the "righteousness" (*dikaiosuné*) of God of which Paul speaks in his letters. Luther came to understand God's righteousness as not a demanding, punishing justice but a saving graciousness extended to humankind in Christ. He came to the conclusion that the theology in which he had been trained had obscured the central message of the Gospel, namely, that of the justification of the sinner by the free grace of God. As the quotation above from his *Small Catechism* indicates, this justifying action of God was effected by means of the death and resurrection of Jesus. For Luther, then, an authentically Christian soteriology must illumine the salvific, justifying grace of God made available in Jesus Christ.

Luther sometimes echoes Anselm by describing the saving work of Christ in terms of satisfaction. In lectures on Paul's letter to the Romans, he says of Christ: "He is the one who has made satisfaction, he is the one who is righteous, he is my defense, he is the one who died for me."[121] Luther also included other themes in his soteriology, most notably the patristic theme of *Christus Victor*. Christ is the One who defeated the enemies of the human race, which for Luther include sin, death, the devil, the law, and the wrath of God. Commenting on Galatians 3:13, he says to his readers, "If you believe that sin, death and the curse have been abolished, they have been abolished, because Christ conquered and overcame them in himself; and he wants us to believe that just as in his person there is no longer the mask of the sinner, or any vestige of death, so this is no longer in our person, since he has done everything for us."[122] Gustaf Aulén put great stress on this victory motif in Luther's soteriology.[123] Christ clothed himself in the person of the sinner, took the law and the curse on himself, and suffered death for us. Because he was a Divine Person, it was impossible for these enemies to hold him, and by his resurrection he broke the power of death and defeated them.

Luther had a paradoxical approach to the law. As an expression of God's will and word, it is something good. So, for example, he incorporates commentary on the Decalogue into his catechisms. But his interpretation of Paul's statements about God's law led Luther to the conclusion that the law acts as a tyrant that provokes sin and increases sin. It is not a means of salvation. This includes the ceremonial prescriptions and the moral precepts of the Bible, as well as the laws of the church: "Therefore the Law, works, love, vows, etc., do not redeem; they only wrap one in the curse and make it even heavier."[124] Luther is at pains to oppose the notion of Christ as a lawgiver. He says that Christ is not a lawgiver but a propitiator and savior.[125] When the law accuses and sin troubles, the Christian looks to Christ and is freed from the law. The "highest art" of Christians is to be able to define Christ not as a lawgiver but as the dispenser of grace, the savior, the One who pities, him who is sheer, infinite mercy.[126] He can even claim that the law attacks and kills Christ because he has taken our sins on himself.[127] Aulén observes that Luther's thought about Christ's victory over the law reflects the idea of "the divine love breaking in pieces the order of merit and justice and creating a new order to govern the relation of man with God, that of grace."[128]

Luther also gives extensive consideration to the wrath of God. His reading of the Old Testament (for example, Psalm 90) convinced him that God's wrath against sin is real. The divine wrath is an immediate and direct reaction to human sin. The wrath of God stands in opposition to divine love. It is the wrath of God and the curse of sin that must give way to the eternal grace and mercy of God in Christ.

Luther often appeals to the Pauline statements in 2 Corinthians 5:21 (God "made him to be sin who knew no sin") and Galatians 3:13 ("Christ ransomed us from the curse of the law by becoming a curse for us") in order to assert that Christ took upon himself the brunt of God's wrath against sin. He interprets Paul's statement in Galatians 3:13 to mean that Christ became the greatest sinner, not in his own person, but in order to bear all sins in his body and to make satisfaction for them.[129] He instructs his readers to "wrap Christ" in their sins, saying, "Whatever sins I, you, and all of us have committed or may commit in the future, they are as much Christ's own as if he himself had committed them."[130] This same idea of Christ enduring and overcoming the wrath of God is implied in Luther's depiction of Christ as the mediator between God and humanity. We are accounted righteous in God's eyes because Christ interposes himself between God and us.

Calvin

In his *Institutes of the Christian Religion*, Calvin stresses that the saving work of God in Christ had its origin in God's enduring love for humanity. And he acknowledges that this redemptive work encompasses the entirety of Jesus' life and ministry. He says that, even though we are sinners who are subject to the wrath of God, God "still finds something in us which in kindness he can love."[131] The entire work of Christ is the effect of God's reconciling love: "It is because he first loves us, that he afterwards reconciles us to himself."[132] He proceeds to say that Christ accomplished this work of reconciliation "by the whole course of his obedience."[133] Calvin's reading of the gospels leads him to argue that "from the moment when he [Christ] assumed the form of a servant, he began, in order to redeem us, to pay the price of deliverance."[134] He observes, however, that Scripture, "the more certainly to define the mode of salvation, ascribes it peculiarly and specially to the death of Christ."[135]

Calvin understands the death of Jesus in terms of penal substitution. He asserts that Christ "substituted himself in order to pay the price of our redemption."[136] Educated in the legal system of sixteenth-century France, he interpreted Christ's redemptive death in forensic categories. While for Anselm sinful humanity was likened to a debtor in civil court, for Calvin it was compared to a felon in criminal court.[137] This is the image that seems to have compelled Calvin in his thought on redemption. From this perspective, the passion and death of Jesus are viewed as the most profound experience of God's punishment of sin, which Christ undergoes as the divinely chosen substitute for sinners. Calvin thinks it is very important that Christ died as a condemned criminal. The circumstances of his death were integral to its salvific significance:

> For in order to remove our condemnation, it was not sufficient to endure any kind of death. To satisfy our ransom, it was necessary to select a mode of death in which he might deliver us, both by giving himself up to condemnation, and undertaking our expiation. Had he been cut off by assassins, or slain in a seditious tumult, there could have been no kind of satisfaction in such a death. But when he is placed as a criminal at the bar, where witnesses are brought to give evidence against him, and the mouth of the judge condemns him to die, we see him sustaining the character of an offender and evil-doer. . . . Our acquittal is this—that the guilt which made us liable to punishment was transferred to the head of the Son of God. (Isa 53:12)[138]

Calvin applies this notion of penal substitution to all of the aspects of Christ's passion. The gospel accounts of Jesus' agony in the garden show that he "had a fiercer and more arduous struggle" than that which accompanies an "ordinary death."[139] Even though the Father could never be angry with the beloved Son, Christ's cry of abandonment from the cross reveals that he "bore the weight of the divine anger, that, smitten and afflicted, he experienced all the signs of an angry and avenging God."[140] Christ descended into hell in order to "engage, as it were, at close quarters with the powers of hell and the horrors of eternal death."[141] In order to satisfy the demands of God's righteous judgment "it was necessary that he should feel the weight of divine vengeance."[142] Because he endured these sufferings in our place and rose from the dead, Christ "gained the victory, and achieved a triumph, so that we now fear not in death those things which our Prince has destroyed."[143] Calvin distinguishes the salvific effects of Jesus' death from those of his resurrection, arguing that by his death sin was removed and satisfaction given to God's justice, while by his resurrection righteousness was renewed and restored.[144] Calvin also places soteriological emphasis on the role of the risen Christ as intercessor for humanity. The risen Lord "constantly appears as our advocate and intercessor in the presence of the Father," and he "directs attention to his own righteousness, so as to turn it away from our sins."[145] He can even speak of Christ reconciling the Father to us through his intercession for us.[146]

The Council of Trent (1545–1563)

Soteriology was not the main item on the agenda for the Council of Trent. In its teaching on justification and on the Mass as sacrifice, the council did, however, incorporate certain soteriological conceptions. The council took up the disputed issue of justification in its first period, issuing its Decree on Justification in 1547.[147] In this decree, the council utilized the medieval terminology of "merit" and "satisfaction" and it employed Aristotelian categories of causality as a way of depicting the dynamics of justification.[148] The meritorious cause of justification is Jesus Christ, who "merited for us justification by his most holy passion on the wood of the cross and made satisfaction for us to God the Father."[149] Through the merit of Christ's passion, the gift of the Holy Spirit is poured out on believers and the virtues of faith, hope, and charity are infused into them.[150] Gerald O'Collins observes that "without offering any definition of 'merit' or 'satisfaction' and without introducing the term 'sacrifice', Trent here interpreted the saving impact of Christ's passion (but not his resurrection) with language that reached back . . . through Aquinas to Anselm."[151]

Trent did employ the language of sacrifice in its doctrinal statement on the Mass as sacrifice, issued in 1562.[152] This decree was issued eleven years after the council's earlier decree on the Eucharist, in which it had addressed issues around the real presence of Christ in the sacrament.[153] Trent's affirmation of the sacrificial nature of the Mass was formulated in response to Protestant criticism of this idea and to the rejection by Reformers of the practice of offering Mass for the living and the dead.[154] Offering Mass for the benefit of the living and the dead appeared to the Reformers to be another expression of works-righteousness, which they found contrary to the authentic teaching of the Gospel. The soteriological statements made in Trent's decree, then, are set within the context of controversies surrounding the understanding and practice of the Eucharist.

Trent maintains the intrinsic connection between the sacrifice of the Mass and the sacrifice of the cross. It cites several verses from the Letter to the Hebrews as biblical warrants for its teaching on the priesthood of Christ and his self-offering on "the altar of the cross."[155] At the Last Supper, Christ acted to bequeath to the church a visible sacrifice by which the bloody sacrifice he was soon to offer on the cross would be represented and its memory perpetuated. In the sacrifice of the Mass, "the same Christ who offered himself in a bloody manner (cf. Heb 9:14, 27) is contained and offered in an unbloody manner."[156] Trent describes this sacrifice as "truly propitiatory" (*vere propitiatorium esse*) and a source of grace for those who participate in a spirit of reverence and repentance.[157] It says that the Lord is "appeased by this oblation" (*huius quippe oblatione placatus Dominus*) and thus grants grace and pardon to sinners. The victim who is offered by the priest at the Mass is the same one who offered himself on the cross; it is only the manner of offering that is different. The council goes on to assert that the sacrifice of the Mass is rightly offered "for the sins, punishments, satisfaction and other necessities of the faithful"—both living and dead.[158] In the canons attached to this teaching, Trent anathematizes those who would deny that in the Mass a sacrifice is offered to God, or who would understand this offering as merely a sacrifice of praise and thanksgiving and not a propitiatory sacrifice.[159]

Trent did not define what it meant by the terms "sacrifice" and "propitiation." Its primary focus was the theology and practice of the Eucharist, not the theology of redemption as such. David Power observes that in the decree the term "propitiation" is a descriptive word and that has a twofold reference: first, it hearkens back to Christ's command, "Do this in memory of me" (Luke 22:19; 1 Cor 11:24); second, it refers to the action of the priest in the celebration of the Eucharist, when he acts in virtue of this memorial command. Power argues that "to offer propitiation in the sense that Trent gives it is to perform an act that obtains some remission of sin for either living or dead, distinct from the grace obtained through the reception of communion."[160] It is clear, however, that the language of sacrifice, propitiation, and appeasement/placating is employed in Trent's teaching to refer to the redemptive act of Christ's death on the cross.

In his study of Christian soteriology, O'Collins makes special note of this inclusion of penal elements in the teaching of Trent.[161] As he puts it, "Satisfaction was now officially depicted as involving punishment."[162] Trent does not speak of Christ experiencing "the weight of divine vengeance," as does Calvin. But it is evident that there has been a shift away from Anselm's notion of satisfaction as the action of God, in and through Christ, to restore the right order of a creation disfigured by sin, and toward an understanding of satisfaction in terms of divine punishment, propitiation, and appeasement. O'Collins points out that the idea of God's anger being appeased at the expense of his Son was later promoted among famous French Catholic preachers of the seventeenth century, such as J. B. Bossuet (1627–1704) and Louis Bourdaloue (1632–1704). "French religious eloquence, both in the seventeenth century and later, turned God into a murderer who carried out a cruel vendetta before being appeased and then exercising the divine mercy."[163] Such a conception of redemption, O'Collins insists, is contrary to the teaching of the New Testament and to the theology of Anselm.

Concluding Remarks

In his discussion of medieval and Reformation soteriology, Brian McDermott observes "how close the correlation is between the theology of salvation developed in a particular era and the operative theories of human relations, particularly regarding the rupture of relationship and its restoration."[164] I would add that this correlation pertains to the operative *images* and the *theories* of human relations. It is evident in the theologians we have treated in this chapter. Anselm's theory of satisfaction can be rightly understood only against the backdrop of a feudal society in which honor was integral to the maintenance of order. And Calvin's immersion in the French legal system led him to picture Jesus as standing before the bar of divine justice, putting himself in the place of humanity in order to absorb all of the punishment due to sin. Abelard, Aquinas, and Luther incorporated a variety of soteriological conceptions into their theologies, but they, too, were influenced by their experience of rupture and restoration in human relationships.

Difficulties arise when the operative images and theories of human relations in any particular era obscure, rather than illumine, the biblical testimony to God's saving work in Christ. This seems to be the case when the redemptive work of God in Christ is depicted in terms of penal substitution. In this regard, O'Collins says, "One must insist that the New Testament never speaks of redemption altering God's attitudes towards human beings and reconciling God to the world. The sending or coming of God's Son and the Spirit presupposes God's loving forgiveness."[165] In every age, the experience and understanding of human relations informs theologians' interpretations of the biblical witness about God's saving love. It is also true, however, that theologians must allow their experience and understanding to be challenged and purified by this biblical testimony. In a particular way, Christian theologians need to let their soteriologies be informed by the biblical witness to the primacy of divine love in the work of salvation.

CHAPTER 5

Three Twentieth-Century Theologians

n this chapter we move ahead to the twentieth century to explore the ways in which three prominent Catholic theologians treated the saving work of Christ. They are: the German Jesuit Karl Rahner (1904–1984); the Swiss theologian Hans Urs von Balthasar (1905–1988); and the Belgian Dominican who taught for many years in the Netherlands, Edward Schillebeeckx (1914–2009). Each of these thinkers reflected on the various perspectives on soteriology that we have examined thus far. Each was schooled in the rigid approach to Christology and soteriology found in the neoscholastic manuals prominent in the late nineteenth and early twentieth centuries. They each found this manualist theology to be deficient in its treatment of the person and saving work of Christ. Though the soteriological perspectives of Rahner, Balthasar, and Schillebeeckx are distinct, each of these thinkers has made a significant impact on Christian theology and has attracted a large following.

Karl Rahner

God and Human History

It is important to begin with Rahner's overarching vision of God's relationship to the human family and human history.[1] The starting point lies with God's desire to offer God's self freely to human beings who have been created in such a way that we are open to God's self-communication should God decide to give it. While we are only aware of this divine intention from the history of revelation—particularly from reflection on the life, death, and resurrection of Jesus—for Rahner, what has been revealed in history really does tell us something about God's ultimate designs for the human family. God creates in order to have a recipient of grace. The primary meaning of grace is God's self-communication—God giving God as One to be known and loved. In an early essay Rahner says, "God wishes to communicate himself, to pour forth the love which he himself is. That is the first and last of his real plans and of his real world, too. Everything else exists so that this one thing might be: the eternal miracle of infinite love."[2] Rahner proceeds to say that this is the reason God created human beings: "God makes a creature whom he can love."[3] Adhering to fundamental principles of Catholic theology, Rahner upholds the gift-character of both creation and God's offer of grace. But he asserts that God's self-revelation in history discloses that God creates because God wants to offer grace. According to Rahner, then, the ultimate reason for the universe is that God wanted to give God's self in love. That is the reason why there is anything at all.

Rahner argues that if God decides to offer grace, it must be offered to all people. It must be a universal offer because of the unity and common destiny of the human race. Rahner takes the teaching about the universal salvific will of God found in First Timothy 2:4 ("This is good and pleasing to God our savior, who wills that everyone be saved and come to knowledge of the truth") to "possess binding dogmatic force."[4] The offer of grace is present in the life of every person and can be accepted even by those who do not know about or believe in Christ.[5] For Rahner we live in a world of grace, and every person is affected by the nearness of God—even those who take no notice of God's presence in their lives.

Rahner also argues that God's offer of grace must be incarnational—addressed to spirit and matter—since each human being is a unity of spirit and matter. God's self-communication has an intrinsic tendency to be embodied, to become tangible in history. If grace is to be offered, it must occur incarnationally, though the event of the incarnation of the Word of God does not have to take place at the beginning of human history. God's self-communication is incarnational even before Christ because it becomes tangible, especially in the people, history, and teachings of Israel. This means that for Rahner, grace leads to incarnation. Ultimately, God's self-communication leads to its personal embodiment in the incarnation of the Son of God. In the previous chapter, we saw that Aquinas argued that we do not have sufficient knowledge of God's will to assert that God would have become incarnate even if there had been no sin. Rahner's understanding of grace leads him to answer this question about the motive of the incarnation differently. Like Duns Scotus, he answers in the affirmative: God would have become incarnate even if there had been no sin. If Christ comes into the picture only because of sin, then the incarnation becomes a kind of "second effort" on God's part. While Rahner does integrate the forgiveness of sin and overcoming of evil into his soteriology, he holds that salvation means something more than that. Redemption precedes sinfulness.[6] Drawing on the Greek patristic tradition, Rahner argues that ultimately salvation means participation in the life of God. Thus, he suggests that God's becoming human, God's gift of Self to us in the most personal way in our human history, is intended from the beginning. The incarnation is "the summit and height of the divine plan of creation."[7] Once sin enters into the picture, the incarnation takes on additional redemptive dimensions.

The Life and Ministry of Jesus

Throughout the course of his theological career, Rahner emphasized the necessity of affirming the true humanity of Jesus. He thought that there was a tendency within Catholic Christology of the early twentieth century, and within much of popular Catholic piety, to think of Christ simply as God in human disguise. This view, he thought, reflected Monophysite tendencies that were rejected by the christological councils of the early church. Rahner stressed that if Jesus was to be mediator of salvation, his humanity had to be genuine. Jesus must stand before God as a true human being on our side, in free obedience to the will of the Father. Rahner argued that, precisely because of the union of the divine and human natures in the one person of Christ, his humanity must be truly real and full. This is because radical dependence on God and genuine human autonomy vary in direct, not in inverse proportion. When the divine draws close, the human is not annulled or abbreviated but is brought to fulfillment.[8]

The integrity of Jesus' humanity implies a real human history.[9] Rahner argued against the view, espoused by Aquinas and many other medieval theologians, that Jesus enjoyed the beatific vision from the first moment of his conception.[10] Such a vision of God would include a knowledge of all realities past, present, and future. Rahner does uphold the uniqueness of Christ's human knowledge.[11] He argues that because of the union of the divine and human in Christ, his human consciousness of God and of himself was unique. Rahner speaks of Christ's "consciousness of a radical and unique closeness to God, an unreflexive consciousness in the depths of his being which continued throughout the whole history of his life (as shown in the unique nature of his behavior towards the Father)."[12] But, Rahner continues, "the objectifying and verbalizing consciousness of Jesus has a history."[13] Here Rahner distinguishes between "unreflexive" consciousness—implicit knowledge that can become more explicit through life experience—and "objectifying" consciousness—conceptual knowledge of things we can specify. Thus for Rahner, Jesus was conscious of his unique immediacy to the God whom he addressed as "Abba," and he was aware of his unique redemptive mission. But this unique consciousness did not provide detailed, objective knowledge about the future. Jesus grows in knowledge in a more ordinary sense; he "learns and has new and surprising experiences."[14] Rahner thinks, for example, that Jesus learns of his approaching death by experiencing the effects of his mission. As he puts it, "the experience grew stronger in him that his mission was bringing him into mortal conflict with the religious and political society."[15] The lack of a detailed, objective knowledge about future events does not detract from Jesus' perfection. Rather, it enables him to exercise freedom in the human sphere. Rahner asserts that "a genuine human consciousness must have an unknown future ahead of it."[16] Rahner wants to emphasize that, while Jesus was truly divine, as truly human he lived our life and died our death.

Rahner presents in summary form the findings of mainline biblical scholars about the public ministry of Jesus.[17] Jesus was a radical reformer who opposed justification by works, "which was supposed to give man security against God."[18] He knew himself to be radically close to God. His preaching and call to reform emerged from his conviction about the closeness of God's kingdom. This nearness of the reign of God was inseparably connected with his person; in other words, acceptance of the kingdom entailed following Jesus.

> Jesus experiences in himself that radical and victorious offer of God to him which did not exist before in this way among "sinners," and he knows that it is significant, valid and irrevocable for all men. According to his own self-understanding he is already before the resurrection the one sent, the one who inaugurates the kingdom of God through what he says and what he does in a way that it did not exist before, but now does exist *through* him and *in* him.[19]

The hostile reaction to his proclamation by some, including those in religious and political authority, led him to recognize that his mission was bringing him into mortal danger. "But he faced death resolutely and accepted it at least as the inevitable consequence of fidelity to his mission and imposed on him by God."[20] Rahner does not clarify what he means here when he says that Jesus' death was "imposed on him by God." He concludes that, from a historical point of view, there is much about Jesus' public life and ministry that must be left open. Among the matters about which we do not have definitive knowledge is "whether and to what extent and in what sense the pre-resurrection Jesus explicitly ascribed a soteriological function to his death."[21]

Death and Resurrection

Rahner's treatment of Jesus' death is related to his theology of death, which in turn is based on his theology of freedom. Rahner understands human freedom to be, at its roots, the capacity for definitive self-disposal before God. Freedom is not only the ability to choose among various options; more fundamentally, it is also the capacity to make something of oneself before God, to become a certain kind of person. Rahner argues that in and through death human beings have the possibility of attaining the fullness of freedom and achieving a definitive disposal of themselves before God. He says that "through death there comes to be the final and definitive validity of man's existence which has been achieved and has come to maturity in freedom."[22] While there is a painful and frightening dimension of death that is a consequence of sin (the passive dimension of death), death can also be the act that culminates a life of entrusting oneself to God, or of deciding against God (the active dimension of death).

Rahner views the death of Jesus as the paradigmatic instance of right dying and the means of the transformation of death. Jesus makes a choice for the Father in the face of the darkness of his passion. This choice sums up his life of freedom, of complete self-disposal before God. Rahner likes to cite the final words that Luke attributes to the dying Jesus ("Father, into your hands I commend my spirit"; Luke 23:46, cf. Ps 31:6) as the most illuminating biblical statement about what really took place in Jesus' death. Reflecting on this Lucan verse, Rahner writes, "And so you let yourself be taken from yourself. You give yourself over with confidence into those gentle, invisible hands. We who are weak in faith and fearful for our own selves experience those hands as the sudden, grasping, merciless, stifling grip of blind fate and death. But you know that they are the hands of the Father."[23]

Rahner stresses the unity of the death and resurrection of Jesus. His death of its very nature culminates in resurrection. Rahner views Jesus' resurrection more as the completion of his living and dying, rather than as the correction of what was done to him. In an essay on Easter, Rahner asserts that the resurrection of Christ was "the appearance of what took place in Christ's death: the performed and undergone handing over of the entire reality of the one corporal man to the mystery of the mercifully loving God through Christ's collective freedom, which disposes over his entire life and his entire existence."[24] In *Foundations of Christian Faith*, he argues that "the death of Jesus is such that by its very nature it is subsumed into resurrection. It is a death into resurrection."[25] Though Rahner usually places his soteriological focus on Jesus' death, he does acknowledge that discussion of the salvific significance of Jesus must include both his death and resurrection. Through his resurrection the person and mission of Jesus are validated. The resurrection means "the permanent, redeemed, final and definitive validity of the single and unique life of Jesus who achieved the permanent and final validity of his life precisely through his death in freedom and obedience."[26] He calls Jesus' resurrection "the eschatological victory of God's grace in the world."[27]

Soteriological Perspective

Rahner emphasizes that the only ultimate salvation for humanity is God in God's very Self. He says, "Salvation here is to be understood as the strictly supernatural and direct presence of God in himself afforded by grace."[28] And it is only through God's gift of Self that sin is forgiven and evil overcome. In an essay on reconciliation, Rahner includes a section on "the hopelessness of guilt."[29] He points out that even when we express sorrow for something we have done and seek to change our ways, we cannot undo the wrong we have committed. He speaks of people's experience "that they are and will for all eternity remain persons who have betrayed their love and fidelity."[30] By their own power, they cannot separate themselves from their past evil deeds. Rahner argues that this experience of the hopelessness of guilt reveals that the basis of hope for forgiveness can be found only in grace, in "something that utterly transcends their own freedom."[31] Real forgiveness can only come through the self-communication of God, "who contrary to all personal experience of freedom is able to overcome the eternity of the evil deed."[32]

In his treatment of the way in which God overcomes evil—how God reconciles the world to himself in Christ—Rahner persistently emphasizes the loving initiative of God in the entire Christ event. He wants to oppose any notion of Christ appeasing an angry God through his death. He asserts that "it is precisely a God who loves the sinner originally and without reasons who is the cause of his reconciliation."[33] He thinks that the way in which Anselm's soteriology was often presented in theology and preaching obscured this loving divine initiative. The theory of satisfaction was transformed into a theology of appeasement. In an essay on soteriology, Rahner reflects on Jesus' death and insists, "God is not transformed from a God of anger and justice into a God of mercy and love by the cross; rather God brings the event of the cross to pass since he is possessed from the beginning of gratuitous mercy and, despite the world's sin, shares himself with the world, so overcoming its sin."[34] It is not clear what exactly Rahner means when he says that "God brings the event of the cross to pass." In *Foundations of Christian Faith*, Rahner makes a similar assertion about God's loving initiative in salvation, but there he says that "the pure initiative of God's salvific will establishes the life of Jesus which reaches fulfillment in his death."[35] The latter way of articulating the point links God less directly to the crucifixion of Jesus.

Rahner employs principles of sacramental causality in discussing what God has done "for us" in Christ. A classic principle in sacramental theology is that sacraments cause grace because and insofar as they signify grace. The grace that is effected in sacraments is effected by being signified, by being "symboled forth." Rahner, then, can speak of the unitive event of Jesus' death and resurrection as the sacrament—the efficacious sign—of God's salvific grace and of its victorious and irreversible activity in the world.[36] In Jesus' life, death, and resurrection we have the absolute, definitive self-communication of God, the complete human acceptance of God's self-communication and God's validation of this acceptance. Rahner says that "we are saved because this man who is one of us has been saved by God, and God has therefore made his salvific will present in the world historically, really and irrevocably."[37] Before Jesus' death and resurrection a positive ending of human history was not assured with tangible, historical certainty. But because Jesus died and rose again, God's loving self-communication will be victorious in human history as a whole. Jesus has made God's saving grace present and effective in human history in a definitive and irreversible way.

Given that God has saved humanity in Christ, can an individual reject God's self-communication in a definitive manner, resulting in eternal perdition? Rahner asserts that a person who is still living in history must reckon seriously with the possibility of final loss as a consequence of rejecting God. Acceptance or rejection of God's self-communication happens primarily through the way one acts toward his or her neighbor. Rahner upholds the traditional teaching against a positive, theoretical doctrine of apocatastasis.[38] At the same time, Rahner points out that, for the Christian, statements about eternal salvation and statements about eternal loss are not parallel. "For since we are living in the eschaton of Jesus Christ, the God-Man who was crucified for us and who has risen for us and who remains forever, we know in our Christian faith and in our unshakable hope that, in spite of the drama and ambiguity of the freedom of individual persons, the history of salvation as a whole will reach a positive conclusion for the human race through God's own powerful grace."[39] The salvation of the world as a whole is a *promise;* eternal loss for the individual is a *possibility.* The church has never officially declared that any particular individual has, in fact, suffered eternal loss. Rahner interprets biblical statements about hell and eternal loss as warnings to individuals to take into account the possibility of eternal loss, rather than as literal descriptions of hell.

Rahner interprets the benefits of salvation in Christ in relational terms. Growth in acceptance of God's self-communication leads to greater dependence on God, which in turn results in enhanced personal freedom. Above all, this graced freedom enables us to deepen our love for neighbor, a love that Rahner stresses is inextricably united with love for God. For the Christian, being saved in Christ also entails a dynamic personal relationship with Jesus Christ. Rahner asserts that salvation "does not mean a reified and objective state of affairs, but rather a personal and ontological reality." It entails "an abiding personal relationship to the God-Man in whom and in whom alone immediacy to God is reached now and forever."[40]

We will encounter Rahner's thought again in chapter 7, when we discuss salvation in light of an evolutionary view of the world, and in chapter 8, when we address the question of Jesus as universal savior.

Hans Urs von Balthasar

Foundational Principles

Hans Urs von Balthasar is notable for his project of articulating the meaning of the Christian revelation under the rubric of the three transcendentals (fundamental and comprehensive characteristics of being as such): beauty, goodness, and truth.[41] He begins with the transcendental of beauty, moves on to consider that of goodness, and then addresses the truth of revelation. By starting with beauty, Balthasar focuses on the revelation of God's glory, objectively and definitively manifested in Christ. God takes the initiative to reveal God's self and act in a sovereign way to redeem humanity. Balthasar says that we can speak about a "theological aesthetics" because "on his own initiative and independently of man's anthropological structures God takes form and allows himself to be seen, heard, and touched."[42] Balthasar highlights the uniqueness of the form (Gestalt) of Christ in history. It is unlike any other form; it is the Form of all forms. The believer is able to perceive its "objective, demonstrable beauty."[43] As the manifestation of God's glory, the form of Christ is the culmination of the beautiful and, therefore, it displays perfect harmony.

Though the theme of God's saving work in Christ permeates Balthasar's entire corpus, he addresses soteriology particularly under the transcendental of goodness.[44] Balthasar does theology through dramatic narrative; he narrates the story of the life-and-death drama of God's action in human history. Not unlike patristic theologians who heralded the victory of Christ over the powers of evil, Balthasar envisions God's saving work in Christ as a cosmic drama wherein God overcomes that which enslaves humanity. He speaks of the "eminently dramatic constitution" of human life.[45] The drama of human living is grounded in the tension between our natural desire for God and a negative desire to be for ourselves. Balthasar describes the very constitution of the human being as "agonal"—replete with struggle or agony. "Only with the assistance of grace can he [the human person] win through to the self-conquest that is required of him."[46] Balthasar's view of human existence then leads him to depict "the fundamental theodramatic law of world history" in this way: "the greater the revelation of divine (ground-less) love, the more it elicits a groundless (John 15:25) hatred from man."[47] This statement implies a fundamental clash between God and sin, and it suggests that the cross will have a central place in the soteriology of Balthasar. The saving grace of God in Christ "has itself adopted an agonal form as a result of the world's sin."[48] Balthasar is convinced that Christian soteriology must be dramatic in form and content. Though he is critical of certain dimensions of Anselm's theory of satisfaction, he acknowledges that "the dramatic dimension of the world's redemption in Christ came out in his theology as never before, in terms not only of content but also of form."[49]

The Incarnation

Inspired particularly by the Gospel of John, Balthasar's Christology is a "Christology from above" that takes as its starting point the incarnation of the Son/Word of God. And Balthasar relates what happens in the incarnation to the inner life of the Trinity. The incarnation is the condescension of God—the *kenōsis* (self-emptying) of God—who comes to be with us, to accompany us even into the darkest places of our sinful and wounded existence. Balthasar argues that the self-emptying of God in the incarnation is grounded in a more original *kenōsis* that takes place within the life of the Trinity, in the eternal generation of the Son. In this generation, "the Father strips himself, without remainder, of his Godhead and hands it over to the Son; he 'imparts' to the Son all that is his."[50] This *kenōsis* within the Trinity underpins all of the divine self-emptying that takes place in creation and salvation history. Balthasar declares that "it is the drama of the 'emptying' of the Father's heart in the generation of the Son that contains and surpasses all possible drama between God and the world."[51] Envisioning God in terms of this eternal and historical self-emptying entails a new way of seeing God: "God is not, in the first place, 'absolute power', but 'absolute love', and his sovereignty manifests itself not in holding on to what is its own but in its abandonment—all this in such a way that this sovereignty displays itself in transcending the opposition, known to us from the world, between power and impotence."[52]

Believers perceive this divine self-emptying in the entire story of Jesus. The incarnation meant not only the act by which the Son entered into human existence but also "the acceptance of an entire human life, prone to suffering."[53] For Balthasar, we must envision the incarnation as ordered to the cross. The latter is the "final cause" of the former. Balthasar says that the day exists when the Son is dead and the Father is inaccessible; he asserts that "it is for the sake of this day that the Son became man."[54] He appeals to patristic sources in making this point, especially the statement by Gregory of Nyssa, "Anyone who ponders the mystery will be more inclined to say that it was not his death that resulted from his birth, but that he accepted to be born so that he might be able to die."[55] Balthasar describes Jesus' entire life as "saturated with his death," and he says that the final goal of the *kenōsis* of the incarnation was "the particular death of Jesus, designed to outstrip and 'conquer' death itself."[56] Willing to go to the lengths of death on the cross in his obedience to the will of the Father, Jesus "unveils a totally unexpected picture of God's internal, Trinitarian defenselessness: the wisdom of God that is folly yet wiser than the wisdom of men (1 Cor 1–2)."[57]

The Life and Ministry of Jesus

Balthasar reads the gospel accounts of the ministry of Jesus through the lens of the Johannine narrative. He argues that Jesus' ministry was provocative because of the enormity of his claims. Jesus claims to be "the way and the truth and the life" (John 14:6). He says that "no one has gone up to heaven except the one who has come down from heaven, the Son of Man" (John 3:13). Statements like these (which Balthasar seems to regard as authentic sayings of the historical Jesus) reveal that Jesus is the absolutely singular one. Balthasar observes, "The whole gospel is full of this resounding 'I'."[58] He adds, "Jesus' life stands under the sign of his claim to be preaching the ultimate prophetic inspiration above and beyond Moses and the previous prophets; his 'I am' and 'But I say to you' is a direct resonance of the 'I' laid claim by God himself in the Old Testament."[59] The gospel evidence, rooted in Jesus' own preaching, shows that in him the definitive end—the eschaton—has arrived. Religious and political leaders react against the enormity of Jesus' claims and accuse him of hubris, insanity, and demonic possession. The apostles, on the other hand, are brought to faith because of the power of the person of Jesus. In Balthasar's terms, they are moved to perceive the uniqueness of the form of Christ.

The life, ministry, and death of Jesus are, above all, imbued with and impelled by his perfect obedience. Balthasar observes that Jesus "willed to become the one who, in a remarkable and unique manner, is obedient to the Father—in a manner, namely, where his obedience presents the eternal kenotic translation of the eternal love of the Son for the 'ever-greater' Father."[60] This tenacious obedience to the will of the Father is a function of what Jesus, in his self-emptying and self-abasement, willed to become.[61] It means that in his earthly life the Son allows himself to be guided by the Spirit. In his passion Jesus displays complete *disponibilité*—he is utterly at the disposal of the will of the Father. This complete availability means that "Jesus is free from every bond, whether exterior or interior."[62] His ministry and his approach to his passion disclose the fullness of his self-surrender to the Father.

Death, Descent to the Dead, and Resurrection

The *kenōsis* of the incarnation is expressed most fully in Jesus' passion and his descent to the dead. In these moments Jesus, the Word made flesh, bears the brunt of sin and the alienation from God that results from sin. Balthasar interprets the Gethsemane scene as the beginning of Jesus' progressive isolation from his friends and from the Father. Here Jesus enters into the eschatological tribulation—the clash between the power of God and the powers of darkness. He experiences "the entry of the sin of the world into the personal existence, body and soul, of the representative Substitute and Mediator."[63] Jesus' role as "substitute" is very important for Balthasar's soteriology. His anguish in the garden represents a cosuffering with sinners of such a kind that Jesus absorbs the real loss of God that threatens sinners. The sin of the world is laid upon him and he experiences the fear characteristic of those consigned to Gehenna (the *timor gehennalis*).[64] Jesus becomes the object of God's wrath against sin. Balthasar answers a question about this divine wrath that he poses for himself: "Can we seriously say that God unloaded his wrath upon the Man who wrestled with his destiny on the Mount of Olives and was subsequently crucified? Indeed we must."[65]

Balthasar interprets the "handing over" of Jesus to death on two levels.[66] On the human plane, Jesus was handed over by his betrayer. But on a deeper level, Balthasar connects this handing over with the Hebrew tradition of God delivering his chosen people into the hands of their enemies when they were unfaithful.[67] Jesus is handed over by his betrayer, who is the visible agent of all sinners, yet mysteriously this is also connected with the justice of God. At the same time, Balthasar insists, we must complement Jesus' being handed over with the complete self-gift that Jesus makes in his passion. The diverse expressions of this mystery found in the New Testament ground Balthasar's Trinitarian interpretation of Jesus' deliverance unto death:

> From this point on there arises the Trinitarian theme which develops in three forms, simultaneously: God the Father hands over his Son ("does not spare his Son"), thanks to his love for us (Romans 8, 32; John 3, 16), but it is due to Christ's love for us (Romans 8, 35; Galatians 2, 20; Ephesians 5, 1, etc.), in such a way that in Christ's gratuitous self-gift (John 10, 18) the Father's unconditional love becomes plain.[68]

Balthasar insists that on the cross Jesus experiences the abandonment by God that properly belongs to sinners but which he, as the One who was "made sin for our sake" (2 Cor 5:21), endures in our

stead. Balthasar is not afraid to make the strongest possible statements in this regard. The cross is the achievement of the divine
judgment on sin, where sin is condemned in the flesh. Balthasar,
not unlike Anselm, believes that the full demands of divine justice
must be taken into account in soteriology. God must reject sin and
act to undo the havoc that sin has wreaked on God's good creation.
But God does this by becoming human and thus becoming, in one
person, both the subject and the object of judgment. The Son suffers
the remoteness from God—the radical separation—that is caused by
sin. Balthasar says of Christ that his "atoning torment must have
consisted in unfathomable depths of forsakenness by the Father."[69] He
asserts that "the forsakenness that prevails between the Father and
his crucified Son is deeper and more deadly than any forsakenness,
temporal or eternal, actual or possible, that separates a creature from
God."[70] Jesus endures this abandonment in order to atone for every
sin. At the same time, this experience of "wrathful alienation" is a
moment in which the Father and Son are united in one love and thus
"are closer together than ever."[71]

The self-emptying of Jesus, and his endurance of the effects of sin,
reaches its ultimate end in his descent to the dead. In these reflections, Balthasar is particularly dependent on the insights of Adrienne
von Speyr. Von Speyr was a physician who converted to Catholicism
under Balthasar's direction and whose mystical visions related to the
mystery of Holy Saturday became a source for his theology.[72] Rather
than envisioning Christ's descent as the triumphant entry of the Victor to open the gates of hell and liberate the just, Balthasar views it
as the crucified Christ's being with the dead. He is in solidarity with
those who have lost their way from God. Christ's solidarity with the
lost completes his standing for (substituting for) sinful humanity before God. In order to pay the entire penalty imposed on sinners, Christ
willed not only to die but also to go down, in his soul, *ad infernum*.[73]
Stripped by the cross of every power and initiative of his own, the
dead Christ serves as a sermon to the dead. He is dead together with
them. "And exactly in that way he disturbs the absolute loneliness
striven for by the sinner; the sinner who wants to be 'damned' apart
from God, finds God again in his loneliness, but God in the absolute
weakness of love who unfathomably in the period of nontime enters
into solidarity with those damning themselves."[74]

Pursuing his Trinitarian interpretation of the paschal mystery, Balthasar envisions the resurrection of Jesus as the reunion of the Son with the Father after the Son has fulfilled his mission.[75] Easter also represents the completion of the Father's action as Creator: "One can say, therefore, that the entire action of the living God in all ages has had as its goal the resurrection of the Son, that the completion of Christology found in the Father's act is at the same time the fulfillment of the act of creation itself."[76] Balthasar identifies two fundamental movements that are at work in the paschal mystery—abasement (*kenōsis*) and exaltation: the supreme abasement of the Son in the incarnation and death of Jesus and the exaltation of the Son in the resurrection. Both are rooted in divine love, the love in which the Father and the Son are united in this movement of self-emptying and exaltation. This twofold movement intrinsic to God's saving action is revelatory of the love of the Trinity: "Basically, in Jesus Christ's death, descent into hell and resurrection, only one reality is there to be seen: the love of the Triune God for the world, a love which can only be perceived through a co-responsive love."[77]

Soteriological Perspective

Balthasar's soteriology is fundamentally a theology of substitution.[78] He also employs the terms "solidarity" and "representation," but his interpretation of these ideas leans in the direction of substitution. He approves of a statement by theologian Jean Galot in this regard: "There is solidarity it is true, but it extends as far as substitution: Christ's solidarity with us goes as far as taking our place and allowing the whole weight of human guilt to fall upon him."[79] In his reading of the New Testament accounts of God's saving work in Christ, he focuses on the idea of "exchange" (*commercium*), which is connected to substitution. Citing 2 Corinthians 5:21 and Galatians 3:13, he emphasizes that the New Testament shows us that Christ "gives himself 'for us' to the extent of *exchanging places with us*."[80] Jesus, the Word made flesh, takes our place in bearing the consequences of sin. In so doing, he atones for the sin of the world. At the same time, Balthasar highlights the New Testament teaching that the entire redemptive process has its origin in God's merciful love: "It is God's immense love for the world that has caused him to give up his only Son (John 3:16) and thereby to reconcile the world to himself (2 Cor 5:19; Col 1:20)."[81]

Balthasar's reflections on the mystery of Holy Saturday suggest the notion of universal salvation. If the crucified Christ sojourns to the farthest regions of hell to disturb the loneliness of even the most hardened sinners, does that mean that all people will be saved? Balthasar wrote a book on the topic of apocatastasis not long before he died in which he examined the tradition on this topic (particularly the patristic tradition) and offered his own ideas.[82] His position on this question closely resembles that of Rahner—he quotes Rahner several times in his book. Balthasar argues that eternal loss is a possibility that each person must seriously consider for himself or herself alone, though not for others, since hell is in essence the sinner utterly alone. But through the cross and resurrection of Christ, the saving love of God has been revealed and effected. This means that the believer may hope that all will be saved. In fact, Balthasar argues, Christians *must* hope that all will be saved. To hope for one's own salvation and not for the salvation of all would be unchristian, since Christ died for all. He proposes the following thesis: "Whoever reckons with the possibility of even only *one* person's being lost besides himself is hardly able to love unreservedly. . . . Just the slightest nagging thought of a final hell for others tempts us, in moments in which human togetherness becomes especially difficult, to leave the other to himself."[83]

For Balthasar, the life of grace is made possible by Christ's redemptive act. This act has resulted in a transformation on the level of being. He says that "there can be no doubt that those for whose sins Christ suffered and atoned have undergone an ontological shift."[84] This transformation leads to participation in the life of the church, particularly the Eucharist. The exemplar of the church is Mary, whose "yes" to God at the annunciation and at the foot of the cross sustains the Body of Christ. Standing near the cross, "her consent becomes the most excruciating affirmation of her Son's sacrifice."[85] Here we meet the theme of obedience in Balthasar again—the obedience of Christ, the obedience of Mary, and the obedience to God's will to which believers are called. In the Eucharist, "the community is drawn into Christ's sacrifice, offering to God that perfect sacrifice of Head and members."[86] Influenced by the mysticism of Adrienne von Speyr, Balthasar places contemplation at the center of Christian life. He advocates work for social justice but is critical of liberationist theology and of Vatican II's *Gaudium et Spes* (the Pastoral Constitution on the Church in the Modern World), concluding that both are overly optimistic about what human beings can accomplish in the world. While the Christian must work for justice in the world, "the best that can be achieved is a temporary balance, not between intolerable misery and senseless luxury or a Titanic will-to-power, but between a bearable poverty and a comfortable existence that is concerned about the world in its wholeness."[87]

Edward Schillebeeckx

We have already encountered the thought of Schillebeeckx in chapter 2. There we examined the concepts of salvation that he gleaned from his in-depth study of the New Testament. Of the three authors discussed in this chapter, Schillebeeckx's views on soteriology are shaped most specifically by his engagement with the biblical material and the findings of New Testament scholarship.[88] He points out that the soteriological concepts found in the New Testament "give us a good idea of the New Testament understanding of what redemption through Christ Jesus is from and what it is for."[89] Schillebeeckx argues that for New Testament authors redemption in Christ is always both a grace and a requirement; it is the free gift of a gracious God but also a task to be undertaken by believers.

Robert Schreiter observes that Schillebeeckx's "whole Christological project is about discovering a new soteriology for a postmodern world."[90] Schillebeeckx himself says that "the question of salvation is the great driving force in our present history, not only in a religious and theological context, but also thematically as well."[91] The starting point for Schillebeeckx's soteriology is human experience of the world in which we live. While he would affirm that this world is essentially good, he also sees it as a world that is indelibly scarred by the scandal of evil and human suffering. In the background of his reflection on salvation from God in Jesus is his awareness that human history is marked by a "barbarous excess" of evil and suffering.[92] From that vantage point, he endeavors to formulate a soteriology within the matrix of the human search for meaning and liberation.

In his discussion of this search for meaning and liberation in a suffering-filled world, Schillebeeckx adduces the category of negative

contrast experience. This refers to our natural human reaction to evil
and suffering, to things that we instinctively know should not be.
When normal people experience or even just hear about torture, ethnic
cleansing, child abuse, and the like, they instinctively react, even before they think about it. Schillebeeckx argues that contrast experiences
have both a negative and a positive dimension. The negative moment
is the reaction to and protest against such evil. Schillebeeckx observes,
"What we experience as reality, what we see and hear of this reality
daily through television and other mass media, is evidently not 'in
order'; there is something fundamentally wrong."[93] More positively,
this reaction points to a hope for, and even an insight into, something
better. It reflects an awareness of goodness and value that should be
present. For Schillebeeckx there is an element of longing, even of
transcendence, in every contrast experience—a movement toward
the good. Schillebeeckx names the knowledge that is implicit in our
reaction to evil and suffering as "a critical epistemological force which
leads to new action, which anticipates a better future and seeks to put
it into practice."[94] He is convinced that talk about the experience of
salvation from God in Christ must always be connected with human
flourishing, which entails the overcoming of evil and suffering.

The Ministry of Jesus

Schillebeeckx does not attempt to construct a theory about the
saving work of Christ. He favors narrative over theory, particularly
when faced with the mystery of evil and suffering. He thinks that
theories are of little help when dealing with suffering, observing that
"people do not argue against suffering, but tell a story."[95] Commenting on the Christology of Schillebeeckx, John Galvin points out that
"unlike theories, which tend to domesticate problems and thus to
perpetuate them, the telling and retelling of stories preserves dangerous memories, awakens liberating hopes, and provides a framework
for expressing the specific anticipations of a better future in parables
and symbols."[96] In his Christology, then, Schillebeeckx attempts to
retell the life story of Jesus as the liberating story of God. The entire
story of Jesus, from beginning to end, is about the definitive offer of
salvation from God. As Schillebeeckx puts it, "Where Jesus appears,
salvation begins to live."[97]

Schillebeeckx is critical of treatments of Jesus' saving work that envision his public ministry as merely a prelude to his death and resurrection. He insists that Jesus' death is the direct outcome of his ministry, and thus the shape and content of this ministry should be carefully elucidated in soteriology. If one's entire soteriological focus is on Jesus' death, one will be left with a distorted picture of Jesus and of God. Schillebeeckx, then, devotes a great deal of attention to Jesus' proclamation of the reign of God. The message of the kingdom that Jesus preached and acted on presented a God who has made the concerns of humankind God's own, and whose coming rule means life and wholeness for people. Jesus' proclamation of the kingdom leads to special concern for the most vulnerable people of the world. Schillebeeckx's reading of the gospel accounts of Jesus' public ministry leads him to speak of the reign of God as "the saving presence of God, active and encouraging, as it is affirmed or welcomed among men and women." This saving presence of God "takes concrete form above all in justice and peaceful relationships among individuals and peoples." It entails "a changed new relationship of men and women to God, the tangible and visible side of which is a new type of liberating relationship among men and women."[98] The God of the kingdom preached by Jesus is the God of life, the God whose presence means life for human beings.

Jesus makes this reign of God present in his acts of healing and his table fellowship. Drawing on his study of New Testament exegesis, Schillebeeckx concludes that there is a historically firm basis for affirming that Jesus acted as a healer and an exorcist. Through these actions, Jesus' caring and abiding presence among people was experienced as salvation coming from God.[99] Jesus also discloses the meaning of God's reign through his table fellowship with all kinds of people. Through his communion with others at table, including those considered disreputable, Jesus brings them into communion with God. Schillebeeckx observes, "To a great extent Jesus' action consisted in establishing social communication above all where excommunication or expulsion was officially in force."[100]

Schillebeeckx maintains that Jesus' proclamation of God's reign was rooted in his unique intimacy with the God whom he addressed as "Abba." He names this "Abba experience" "the source and secret of his [Jesus'] being, message and manner of life."[101] This experience entailed "an immediate awareness of God as a power cherishing people and making them free."[102] Schillebeeckx thinks of Jesus' Abba experience as a contrast experience. Jesus had firsthand knowledge of the pain of the world, so evident in the people who sought his help, as well as in the forms of injustice present in his society. But the fundamental inspiration for all that Jesus said and did was his experience of God as the loving opponent of evil. Schillebeeckx names this God revealed in Jesus' public ministry "Pure Positivity." The God whom Jesus discloses in word and deed is purely the source and ground of life, of the good. Neither death nor any other form of negativity finds its source in God. This conviction will influence the way in which Schillebeeckx addresses the traditional teaching about the salvific significance of Jesus' death.

Death and Resurrection

Schillebeeckx understands Jesus' crucifixion to be "the intrinsic historical consequence of the radicalism of both his message and his lifestyle, which showed that all 'master-servant' relationships were incompatible with the lifestyle of the kingdom of God."[103] He argues that the rejection of Jesus began not in the final days of his ministry in Jerusalem but in the conflicts that arose from his ministry in Galilee. He concludes that Jesus was rejected not for having divine pretensions (as Balthasar suggests) but for "his sovereign and free human way of life."[104] Like Rahner, he proposes that while at the outset of his ministry Jesus did not expect that his life would end in violent death, he became increasingly aware of the mortal danger into which he was headed. He says, "From a particular moment in his career he must have come to terms with the possibility, in the longer term the probability, and in the end the actual certainty of a fatal outcome."[105]

Schillebeeckx offers a nuanced description of the way in which Jesus integrated his impending death into his life and mission. This is pivotal for his approach to soteriology. On the one hand, he is concerned not to place what he considers later Christian affirmations of the salvific importance of Jesus' death found in the New Testament on the lips of the historical Jesus. He doubts that the historical Jesus spoke explicitly of his impending death as having salvific significance for the world. This position is related to Schillebeeckx's insistence on the negativity of Jesus' death and his criticism of the Christian tendency to glorify the cross. He insists that the cross, in and of itself, must be soberly viewed in all of its negativity. Jesus was crucified by human injustice and in that sense the cross is "the index of the anti-divine in human history."[106]

On the other hand, Schillebeeckx also wants to take into consideration reliable New Testament evidence indicating that Jesus did not approach his death as an event entirely devoid of meaning. For example, he appeals to the Last Supper tradition of Jesus passing the cup to his disciples (Mark 14:25) as a sign of Jesus' deep trust that his fellowship with the disciples was stronger than death. This symbolic action shows that "Jesus felt his death to be in some way or other part and parcel of the salvation-offered-by-God, as a historical consequence of his caring and loving service of and solidarity with people."[107] As one final act of fidelity to God and service to others, his death took on a meaning that it would not otherwise have had.

Schillebeeckx writes in direct opposition to Christologies that attribute the cross, or the handing over of Jesus to death, to the action of God (the Father).[108] Thus, his treatment of Jesus' death is quite distinct from that of Balthasar. Jesus was crucified by people who were threatened by his words and his behavior. His execution represented human rejection of the salvation from God that was offered in Jesus. Schillebeeckx insists, "God . . . did not put Jesus on the cross. Human beings did that."[109] He also rejects the notion, so prominent in the theologies of Balthasar and Jürgen Moltmann, that Jesus suffered divine abandonment on the cross. Schillebeeckx asserts that "on exegetical grounds we must resolutely reject the possibility that Jesus himself had been abandoned by God."[110] He argues that the opening line of Psalm 22, quoted in Mark 15:34 and Matthew 27:46, evokes the entire psalm, which concludes in a spirit of trust and thanksgiving. Thus the cross is the ultimate contrast experience: it involves the terrible suffering of a violent death that should not have been, but at the same time, it is an experience filled with trust and hope in God. On the cross, Jesus continues to hold God's hand in radical trust. God is silently present to Jesus at this moment, just as God is silently present to all those who suffer. God's silent presence to Jesus does not dispel the darkness of Calvary. But Schillebeeckx contends we must say that for Jesus and all those who suffer, "God *nevertheless remains near at hand* and that salvation consists in the fact that man still holds fast to God's invisible hand *in* this dark night of faith."[111]

In the resurrection of Jesus the power of God, who was faithfully present to Jesus at Calvary, erupts from within. Schillebeeckx differs from Rahner in that he places emphasis on the resurrection as correction rather than completion. Like Rahner, Schillebeeckx affirms that the resurrection is God's endorsement of Jesus' life. It is anticipated by the profound communion with God that Jesus experienced throughout his life. The resurrection is "God's yes to the person and life of Jesus."[112] But Schillebeeckx focuses more of his attention on the resurrection as a new, creative act of God that corrects what was done to Jesus. He fears that if one views the resurrection as simply the other side of Jesus' death it will minimize the negativity of this death. In raising Jesus from the dead, God breaks through humanity's rejection of definitive salvation offered by Jesus: "In the risen Jesus God shows himself to be the power of anti-evil, of unconditional goodness that in sovereign fashion refuses to recognize, and breaks, the overweening power of evil."[113]

Soteriological Perspective

Because Schillebeeckx prefers narrative over theory in his Christology and soteriology, he does not provide a precise analysis of how God effects salvation in Christ. Rather, the entire story of Jesus, from beginning to end, is the story of salvation. He resolutely rejects the notion that God required the death of Jesus as compensation for sin.[114] In a famous passage, he says that we cannot find a reason for the death of Jesus; thus, "we have to say that we are not redeemed *thanks* to the death of Jesus but *despite* it."[115] He qualifies that statement by adding that, because in the resurrection of Jesus God has so overcome the negativity of this death, in faith we can say that even the negative aspects of our history have an indirect role in God's saving work. So the statement "despite the death" does not say enough. Schillebeeckx, however, asserts that "the terms in which we could fill this unfathomable 'does not say enough' in a positive way, with finite, meaningful categories, escape us."[116]

While Schillebeeckx does not develop a precise theory about God's saving work in Christ, three soteriological themes can be discerned in his writings. First, he speaks often of solidarity and communion: Jesus' communion with God, Jesus' solidarity with humanity, and God's solidarity with humanity in Jesus. Even in the darkness and terror of Calvary, Jesus maintains communion with God. Schillebeeckx says that "this belonging to God in an 'anti-godly' situation seems to effect our salvation."[117] Ultimately it is communion with God that saves. Schillebeeckx also speaks of Jesus' solidarity with humanity in his living and dying. He writes, "On the cross Jesus shared in the brokenness of our world. This means that God determines in absolute freedom, down the ages, who and how he wills to be in his deepest being, namely a God of men and women, an ally in our suffering and absurdity."[118] He also asserts that "in the dying Jesus God is present, and indeed present as pure positivity, as he was with the living Jesus."[119] Second, Schillebeeckx highlights the significance of Jesus' free acceptance of his death. His detailed study of the New Testament leads him to conclude that "the all-embracing sign of grace . . . is Jesus' love to the point of death: his suffering and dying as a breaking of the life which he entrusts to God, in grief, but with all his heart."[120] Jesus' acceptance of his unjust death gives it a meaning and significance that it would not otherwise have. Third, we have seen that Schillebeeckx places great stress on the resurrection as God's overcoming of the powers of evil. Schillebeeckx's approach to soteriology bears some similarities to the *Christus Victor* theme of patristic theology. He maintains that "through the resurrection of Jesus from the dead he [God] conquers suffering and evil and undoes them."[121] And he observes that the resurrection is "the germ of the establishment of the kingdom of God."[122]

With regard to the question of universal salvation, Schillebeeckx takes an approach that is slightly distinct from the positions of Rahner and Balthasar.[123] Like them, he says that heaven and hell are asymmetrical affirmations of faith. Christian belief in heaven has a definitive quality about it that is not true about the teaching regarding the possibility of eternal loss. There is a heaven because in Jesus God overcomes death for those who anticipate the kingdom of love and freedom in history. The foundation of eternal life is living communion with God. Hell is not the invention of God but of human beings who choose evil. For evildoers the absence of living communion with God is "the foundation of non-eternal life."[124] But we cannot know whether there are in fact people who definitively choose evil. Still, theories that claim that in the end everyone will be saved represent "too cheap a view of mercy and forgiveness" and "they trivialize the drama of the real course of events in the conflict between oppressed and oppressors, between the good and the evil in our human history."[125] Eschewing the scenario that "alongside" heaven there are people in hell suffering eternal torment, Schillebeeckx suggests the possibility that hell means no longer existing at death. As a result of one's evil behavior, there is no ground for eternal life. He proposes the possibility that such people will be annihilated at death and no one will remember them. This is the "limited logic" of evil: "Through its own emptiness and weightlessness the wicked world which was formerly so powerful and evil disappears by its own logic into absolutely nothing, without the blessed having to feel offended by some barracks next to heaven where their former oppressors are tortured for ever."[126]

Schillebeeckx speaks of the life of grace as one of active resistance to evil and furthering the reign of God. Christians are called to live in solidarity with the suffering people of the world. They are summoned to praxis—reflective action that alleviates human suffering and fights against the causes of suffering. This praxis has both mystical and political dimensions; it entails "the harmonizing of a contemplative approach with a concern for liberation."[127] Schillebeeckx argues that for the Christian believer, Jesus' ministry, death, and resurrection "take on a critical and productive, liberating power."[128] They show us that the desire for the *humanum*—the flourishing and wholeness of humankind—"is something which is very close to the heart of God."[129] Schillebeeckx speaks of salvation in Christ as liberation that impacts on all the dimensions of life. Through Christ we are liberated. We are liberated to accept that despite guilt we are accepted by God; to live in this world without despair; to commit ourselves to others; to accept experiences of peace, joy, and communication as fragments of the saving presence of the living God; to join in the struggle for social justice; and to be free for doing good to others.[130]

Reflections

This chapter shows that there are differences—some subtle, others more obvious—among the soteriologies of Rahner, Balthasar, and Schillebeeckx. Indeed, to a certain degree, these thinkers are mutually critical of one another. Balthasar is critical of Rahner for understating the clash between God and sin. He views Rahner's soteriology, with its use of sacramental causality, as too "smooth"; it ignores the drama and conflict entailed in God's saving action in Christ.[131] While (to my knowledge), Schillebeeckx does not explicitly critique Rahner's soteriology, his treatment of the death of Jesus is distinct from that of Rahner. He is wary of conceiving of death as the culminating act of human freedom and of envisioning Jesus' death as a death into resurrection.[132] Both Rahner and Schillebeeckx are critical of the substitution motif that is so central to Balthasar's soteriology.[133] And Schillebeeckx, as we have seen, rejects the notion that Jesus was abandoned by God at Calvary, a theme that Balthasar exploits. Balthasar, on the other hand, asserts that Schillebeeckx's presentation of Jesus' solidarity with the human race entails a weak understanding of solidarity without real ontological effect. Such a view, according to Balthasar, imperils the doctrine of the salvation of the human race in Christ.[134]

In my view, Balthasar's soteriological account is problematic. His intention is clearly to present a God whose saving action integrates justice and mercy and who (in Christ) takes the burden and consequences of sin on God's self. But his portrayal of the Father's relationship to Jesus, particularly the Father's abandonment of the Son, inevitably raises the specter of a punishing God. Balthasar's dramatic account gives the reader the impression that the Father is cruel in the way he relates to the Son.

Schillebeeckx's insistence on the relationship between Jesus' kingdom ministry and his death on the cross is of essential importance. He constantly reminds us that the God revealed by Jesus is the God of life. This image of the God of the kingdom must inform our discussion of God's relation to Jesus' death. Schillebeeckx's account of the resurrection of Jesus, with its focus on the God who acts to overcome evil and suffering, is also compelling. His soteriology would have been enriched, I believe, if he had given greater attention to the theology of the incarnation, through which he would have been able to give more ontological depth to the notion of God's solidarity with humankind in Jesus.

Rahner's use of sacramental causality in depicting God's saving action in Christ does not settle all of the issues, but it is a creative means of accentuating God's loving initiative in the entire drama of salvation, and it represents an enduring contribution to Christian soteriology. It elucidates the Christian belief that God's loving self-communication will have the final word in human history.

CHAPTER 6

Liberationist and Feminist Views of Salvation

n our discussion of the soteriology of Edward Schillebeeckx, we saw that he begins his theological reflection on salvation with human experience of the world. This world, though it is the good gift of an all-good Creator, is marked by what he terms a barbarous excess of evil and suffering. Schillebeeckx is convinced that any worthwhile account of the saving work of Christ must speak to the human search for meaning and liberation in a suffering-filled world.

The theological reflections that we are exploring in this chapter are grounded in this same conviction that the Christian proclamation of salvation must address the stark reality of the suffering that characterizes the lives of billions of people across the globe. These theologians approach the question of salvation from the vantage point of the poor and of women. They strive to understand what it means to confess Jesus as "Savior" or "Redeemer" when people live in situations of injustice, deprivation, and oppression. The emergence of liberationist and feminist theologies during the past fifty years has awakened Christians and people of other religious traditions to the questions and concerns of those who exist on the "underside" of human history, many of whom are treated as "nonpersons" by the powerful of this world. They have focused our attention on people like the little Haitian girl whom I mentioned in the introduction to this book. Liberationist and feminist theologians have illumined the ways in which formulations of the Christian tradition in general, and the tradition of soteriology in particular, have served to legitimize and bolster the oppression of impoverished and other marginalized people.

Because of limitations in space, I will discuss themes in liberationist and feminist soteriologies together in this chapter. A treatment of this length cannot do justice to the wealth and diversity of either of these two theological streams. There are, however, "family resemblances" among these theologies that allow them to be addressed in concert. Many feminist theologians understand their work as an expression of, or at least as related to, liberationist theology.[1] Feminist theologians often express their kinship with liberationist theologians because they point out that most of the poorest people of the world are women, or women with their dependent children.[2] And both of these streams of theology emphasize that the good news of salvation in Christ should make a difference for the lives of people in the here and now—not only in the hereafter. I will discuss major principles and themes in liberationist and feminist soteriologies under three headings: (1) vision and method; (2) critique of the Christian tradition of soteriology; (3) constructive approaches. In order to give representative examples of constructive liberationist and feminist approaches to soteriology, I will explore the thought of Gustavo Gutiérrez and Elizabeth Johnson.

Vision and Method

Liberationist theologians argue that the good news of salvation in Christ must speak to the experience of the poor. And by "poor" they mean primarily the economically poor. They strive to give voice to the experience of poverty by first listening to the voices of impoverished and marginalized people. They emphasize that the situation of massive, oppressive poverty stands in contrast to the reign of God proclaimed by Jesus. Writing from the vantage point of the poor in El Salvador, Jon Sobrino speaks of doing theology from the viewpoint of "the victims of this world."[3] He argues that any statement about Jesus Christ will have something to say about Christ's crucified people; conversely, any statement about the crucified people of the world will shed light on Christ.[4] Liberationist theologians argue that economic poverty is the most fundamental cause of suffering in the world and the most basic form of human suffering. Gustavo Gutiérrez points out that the poor are often idealized by the economically advantaged, labeled as simple people who are content with their lot and close to God. Such idealization is oblivious to the daily, life-and-death struggles of the poor. Gutiérrez attempts to describe the real world of impoverished people, repeatedly emphasizing that economic poverty leads to unjust and premature death.[5] He observes that modern means of communication have heightened everyone's consciousness of the glaring disparity between the rich and the poor across the globe. He says, "The faces of the poor must now be confronted."[6] Moreover, greater insight into the causes of poverty makes us aware that it is not so much a misfortune as it is a consequence of injustice. Gutiérrez asserts, "Christians cannot forego their responsibility to say a prophetic word about unjust economic conditions."[7]

Feminist theologians maintain that the good news of salvation in Christ must speak to the experience of oppressed women, many of whom are economically poor. They give voice to the suffering of women past and present who have been subjugated in male-dominated societies, where sexism is pervasive. Like liberationist theologians, they envision this suffering to be the result of systemic oppression. Feminist thinkers argue that sexism is expressed in both personal attitudes and social structures. The attitude that men are inherently superior to women is labeled "androcentrism." The social structure that is the product of this attitude, and also a factor in perpetuating it, is termed "patriarchy." Feminist theologians believe that much of the Christian tradition has been developed with an androcentric bias. They assert that patriarchal structures permeate the church as well as secular society.

Feminist theologians often appeal to a critical principle that is used as a lens through which to evaluate the Christian tradition and formulate more constructive and freeing theological expression. Rosemary Radford Ruether articulated this principle as such: "The critical principle of feminist theology is the promotion of the full humanity of women. Whatever denies, diminishes or distorts the full humanity of women is, therefore, appraised as not redemptive." Ruether goes on to say that "whatever diminishes or denies the full humanity of women must be presumed not to reflect the divine or an authentic relation to the divine, or to reflect the authentic nature of things, or to be the message and work of an authentic redeemer or a community of redemption."[8] Feminists argue that this principle is not a novelty but is, rather, a retrieval of the classical doctrine of the human being as *imago Dei*, though now extended to women. It is clear that Ruether's formulation of this critical principle pertains directly to theologies of salvation.

Liberationist and feminist theologians envision the work of theology as an involved and engaged enterprise. While they affirm the classical Anselmian description of theology as "faith seeking understanding," they argue that this definition does not go far enough. In their minds, theology is also "faith seeking transformation." Theology has a role in helping to transform unjust relationships and structures. As such, it is an advocacy theology, entailing the work of reflecting on Christian faith and practice in a way that is in solidarity with those who are oppressed. Gutiérrez says that theology "does not stop with reflecting on the world, but rather tries to be part of the process through which the world is transformed."[9] The doing of theology is related to praxis (reflective action), so that the theologian "will be engaged where nations, social classes, people struggle to free themselves from domination and oppression by other nations, classes, and people."[10] Elizabeth Johnson observes that a similar engaged approach to theology is characteristic of Christian feminist theology: "Amid incalculable personal, political and spiritual suffering resulting from women's subordination in theology and practice, Christian feminism labors to bring the community, its symbols and practices, into closer coherence with the reign of God's justice."[11] Johnson points out that the vision that guides feminist theology "is that of a new human community based on the values of mutuality and reciprocity."[12]

These thinkers directly address the presence and effects of sin in the world—personal and social sin. By envisioning the suffering of the poor and marginalized as a consequence of injustice, they place sin, and the need to overcome sin, at the center of their theologies. In his landmark work, *A Theology of Liberation*, Gutiérrez asserts that sin, which he conceives of as a breach of communion with God and one's fellow human beings, is the ultimate cause of poverty, injustice, and oppression. He argues that while the structural causes of poverty must be analyzed and remedied, "behind an unjust structure there is a personal or collective will responsible—a willingness to reject God and neighbor."[13] Thus Christian soteriology must confront the issue of the way in which God overcomes sin through the Christ event. And if Christ is the savior, the salvation that he offers and effects must have something to do with redeeming not just individuals but structures as well. We will see, however, that feminist theologians argue that sin has different contours for women than it does for men.

While there is remarkable diversity among Christian liberationist and feminist theologies, they usually incorporate four methodological moments, or tasks. First, the social situation is analyzed and evaluated. Quite often, tools from the social sciences are employed in this analysis. The goal is to uncover the root causes of oppression. Second, the Christian tradition is read with a critical eye (the "hermeneutic of suspicion") in order to ascertain ways in which operative interpretations of this tradition have contributed to the oppressive situation. (The next section of this chapter will focus on critiques of the tradition of soteriology formulated by liberationist and feminist theologians.) Third, the tradition is studied again to discover elements in it that contribute to the transformation of the oppression that is experienced by women, the poor, and other marginalized people (the hermeneutic of retrieval). Such liberating elements have often been dormant or neglected in mainstream Christian tradition. Finally, this engagement with the social situation and the tradition leads to new, constructive expressions of Christian belief and practice.

Critique of the Christian Tradition of Soteriology

Liberationist and feminist theologians engage in vigorous critique of the ways in which the saving work of Christ has been understood and expressed in Christian tradition. This critique is quite wide ranging; I will simply enumerate some common themes here. First, like Schillebeeckx, those who theologize from the vantage point of the poor and women are critical of soteriologies that ignore or give scant attention to the public ministry of Jesus. They argue that the Christian tradition, as it developed, came to focus on the incarnation and death of Jesus, with occasional attention given to the resurrection. We saw that this was the case in Anselm's theory of satisfaction. Discussions of Jesus as bringer of salvation tended to pass over his proclamation of the reign of God. In the view of these theologians, neglect of Jesus' public ministry leads to a distorted understanding of his saving work and of the nature of the salvation that he offers.

Jon Sobrino is strong on this point. He argues that in the early centuries of the church leading up the christological councils, "Jesus' public life—his story—declined in importance and disappeared, to the extent that everything was reduced to the final event, that he 'suffered and died under Pontius Pilate.'"[14] Sobrino insists that for Christians, God must be understood according to the "key" provided by Jesus' life, "which is none other than the historical project of the *Kingdom of God*, with the specific contents he gave it."[15] It is the story of Jesus, especially his mission of proclaiming God's reign, that gives substance to the Christian meaning of salvation. Jesus' public ministry discloses the liberating character of God's offer of salvation, directed especially to the victims of oppression.

Related to this critique is the observation, offered by many feminist theologians, that the inculturation of the Gospel in the Greco-Roman world resulted in a portrayal of Jesus crafted along the lines of the imperial ruler. The prophetic, liberating Jesus who healed the sick, dined with sinners, told provocative stories, and challenged those in religious and political authority disappeared from view. In a heavily patriarchal culture, Christ took on the image of the absolute king of glory; this imperial model supplanted the prophetic portrait of Jesus found in the gospels. Elizabeth Johnson asserts that "christology in its story, symbol, and doctrine has been assimilated to the patriarchal world view, with the result that its liberating dynamic has been twisted into justification for domination."[16] The result is that "the powerful symbol of the liberating Christ lost its subversive, redemptive significance."[17] Ruether offers similar observations, arguing that in his ministry Jesus focused on the coming reign of God as vindication for the poor and oppressed. This focus was lost when the image of Jesus became "patriarchalized" in the early church.[18]

A second line of critique among liberationist and feminist theologians addresses the symbol of the cross. These theologians maintain that Christian theologizing and preaching about the cross have often served to discourage the oppressed from asserting themselves and, in some cases, have been exploited to legitimize oppression. Christians have repeatedly been exhorted to imitate Christ the Victim, the One who sacrificed himself for others. At times, this version of spirituality has bordered on a cult of suffering. In her study of theologies of the cross, Cynthia Crysdale notes the way in which the spirituality of "a dead Jesus" was preached by European missionaries who accompanied colonizers in Latin America, South Africa, and Asia. Whatever were the true motives of these missionaries, "the cross nevertheless served as an agent of domination."[19] Feminist theologians point out that the spirituality of the cross has often proven dangerous for women, leading them to acquiesce to situations of violence, especially violence at the hands of abusive men. The interpretation of the death of Jesus in sacrificial terms is, therefore, problematic for many feminist theologians. They argue that this construal of redemption entails a sadistic portrait of a god who demands the death of an innocent son, and it reinforces acquiescence and submissiveness among the oppressed.

Some feminist thinkers assert that Christian rhetoric about the cross as sacrifice has directly contributed to violence in society, even to the abuse of children. Rita Nakashima Brock maintains that the idea that Jesus, the one perfect child, is sacrificed for others is based on implicit elements of child abuse. "The punishment earned by us all is inflicted on the one perfect child. Then the father can forgive his wayward creation and love it."[20] The more benign version of this scenario, in which the Father does not punish but only allows the Son to suffer the consequences of evil, is no less problematic. Brock says, "Such doctrines of salvation reflect and support images of benign paternalism, the neglect of children, or, at their worst, child abuse, making such behaviors acceptable as divine behavior—cosmic paternalism, neglect, and child abuse as it were."[21] Elizabeth Schüssler-Fiorenza mounts a similar, sweeping critique against sacrificial interpretations of the death of Jesus. She says, "By ritualizing the suffering and death of Jesus and by calling the powerless in society and church to imitate Jesus' perfect obedience and self-sacrifice, Christian ministry and theology do not interrupt but continue to foster the circle of violence engendered by kyriarchal social and ecclesial structures as well as by cultural and political discourses."[22]

Third, related to this criticism of a sacrificial interpretation of Jesus' death is a reaction against transactional or "payment" construals of redemption. The idea that Christ "paid the debt" for us through his suffering and death is viewed as theologically problematic. Johnson asserts that the interpretation of the death of Jesus as required by

God in repayment for sin "is virtually inseparable from an underlying image of God as an angry, bloodthirsty, violent and sadistic father, reflecting the very worst kind of male behavior."[23] She insists that Jesus' death was an act of violence committed by threatened human beings. Crysdale argues that a transactional notion of redemption, in which Jesus becomes the sacrificial scapegoat who takes on the violence of our sins, "ultimately makes of God a bloodthirsty deity and perpetuates the myth of redemptive violence (on God's part) and redemptive suffering (on our part)."[24] It reinforces the false idea of suffering as the *means* to union with God, rather than suffering as a *consequence* of courageous fidelity to God. Sobrino, again emphasizing the importance of remembering the entire story of Jesus' life and ministry, maintains that a soteriology that focuses on Jesus' death as the redemptive shedding of blood "turns into magic or the arbitrary cruelty of a god."[25] If Jesus' death is envisioned as the outcome of his manner of living and relating to others, it spells love—faithful love to the end. But if the cross is isolated from his ministry and interpreted as a transaction between Jesus and God (the Father), it leads to a magical or even cruel view of redemption.

A fourth area of critique pertains to the notion of sin. We saw above that feminist and liberationist theologians address the reality of sin directly—sin as personal and sin as embedded in social structures. But many of these thinkers contest the traditional understanding of sin, or the root of sin, as pride. Pride and prideful rebellion against God have traditionally been viewed as the root of all sin. The Augustinian tradition about original sin has been particularly influential here. For Augustine, humility was a central virtue of Christian life, a fitting response to the humility of God displayed in the incarnation. But for people who live in oppressive situations, rhetoric about the dangers of pride can be misleading, even damaging. It can discourage healthy, legitimate self-assertion by those who are dominated by other people or oppressed by unjust structures. Feminist theologians have consistently raised this issue, arguing that the "original sin" for women is not pride but self-abnegation, or lack of healthy self-assertion. Johnson says that for women the original sin is "more likely" to be the loss of center, diffuseness of personality, lack of a sense of self leading them to take direction unthinkingly from others.[26] Crysdale points out that Christian rhetoric about sin as pride includes a call to repentance and humility, the antidote to such attitudes. But "for those on the underside of power, who have already been socialized into self-blame, ruminations against pride only reinforce previously existing guilt."[27] Redemption for such people entails the healing of wounds and empowerment to assume responsibility for their lives and confront the sources of their suffering in an energetic manner. Writing from a feminist perspective, Mary Grey cautions against construals of this difference in tendencies to sin strictly along the lines of gender. She asks, "Is there not something bourgeois and middle-class about an analysis of sin that sees dominance and pride as masculine, submission and passivity as feminine?" She proceeds to argue that "there is evidence which we cannot ignore that women in power behave in exactly the same over-assertive, over-ambitious manner as men, even toward other women."[28] Thus, it may well be the case that for women *and* men who exist in conditions of deprivation and oppression, salvation is experienced and lived out more in terms of healing and empowerment and less in terms of humility and self-denial.

A final point of critique I will mention concerns the kind of theological account of Christ's saving work. Liberationist and feminist theologians are critical of soteriologies that purport to develop a comprehensive theory of salvation in Christ. We have already seen that the many metaphors used in the New Testament and patristic descriptions of Christ's saving work gradually developed into theories, especially with Anselm. Crysdale and others argue that Anselm's metaphor of satisfaction was "codified as reality" and understood as literal truth. She believes that this entailed a misinterpretation of Anselm. Moreover, it reduced the narrative and multivalent power of symbols and stories to variations on a single theme.[29] Lisa Sowle Cahill also emphasizes the importance of incorporating a plurality of symbols and images into Christian soteriology, since no single image can exhaust the mystery of salvation in Christ. In her discussion of Anselm, Cahill maintains that "it is important to balance soteriologies that focus on the cross and suffering with those highlighting recapitulation, divinization, inauguration of the reign of God and resurrection."[30] Elizabeth Johnson goes further in this critique. She argues that traditional soteriologies like that of Anselm, and even modern accounts such as that of Rahner, represent "totalizing narratives." This approach to soteriology "subtly utilizes patterns that embrace everything," and it "attempts to interpret all of history, including its disruptions, in an intelligible way."[31] For Johnson and other theologians influenced by postmodernist thought, totalizing narratives do not do justice to the excessive character of historical suffering. They fail to address events (e.g., the Shoah) that cannot be made to fit into any overarching "plan" of God. Thus, as we will see below, Johnson advocates "contingent historical narrative" instead of totalizing approaches that purport to provide a comprehensive theory of the history of salvation. Feminist and liberationist theologians, then, prize the wealth and diversity of metaphors for redemption found in Scripture and the theological tradition. They caution against soteriological theories that seek to offer an all-embracing account of God's saving action in history.

Constructive Approaches

With these critiques of the Christian tradition of soteriology, how do liberationist and feminist theologians proceed in discussing the saving work of God in Christ? Their accounts are quite diverse, with variations related to social location and theological assumptions. Here I will summarize the approaches of two prominent theologians—Gustavo Gutiérrez, a Peruvian liberationist theologian, and Elizabeth Johnson, a feminist theologian from the United States. Their discussions of Christ's saving work incorporate many of the concerns and convictions of liberationist and feminist thinkers.

Gustavo Gutiérrez

As is clear from the quotations in the first section of this chapter, Gutiérrez reflects on the Christian tradition from the vantage point of the economically poor and other marginalized people of the world.[32] He is convinced that the Christian message to such people should be one of salvation as *liberation.* He distinguishes three levels of liberation, which he argues are intertwined with one another.[33] The first level is social and political liberation: the formation of a just economic and political order. This dimension pertains to freeing the poor from oppression. The second level of liberation is the psycho-social dimension, that is, empowering people to assume conscious responsibility for their lives and their destiny. For those inclined to promote their own self-interest with little concern for others, this aspect of liberation entails a movement away from self-preoccupation toward concern for others, especially those in need. For people living under oppression, it entails a movement toward greater self-possession and creative initiative. Gutiérrez identifies the third level as that of liberation from sin, which is the ultimate root of injustice and oppression. He asserts that the three levels of liberation that he has delineated entail "a single, complex process, which finds its deepest sense and its full realization in the saving work of Christ."[34]

In his work *A Theology of Liberation*, Gutiérrez included a chapter on liberation and salvation.[35] He argued there for the need to move from a "quantitative" view of salvation to a "qualitative" understanding of salvation.[36] What he meant by that contrast was a shift away from theological speculation about the salvation of those who do not profess belief in Jesus Christ or allegiance to the church toward consideration of what salvation in Christ means for life in this world and the next. He writes, "Salvation is not something otherworldly, in regard to which the present life is merely a test. Salvation—the communion of men with God and the communion of men among themselves—is something which embraces all human reality, transforms it, and leads to its fullness in Christ."[37] He stresses that history is one—there is no salvation history that is separate from secular history. "Rather there is only one human destiny, irreversibly assumed by Christ the Lord of history."[38] Gutiérrez maintains that "the history of salvation is the very heart of human history."[39] The description of salvation as the communion of human beings with God and one another is a key idea in his soteriology.

Though most liberationist treatments of Jesus take as their starting point the public ministry of Jesus of Nazareth, Gutiérrez blends reflection on the mystery of the incarnation with discussion of the historical Jesus. He emphasizes that Jesus was born into lowliness. He describes the incarnation as "an incarnation into littleness and service in the midst of the overbearing power exercised by the mighty of this world; an irruption that smells of the stable."[40] The humility of the incarnation is further expressed in the fact that Jesus lived in Galilee, an area distant from the center of religious and political power. Gutiérrez observes that "it is from among the poor and despised that the message comes of the universal love that the God of Jesus Christ has for humankind."[41]

In his public ministry, Jesus identifies with the least members of society and discloses to them the God of life. Returning to the theme of communion, Gutiérrez observes that one way that Jesus offered life to people was by bringing women and men—especially those who were marginalized—into communion with God and one another. This happened through his deeds of healing and forgiveness as well as in his table fellowship. Jesus' message and manner of life entailed a "messianic inversion"; he turned things upside down by manifesting a new understanding of power as service rather than domination. Disciples are summoned to reject domination over others and instead imitate the master by harnessing their energies for service to the least of the world.

Gutiérrez offers a subtle, dialectical interpretation of Jesus' proclamation of the reign of God. The reign of God is a kingdom of love and justice that is God's plan for human history. This kingdom is both *gift* and *demand*. It is the gift of a gracious God because it is the result of God's unmerited love for all human beings. But Jesus' proclamation of God's reign includes a call to repentance, which means accepting the demands of the reign of God. Gutiérrez points out that nothing makes more demands on us than the experience of gracious love. Acceptance of the reign of God entails a particular concern for the poor. It means "refusing to accept a world that instigates or tolerates the premature and unjust deaths of the poor."[42] Jesus' proclamation of the kingdom is also characterized by *universality* and *preference*. No one is excluded from either the gift or the demand of the kingdom. At the same time, Jesus' proclamation of the reign of God is marked by preference for the least of the world. Gutiérrez is convinced that the gospel accounts of Jesus' ministry make it clear that the despised of the world are those whom God prefers.

Like Schillebeeckx, Gutiérrez believes that the cross of Jesus should not be isolated and considered apart from his public ministry. He says, "Jesus' death is the consequence of his struggle for justice, his proclamation of the kingdom, and his identification with the poor."[43] Jesus is a victim of an unjust act committed by those in power, though he is not a passive victim because he takes up his cross in radical fidelity to his mission. God identifies with this one who is unjustly executed. The cross of Jesus shows that God is close to all of the crucified of history. Gutiérrez comments on the cry of abandonment from the cross found in the Gospels of Mark and Matthew. He argues that the attribution of the opening lines of Psalm 22 to the dying Jesus implies an experience that included both abandonment and communion. These words "speak of the suffering and loneliness of one who feels abandoned by the hand of God."[44] By making the psalm his own, Jesus "offered to the Father the suffering and abandonment of all humankind."[45] In other words, the death of Jesus was an act of radical solidarity with all humanity. Jesus' solidarity with the suffering of human beings "brought him down to the deepest level of history at the very moment when his life was ending."[46] At the same time, Psalm 22 taken as a whole reflects Jesus' abiding communion with the Father, even in his moment of greatest agony. "He who has been 'abandoned' abandons himself in turn into the hands of the Father."[47] The message of the cross is one of "communion in suffering and in hope, in the abandonment of loneliness and in trusting self-surrender in death as in life."[48]

The raising of the dead Jesus by the Father is the signature act of the God of life. Gutiérrez asserts that liberationist theology "is, in a sense, a theology of life confronted with a reality full of death: physical and cultural death, but also death in the Pauline sense, since sin is also death."[49] The resurrection of Jesus is both confirmation and correction. It is the confirmation of Jesus' mission through which the Father endorses the gift of life that was offered in the ministry of Jesus. It is also correction because it is "the death of death."[50] Here Gutiérrez echoes the *Christus Victor* motif of patristic theology. The raising of Jesus is the sign of God's liberation breaking into the world; it reveals that the God of life is more powerful than the forces of death. Christians are called to bear witness to the resurrection through their commitment to their sisters and brothers, especially by their preferential option for the poor.

From a liberationist perspective, soteriology is closely related to eschatology. Aware that liberationist theology has sometimes been accused of promoting a temporal or political messianism, Gutiérrez offers a nuanced approach. As we saw above, he insists that salvation history and human history are not two separate spheres of history. He points to the gospel testimony about the ways in which Jesus made the reign of God present in his ministry, and he argues that to work to transform the world is a salvific work. Though the liberating action of Christ transcends anything that human beings can accomplish, human acts on behalf of justice are integral to this liberation. In describing the growth of the reign of God, Gutiérrez maintains that "without liberating historical events, there would be no growth of the kingdom." At the same time, "the process of liberation will not have conquered the very roots of oppression and the exploitation of man by man without the coming of the kingdom, which is above all a gift. Moreover, we can say that the historical, political, liberating event *is* the growth of the kingdom and is a salvific event, but it is not *the* coming of the kingdom, not *all* of salvation.[51]

Elizabeth Johnson

Johnson develops her approach to the person and work of Christ from the perspective of women, particularly women who live in situations of oppression.[52] Two key theological assumptions that influence her soteriology are divine self-limitation and divine compassion. Building on the work of thinkers like Jürgen Moltmann, Schillebeeckx, and a variety of feminist theologians, Johnson speaks of a divine self-emptying in creation. The *kenōsis* of which Paul writes in Philippians (2:6-11) to describe the entire Christ event is, in her view, characteristic of God's overall relationship with the world. Conceiving of God as Holy Wisdom (Sophia), she asserts that *kenōsis* "is the pattern of Sophia-God's love always and everywhere operative."[53] This divine self-emptying means that God makes room for creation to be by constricting divine presence and power.[54] God's power to save, then, should not be likened to the domineering power of an absolute monarch. God's respect for human freedom and for the natural laws and the contingency that are at work in an evolving universe preclude a unilateral understanding of divine power.[55] While Johnson affirms that the power of God to effect salvation for a beloved creation will not be defeated in the end, she conceives of divine power as "the liberating power of connectedness that is effective in compassionate love."[56] God empowers people through God's faithful presence to and solidarity with them. The experience of women leads to a conception of divine power as power-with rather than power-over; the power of God is "a sovereign love which empowers."[57]

With regard to divine compassion, Johnson adopts a theological position that is in tension with the classical theology of God. According to the classical conception, God cannot suffer in God's self because God is immutable, immune to change. God can be called "compassionate" only in the sense of enlisting God's self on the side of suffering creatures in order to dispel affliction. To speak of God as compassionate in the sense of really suffering-with God's suffering creatures would be to detract from divine transcendence. Johnson respects the concerns that motivate this classical view, but she wants to speak of God's real suffering-with beloved creatures. She argues that the notion of an immutable, impassible God is not meaningful to women. The ability to enter into compassionate solidarity with another, freely to suffer-with another, represents an excellence, not an imperfection, in God. Johnson emphasizes that divine suffering should be conceived as a free, active suffering on God's part, not a suffering that is imposed on God from outside. But, she argues, compassion is a perfection that should be ascribed to God. And she thinks of compassion as a powerful force.

Like Gutiérrez, Johnson integrates discussion of the historical Jesus with reflection on the mystery of the incarnation. She appeals to the notion of solidarity to illumine the meaning and salvific effects of the incarnation. In Jesus, Holy Wisdom has become flesh, has self-emptied to participate in the beauty and tragedy of human history. The incarnation entails "God's plunging into human history and transforming it from within."[58] It discloses the salvific solidarity of God with all human beings, especially with those who suffer. Christian belief in the incarnation assumes that the transcendent God is "capable of personal union with what is not God, the flesh and spirit of humanity."[59] God's personal solidarity with us in Jesus has powerful effects. In the next chapter, we will see that Johnson argues that the incarnation also entails God's salvific solidarity with nonhuman creation.

Like Schillebeeckx and Gutiérrez, Johnson insists that when we speak of the saving work of Christ, we must pay careful attention to the character of his public ministry. She emphasizes that "the whole life of Jesus is important for soteriology. There is no one mathematical point in that life where salvation is given; even while the climax is Jesus' faithful love to the point of death and resurrection, the repair of the world is signaled in his entire life as salvific."[60] She characterizes Jesus' ministry in prophetic terms, interpreting his mission as that of one "sent to announce that God is the God of all-inclusive love who wills the wholeness and humanity of everyone, especially the poor and heavy-burdened. He is sent to gather all the outcast under the wings of their gracious Sophia-God and bring them to shalom."[61] The reign of God that Jesus proclaims and makes present points to that state of affairs in which God's will is done on earth as it is in heaven. And, as Johnson envisions it, the will of God "is nothing less than redemption, the end of sin and suffering and death, the flourishing of all creatures."[62] God's passion for the wholeness of creatures is manifest in Jesus' healings and exorcisms, which lead not simply to spiritual healing but to the relief of bodily suffering. The shalom to which Jesus brings people means life for the whole person. Johnson highlights the inclusivity of Jesus' table fellowship, whereby Jesus reached out to bring those considered distant from God into communion with himself and, in so doing, with God. His table companions included women, who became Jesus' followers, supporters, and first proclaimers of the resurrection. Intrinsic to the salvation that Jesus offered were new possibilities for relationship— relationship characterized not by domination but by friendship and mutuality. Important for Johnson's view of Jesus' saving work is this conviction that Jesus enables and empowers new ways of relating to God and to one another. His way of relating to both the powerful and the marginalized of his day is one reason that Jesus became a threat to the religious and civil leaders.

I noted above that Johnson levels a severe critique at the interpretation of Jesus' death as the payment for sin. She argues that a historical reading of Jesus' ministry shows that his execution was not something he sought or intended in a masochistic desire for victim status. It was rather, the consequence of the kind of ministry he practiced, whereby he was committed to the flourishing of life in solidarity with others.[63] Jesus remained faithful to his mission, even embracing a death that included everything that makes death terrifying: "The friendship and inclusive care of Sophia are rejected as Jesus is violently executed, preeminent in the long line of Sophia's murdered prophets."[64]

In the resurrection of Jesus, God's "pure, beneficent, people-loving Spirit seals him in new unimaginable life as pledge of the future for all the violated and the dead."[65] This transformation in the Spirit releases the presence of Jesus throughout the world. His resurrection is confirmation of Jesus' life: his entire historical existence is redeemed and validated by the God in whom he had trusted. It is also correction, since it reverses the judgment of Jesus' accusers. It shows that, despite the rejection of his ministry, "Jesus' compassionate, liberating words and deeds are the living sacrament of God reestablishing the right order of creation, according to the priority of saving divine compassion for everyone, and especially for the last, the heavy-burdened, and those of no account."[66] The resurrection also discloses that Jesus' death on the cross was "neither passive, useless, nor divinely ordained, but is linked to the ways of Sophia forging justice and peace in an antagonistic world."[67] God did not ordain Jesus' death; his crucifixion was contrary to the divine intentions. But his death was not useless because he was active within it. His death was the supreme expression of his fidelity to God, and his resurrection was an act of God bringing life out of death. So, in some way Jesus' free taking up of his death gives it a meaning it would not otherwise have. In the next chapter, we will see that Johnson asserts that the resurrection of Jesus unleashes hope for the future not just of the human race but of the entire cosmos.

In Johnson's interpretation of the death of Jesus, "soteriology shifts from the model of God as the perpetrator of the disaster of the cross to the model of God as participant in the pain of the world."[68] The crucified Jesus is not the victim whom God sacrifices on the cross but the very presence of God descending into the darkest depths of human pain and suffering. Jesus' death on the cross signifies and effects God's solidarity with suffering people of all times; indeed, it discloses God's solidarity with the entirety of creation, which groans in agony (see Rom 8:18-25). Johnson says, "The cross signifies that God, who is love, whose will stands in contrast to such misery, nevertheless freely plunges into the midst of the pain and tastes its bitterness to the bitter end in order to save."[69] She speaks of the cross as a "parable" that discloses and enacts this divine solidarity with suffering creatures.[70]

We have already seen that Johnson is critical of totalizing accounts of Christ's saving work, opting instead for what she calls contingent historical narrative. Influenced by Schillebeeckx, she focuses on memory, narrative, and solidarity in her approach to soteriology. Christians keep the memory of Jesus' life, ministry, death, and resurrection;

they tell his story. This memory leads believers to active solidarity with people who are suffering. As we have seen, she is convinced that compassionate solidarity is a powerful, indeed an empowering, force. This includes solidarity with both the living and the dead, especially the deceased who have been victims of oppression. She describes the doctrine of the communion of saints as "a symbol of this solidarity that transcends time in a graced connection of witness and care."[71] Keeping the memory of the story of Jesus yields a "concrete release of praxis and hope."[72] The grace of salvation in Christ calls forth human cooperation in the work of salvation, graced human acts that "allow fragments of well-being to gain a foothold amid historical meaninglessness and suffering."[73] Though she is critical of soteriologies that speak of a metaphysical change because of the Christ event, she argues that contingent historical narrative "is not devoid of metaphysical overtones."[74] Johnson says about this narrative: "It reveals a deep structure of being within history whereby life and communion remain possible even in the midst of discontinuity, repression, and suffering because of the God who comes in historical contingency, ineffable but close, bringing forth being."[75]

Reflections

Liberationist and feminist theologians are making an important contribution to the ongoing theological conversation about the saving work of Christ. They remind us that, in its talk about salvation, Christian theology must pay close attention to the real state of the world, especially to the profound suffering of so many of God's children. Like Schillebeeckx, they maintain that theological accounts of the saving work of Christ must speak to the human search for meaning and liberation in a suffering-filled world. These theology streams have heightened our awareness of those who live on the underside of human history and of God's predilection for them. They have made us more aware that theology is not just an intellectual exercise but is directly related to praxis. Amid cultural trends that eschew the notion of sin, liberationist and feminist theologies have been forthright in speaking of the baneful effects of personal and social sin on the lives of people, especially the poor and women. The critiques of the tradition of soteriology offered by these theologians have forced theologians to think more carefully about the ways in which we portray Christ's saving work. In particular, they have challenged theologians to reimagine the symbol of the cross, which has traditionally had a central place in Christian worship, spirituality, and theology. And the appeal to the notions of solidarity and communion by liberationist and feminist theologians has enriched our insight into the mystery of salvation.

In this chapter, I have taken note of the strong critique of the symbol of the cross and, especially, the notion of sacrifice by liberationist and feminist theologians. Their criticism is salutary. It is undoubtedly true that the interpretation of Christ's death as sacrificial has at times portrayed God as a bloodthirsty deity who demanded and even orchestrated the death of God's Son. It has also been used to inculcate a submissive approach to Christian life, especially among the poor and other marginalized people. At the same time, the prevalence of this theme in the Scriptures, the theology of the early church, and the eucharistic tradition suggests that there is truth in it that needs to be retrieved. Gerald O'Collins argues this point with vigor: "Undoubtedly the language of sacrifice and self-sacrifice has at times been misused massively, but the New Testament witness makes it a normative way of characterizing Christ's death and resurrection."[76] Christ's death can be understood as sacrificial in the sense of his utterly free giving of himself to the very end, even when it meant undergoing an atrocious death. He "took up his cross" not by morbidly seeking death but by his tenacious fidelity to his mission of offering life to people from the God of life. If God was present through Jesus, even present *as* Jesus, then Jesus' complete self-offering signified and effected God's definitive self-communication to the human family. In the self-donation of Jesus, God offered God's self personally and irrevocably to humanity. One can say, then, that this self-gift was costly even to God. The focus here is *life*, not *death*, though sometimes in a world scarred by sin the selfless offering of life elicits lethal opposition. Love is not always sacrificial (in the sense of willingly enduring suffering), but it is always self-communicative. And there are times in which the gift of oneself to another is dangerous. Jesus experienced that in his public ministry and eventually at his arrest. He persevered, however, in giving himself to the God he named "Abba" and to the people he was sent to serve. As Aquinas observed, ultimately it was the supreme human and divine charity in Christ that was saving. In that sense, his death was sacrificial—an utterly free gift of Self for the purpose of communicating the life that God desires for all people.

We have seen that Elizabeth Johnson is critical of totalizing soteriological narratives that attempt to interpret all of history, including the disruptions and senseless violence within history, in an intelligible way. Though enriched by Rahner's thought, she suggests that even his soteriology has such a totalizing character, as it attempts to narrate the "metaphysical change in human historicity" enacted by the Christ event.[77] It seems, however, that one can argue that a metaphysical change in human historicity *did* take place through the life, death, and resurrection of Jesus without presuming to construct a soteriology that "subtly uses patterns that embrace everything."[78] The theologian must distinguish carefully between the *reality* of Christ's saving work and a theological *account* of Christ's saving work. Summarizing a contingent, historical approach to soteriology, Johnson says, "In Jesus the Holy One enters into solidarity with suffering people in order to release hope and bring new life."[79] She also views the cross as signifying that the God of love "freely plunges into the midst of the pain and tastes its bitterness to the bitter end in order to save."[80] We have seen how significant the notion of solidarity—compassionate solidarity—is for feminist theologians and for Johnson in particular. Johnson emphasizes that such compassionate solidarity, in its human and divine expressions, has powerful effects.

If in Jesus, then, God has entered into solidarity with suffering people so as to release hope and bring new life, something objective has taken place within human history. Whether or not one wishes to name that a "metaphysical change" in human historicity, a transformative event of enduring significance has taken place. This is not to deny or ignore the stark reality of evil and suffering that continues to scar human history. And it is not to suggest that any theological description of this salvific reality can provide a comprehensive view that embraces (and thereby domesticates) the many senseless events that have nothing to do with the will of God. Nevertheless, the Christian tradition does affirm that, because of God's self-gift to us in and through Christ, a change has taken place in human historicity, a change effected in the real order by a loving God. Theologians can and should employ a variety of metaphors and theological categories to speak of that change. And they should do so with the awareness that not even the most astute and compelling soteriological account will be adequate to capture the reality of Christ's saving work. Nor will it be able to diagram the perplexing mixture of meaningful and meaningless events that comprise the drama of human history. But Christian soteriology can and should strive to articulate the real, transformative effects of God's saving grace poured out in Jesus Christ.

CHAPTER 7

Christh and the Cosmos

To this point in our study of soteriology we have focused mainly on the saving work of Christ as it relates to humanity—to the individual and humankind. We humans are, however, becoming increasingly aware of our intrinsic connection with the cosmos as a whole. The findings of scientific research about the origins of the universe and of life are making us more conscious of our relationship with the entire universe. Science has enabled us to see that human thought and love "are the flowering in us of deeply cosmic energies, arising out of the very physical dynamism of the cosmos."[1] Concerns about the ecological damage that modern humanity has inflicted on the planet have reinforced our awareness that the survival and flourishing of humanity are intimately linked with the well-being of the earth. In this chapter, then, we will explore the ways in which contemporary theologians think about the relationship between the saving work of Christ and an evolving universe. In what way is salvation in Christ related to the story of the universe?

An Emergent Universe

Scientists are teaching us that it is not only humanity that has a story but also the universe itself—one that continues to unfold. A brief, summary account of the discoveries of astronomers and cosmologists makes that clear.[2] According to current astronomical calculations, the origins of the universe date to about 13.7 billion years ago when, in a unique, barely decipherable moment, an unimaginably

small, hot density of energy went through a period of very rapid infla-
tion, often called "The Big Bang" (or: "The Fantastic Flare"). Scientists note that from the very start, the physical constants and initial
cosmic conditions had to be exactly what they were in order for the
universe to develop in the way it did, especially for life eventually to
appear.[3] Early in the first second of this event, the four fundamental
forces of nature emerged: gravitation, electromagnetism, and the
strong and weak nuclear forces. The nuclei of hydrogen and helium
were formed when protons and neutrons united. After about 400,000
years, these nuclei bonded with electrons to form atoms. As the universe continued to expand, galaxies began to take shape, comprised
originally of large clouds of hydrogen and helium. Stars were formed
through processes of nuclear fusion that took place in pockets of gas
that had collapsed, heated up, and fragmented. These newly formed
stars lit up the universe.[4] Carbon, nitrogen, and oxygen—elements
essential to the later emergence of life—were formed in further nuclear reactions. With the supernova explosions of large stars, heavier
elements were produced and spread throughout the universe, leading
to the formation of additional stars and planets.

Our solar system formed from a great molecular cloud of gas
about 4.6 billion years ago. Earth, a relatively small planet, revolves
around a medium-sized star on the edge of a spiral galaxy, the Milky
Way. Scientists estimate that the Milky Way is one of about 100 to
200 billion galaxies and that it contains more than 100 billion stars.
About a billion years after the formation of our solar system, the
first bacterial cells, lacking nuclei, appeared on earth. Photosyn-
thesis and then respiration developed over a period of hundreds of
millions of years. Primates first appeared 85 million years ago, the
homididae family about 15 million years ago, and the genus *Homo*
about 2 million years ago. Modern humans, descended from various
hominid species, evolved about two hundred thousand years ago. The
universe, of which the human species is a part, is of an age and size
that defies comprehension.

The cosmos, then, is not a static entity that merely provides the
"stage" for the drama of human history. The cosmos itself is a drama,
a dynamic history of which the story of humanity is a part.[5] Thomas
Berry suggests that we live not so much in a cosmos as in a cosmo-
genesis—"a universe ever coming into being through an irreversible

sequence of transformations moving, in the larger arc of its development, from a lesser to a great order of complexity and from a lesser to a great consciousness."[6] Nature itself is historical. And everything in this cosmic drama is interrelated. The scientist and theologian Arthur Peacocke observes that the fact that human beings have iron in their blood is traceable to the supernova explosions that released this element billions of years ago, eventually embedding it into the crust of the earth.[7] Her study of scientific accounts of the origins of the universe and of human life leads Elizabeth Johnson to assert, "We evolved relationally; we exist symbiotically; our existence depends on interaction with the rest of the natural world."[8]

Scientists tell us that the drama of evolution has occurred through the subtle interplay of law (necessity), chance (contingency), and temporality (immense lengths of time). The workings of the laws of nature, including that of natural selection, lend regularity to the emergence of the universe. Nature selects more adaptive organisms to survive and reproduce, and it eliminates those that are less adaptive. Events that are unpredictable, whether at the quantum level, within living species (e.g., genetic mutation), or in the cosmos (e.g., extinction of species through bombardment of the planet by an asteroid) lead to entirely new developments. Genuine novelty emerges in the story of the cosmos. John Haught observes, "Contingency, lawfulness, and time are inseparable aspects of the narrative cosmic matrix in which the drama of life unfolds."[9]

There are great costs involved in this evolutionary process. Struggle, loss, pain (in sentient beings), and death are intrinsic to the emergence of the universe and of life. Sixty-five million years ago, dinosaurs became extinct, probably due to the impact of an asteroid hitting the planet. This extinction paved the way for mammals to diversify and develop. Animals prey on one another for food, leading to adaptive changes in structure and behavior that make survival more likely. As Holmes Rolston expresses it, "The cougar's fang has carved the limbs of the fleet-footed deer, and vice-versa."[10] The death of individuals and of entire species makes space on the earth for other life forms. Reflecting on the omnipresence of death in the history of the cosmos, Johnson exclaims, "How stunning to think that massive death is intrinsic to the process of evolution."[11] Edwards summarizes scientific findings about the costs entailed in evolution:

It has become clear from the evolutionary biology of the past two centuries that competition for resources, predation, death, pain and extinction are built into the evolution of life. They are not simply unfortunate circumstances that sometimes accompany the emergence of a world of beauty and diversity. They were already part of the pattern of life long before the emergence of human beings and cannot be caused by human sin, as many Christians of the past thought. The costs of evolution are intrinsic to the process by which life has come to flourish on earth.[12]

Edwards's remark about the costs of evolution not being caused by human sin touches a nerve for Christian theology. It challenges the picture of a life in paradise before the first sin, in which there was complete harmony in creation and human beings lived without struggle and pain. Edwards and other theologians who dialogue with science envision these costs as a necessary part of the genesis of the cosmos, particularly of the emergence of life and human consciousness. Haught views the struggle and loss intrinsic to the evolutionary process as necessary for the emergent beauty of the universe: "A world devoid of evil and suffering may be a theoretically conceivable alternative to the one we have, but it would have been aesthetically trivial in comparison with the dramatically intense universe that is still coming into being and whose meaning remains obscure until the story is fully told."[13]

Critiques of the Christian Tradition

Christian thinkers who have engaged scientific discoveries about the origin of the cosmos and of life have argued that traditional formulations of doctrine and theology need to be shaped anew in order to account for these discoveries. Pierre Teilhard de Chardin (1881–1955), the influential Jesuit paleontologist and geologist, was among the first to argue that Christian theology needed to address the evolutionary origins of the universe more directly. In an essay written in 1933, he spoke of the need to bring Christology and evolution in line with one another. He lamented that "Christology is still expressed in exactly the same terms as those which, three centuries ago, could satisfy men whose outlook on the cosmos it is now physically impossible for us to accept."[14] Teilhard proposed the idea of Christ as the Omega Point in the evolution of the universe. Teilhard was also critical of Christian teaching about original sin as a particular act that took place at the beginning of human history, out of which arose suffering and death in the world. He argued that moral and physical evil are inevitable byproducts of a developing universe that is moving from a condition of multiplicity and disorganization toward a state of unification. He wrote, "Physical and moral disorder, of one sort or another, must necessarily be produced spontaneously in a system which is developing its organic character, *so long as* the system is incompletely organized."[15]

Thomas Berry (1914–2009), Passionist priest and scholar, was another seminal thinker who challenged Christian theologians to engage "the universe story." He thought that attention to the magnificent story of the emergent universe would lead to a stance of awe, humility, and reverence toward the world. Recounting the comments of astronauts who gazed at the universe from outer space, Berry says that "a new poetic splendor suddenly appeared in their writings."[16] With regard to the story of the earth, Berry was convinced that the destruction of the environment by humankind was the most serious problem we face. In wreaking havoc on the natural world, we are also slowly destroying ourselves. He believed that modern people had lost a sense of their intimacy with the rest of the natural world and the entire cosmos. In so doing, we also miss out on a manifestation of God: "We seem not to hear the divine voice sounding throughout the natural world, or the splendor of the divine revealed in natural phenomena. We seem not to realize the consequences of losing these manifestations of the divine."[17] Berry often quoted the observation of Thomas Aquinas that the diversity of creatures is necessary in order to represent more adequately the goodness of God.[18]

Berry identified four orientations within Christianity, especially Western Christianity, which he called "dark and limited aspects of Christianity that have made our western society prone to act so harshly toward the natural world."[19] The first was the emphasis on the transcendence of God, with the corresponding neglect of Christian belief in the immanence of God to creation. For Berry, this focus on divine transcendence functioned to despiritualize and desacralize the natural world. Second, and directly related to our study, Berry criticized the Christian focus on redemption/salvation. He argued that an excessive emphasis on redemption resulted in a neglect of the doctrine of creation.[20] Third, he argued that the anthropocentrism that has been dominant in Christian thought contrasts the spiritual nature of human beings over against the merely physical nature of the rest of creation. This results in a view of Christian perfection that entails detachment from the natural world. Finally, Berry cited as destructive the Christian expectation (drawn from the book of Revelation) of an infra-historical millennial period of peace and justice to be effected by God. He was convinced that the secular culture of the West had adopted this idea, detached it from its religious moorings, and elevated it to a divine imperative to create this perfect world by means of human genius and the "wonders" of technology. The result has been an exploitation of nature that has had devastating effects.

One does not have to agree with all of the criticisms leveled by Teilhard and Berry, or adopt their theological positions, to recognize that they and other creative thinkers present a salutary challenge to integrate an evolutionary worldview into the understanding and practice of faith. I will draw on the work of theologians who have accepted this challenge in order to explore three theological themes: (1) divine action in the cosmos; (2) the place of Christ and his saving work in an evolving universe; and (3) visions of cosmic fulfillment.

God's Action in Creation

How should we envision the relationship between the creative action of God and the process of evolution? Most theologians appeal to the distinction, which is central to the theology of Thomas Aquinas, between *primary* and *secondary* causality. As primary cause, God is the Giver of *esse*—existence itself. God is the Cause of all causes, the One who confers existence on all things, enabling them to be, to act, and to become.[21] God is God's own existence and is the reason why other beings have existence. For Aquinas, creatures have existence through participation in the fullness of God's existence. Primary causality, then, is causality at the level of the transcendent, operating entirely "above" the network of created, innerworldly causes. But for Aquinas, God—as the transcendent Giver of all existence—is also immanent to creation. God is close to every entity in the universe,

present as the ever-constant source of its being, not only at its com-
ing-to-be but also for as long as it continues in existence. Aquinas
employs the images of fire and the sun in depicting God as the per-
during cause of existence:

> Now since it is God's nature to exist, he it must be who
> properly causes existence in creatures, just as it is fire that
> itself sets other things on fire. And God is causing this effect
> in things not just when they begin to exist, but all the time
> they are maintained in existence, just as the sun is light-
> ing up the atmosphere all the time the atmosphere remains
> lit. During the whole period of a thing's existence, therefore,
> God must be present to it, and present in a way keeping with
> the way in which the thing possesses its existence.[22]

Secondary causality operates at the level of the created, the network of innerworldly relations between things. This is the sphere of
reality that science explores. In his discussion of divine providence,
Aquinas argues that with respect to the execution of providence God
works through intermediaries, that is, through secondary causes.
God acts "from the abundance of divine goodness imparting to creatures also the dignity of causing."[23] Theologians who dialogue with
modern science highlight this traditional theological principle, emphasizing that God continues to create the world through secondary
causes, which include the laws of nature, chance events, and the
processes and regularities of nature that are still unknown to us.[24]
Johnson observes that "God makes the world by empowering it to
make itself."[25] Divine causality is not in competition with secondary
causality; rather "the mystery of the living God acts in and through
the creative acts of finite agents which have genuine causal efficacy
in their own right."[26]

In expounding the action of God as Creator of an evolving universe, many thinkers find Karl Rahner's discussion of creation and
evolution to be illuminative.[27] Rahner proceeds from the assumption
of an evolving universe, that is, "that there is a development which
determines the entire cosmic reality and continues on through it."[28]
He conceives of belief in creation as the transcendental experience
of the origination of all being from absolute being. Everything that
exists bears the stamp of the one primordial ground of being, God.

Like Aquinas, he envisions a uniquely close relationship between God and creation. God is distinct from creation, but God establishes this distinction and in so doing keeps creation with God's self in a unique way.[29] Created, finite beings are subject to the constant "pressure" of divine being. This "pressure," or immanent presence and activity of God, gives creatures the capacity for *active self-transcendence*. This enduring divine activity is not something that could be detected or measured by natural science. It makes possible a *becoming* in creation that is a becoming *more*.

Hydrogen atoms that appeared 13 billion years ago eventually developed into reflective human beings. God's immanent presence within creation makes possible an increase in being that is related to what was there before but not simply accounted for by what was previously existent. God enables creature "A" to surpass itself and become creature "B," though God does not do this as an innerworldly (secondary) cause but as primary Cause who is indescribably close to creation. Drawing on Rahner's argument, and speaking in terms of the Spirit of God, Edwards says that "the Creator Spirit can be understood as enabling the new to emerge from within creation itself, by means of the processes, relationships, and causal connections that can be studied in the natural sciences."[30]

In creating an evolving world, it appears that God limits God's self in order to allow creation to be and to develop. This theme of divine self-limitation, which we noted in the last chapter when discussing Johnson's theology, is prominent in the work of contemporary theologians who dialogue with natural science.[31] God respects the free processes involved in the agency of finite creatures, which include the free decisions of human beings. This makes the history of the cosmos and human history an adventure full of risks. It becomes a history that includes the pain, suffering, and loss within creation referred to above. Johnson argues that divine agency does not determine or dictate all occurrences; rather "divine *kenōsis* opens up space for the genuine integrity of finite systems, allowing chance its truly random appearance."[32] Haught depicts divine wisdom and providence as "an unbounded self-emptying graciousness that grants the world an open space and generous amount of time to become *more*, and in doing so gives it ample opportunity to participate in its own creative self-transformation."[33] He portrays God as "a humble, self-donating liberality that avoids any unmediated manipulation of things."[34] The divine *kenōsis* described by Paul when referring to the incarnation (Phil 2:6-11) is understood to be characteristic of God's interaction with creatures from the origins of the cosmos.

Haught's assertion about God avoiding any unmediated manipulation of things reflects another prominent theological theme in the thought of theologians who engage the work of scientists. They eschew an *interventionist* conception of God's relationship to the world. As primary cause, God does not intervene in creation at the level of secondary, innerworldly causality. God does not intervene to "fill in the gaps" in the chain of innerworldly causes or to replace one of the "links" in that chain. Since God is indescribably close to every creature, holding it in being, God acts from *within* creation in and through finite causes. God works "from inside out" rather than from "outside in." Edwards lays particular stress on this point. He does not want to speak of a divine "intervention" that overturns or bypasses the laws of nature, even with regard to the resurrection of Jesus or the eschatological transformation of the cosmos. He argues that God creates a universe that is transformable from within. He adds, however, that science does not give us a complete picture of the potentialities that are present within creation. Edwards argues that it is possible "to think that the final eschatological transformation of creation, begun in the resurrection, may occur through secondary causes that exist in the natural world but are not mapped, or not mapped well by our scientific theories."[35]

Christ in an Evolving Universe

In the introduction to this study, I mentioned a question posed by John Galvin that is helpful to keep in mind when exploring soteriology: Which aspect of the existence of Jesus Christ is viewed as salvific by a particular author or text? The four main points of reference have traditionally been: the incarnation, Jesus' public ministry, his death, and his resurrection. Throughout this book, we have seen the ways in which various authors have highlighted one or more of these dimensions. Theologians who address the mystery of Christ within an evolutionary view of the world connect all of these aspects of his existence to the well-being and future of the cosmos.

Incarnation

When we explored soteriological themes among theologians of the early church, we saw that some authors emphasized the salvific effects of the incarnation. This view is especially related to the notion of salvation as divinization: in the incarnation God humbled God's self to share in the life of human beings in order that human beings might share in the life of God. The becoming flesh/human of the Son of God was itself transformative of the human situation, even of the cosmos itself. We saw that the reality of the incarnation itself had to be defended by Christian theologians against various forms of dualism—ways of thinking that denigrated matter and the flesh and envisioned salvation as release from the prison of this world. For example, Irenaeus of Lyons, writing against Gnostic interpretations of Christianity, affirmed that the Word truly became flesh (*sarx*; John 1:14) and thus that the material world was the place where God's saving designs were accomplished. The world of matter, of the flesh, was a fitting realm for the Son of God to embrace in the incarnation.

Modern theologians retrieve this fundamental conviction and argue that the reality of the incarnation definitively links God not only with humanity but also with the entire cosmos. In discussing his idea of the universal Christ as the Omega Point of cosmic development, Teilhard argues that the universal Christ could not appear at the end of time if he had not previously entered this world during its development, through the medium of birth, in the form of an element.[36] The notion of "deep incarnation"—a phrase coined by Niels Gregersen—is often adduced here.[37] Gregersen asserts that the term *sarx* in John 1:14 connotes not just human flesh but all that is finite and perishable, the matter that extends throughout the universe. Deep incarnation means "that God became flesh for the purpose of reconciling humanity with God, and of conjoining God and the world so intensely together that there can be a future also for a material world characterized by decomposition, frailty and suffering."[38] Johnson employs this idea to argue that the affirmation that the Word became *sarx* "confers dignity on the whole of earthly reality in its corporal and material dimensions."[39] In the incarnation, God is inextricably connected with matter, with the "stuff" of the cosmos for all time. Thus God's saving action in Christ does not ignore or repudiate the material realm but encompasses it. And matter itself can mediate the presence of God to human beings.

Public Ministry

Our discussion of Jesus' ministry in the second chapter showed that his offer of salvation touched the whole person, spirit and body. The reign of God that he proclaimed and made present entailed the flourishing of creation. God's passion for the wholeness of creatures was evident in Jesus' healing and exorcisms, which led not simply to spiritual healing but to the relief of bodily suffering. His encounter with the leper (Mark 1:40-45 and par.) is emblematic of this dynamic. Stirred in the deepest part of his being by the sight of the leper who approaches him, Jesus does the unthinkable in reaching out to touch him, thereby incurring ritual defilement. He bridges the gap between what human beings view as the holy and unclean. By means of physical touch, he establishes communion with this outcast person and offers him new life by healing his skin disease. Through Jesus' kingdom ministry people in great need—those who have been deprived of life—experience restoration to life.

Contemporary thinkers appeal to the "earthy" character of the ministry of Jesus. They link what he does for the people he encounters with God's concern for the entire cosmos. Johnson points out that as a Jew, Jesus inherited the creation faith of Israel. Therefore his proclamation of the nearness of God's reign assumed that the natural world would be included in this good news.[40] In their encounters with Jesus, suffering people were returned to fuller life in their own finite bodies. Jesus' attention to the bodily, "earthly" needs of people is further disclosed in his feeding of the hungry, his table fellowship with outcasts, and his parables, which were rife with allusions to nature. The ministry of Jesus reveals that "the reign of God embraces all."[41] From an evolutionary perspective, this "all" encompasses the entire planet with all of its ecosystems and, in fact, the entire cosmos.

Death

In the previous chapter, we took notice of the emphasis on solidarity among liberationist and feminist theologians. In particular, Jesus' death by crucifixion is interpreted as the ultimate and enduring act of God's solidarity with all of the suffering of human history. If Jesus is the Word of God incarnate, then God has entered into the darkness and suffering of death; God has known this experience from the inside. This emphasis was particularly evident in the work of Gutiérrez and Johnson.

From an evolutionary perspective, theologians extend this solidarity of God beyond humanity to all creatures. They often appeal to Paul's reflections in Romans 8:18-25 about the "groaning" of all creation: "We know that all creation is groaning in labor pains even until now" (8:22). They link this groaning of creation with the suffering and death that are intrinsic to evolutionary development. The next move is to connect creation's agony with the death of Jesus. While the manner of Jesus' death was not part of an evolutionary process but an unjust act perpetrated by human beings, the fact of his participation in death has ramifications for all of creation.[42] For John Haught, "the cross reveals . . . the unsurpassable beauty of a self-sacrificing God who draws near to creation and embraces the struggles, failure and achievements of the whole drama of life."[43] Taking note of the "cruciform" process of evolution, Ilia Delio speaks of God's closeness to "the violence and atrocities of history, the natural disasters, and the deadly diseases that plague humanity."[44] Johnson affirms that an ecological Christology "interprets the cross, revered as the tree of life, as a sign that divine compassion encompasses the natural world, bearing the cost of new life throughout the endless millennia of dying entailed by evolution."[45] While this affirmation of divine solidarity does not resolve the mystery of suffering within creation, it does make the bold claim that no creature, human or nonhuman, is ever alone in its suffering. God is always present in divine compassion.

Resurrection

Christian affirmation of the resurrection of Jesus has always included an inextricably corporeal dimension. Jesus has been raised up by the Father in all of the dimensions of his personhood. "His human life or total embodied history rose with him and was transfigured into a final mode of existence."[46] As Karl Rahner expressed it, in the risen Jesus "a piece of this world, real to the core" is now with God in glory.[47] Those who proclaimed Jesus as risen from the dead envisioned his destiny as the hope for all. The author of the letter to the Colossians names Christ "the firstborn of creation" (1:15) and "the firstborn from the dead" (1:18). Because he was raised to new life in body and soul, Christ is the crown of God's new creation.

The doctrine of the resurrection of Jesus from the dead entails obvious links with evolutionary thought. The Christian notion of salvation, rooted in the resurrection of Jesus, means the salvation of the cosmos. Ambrose of Milan asserted that "in Christ's resurrection the earth itself arose."[48] Ambrose even suggested that at the end of time all of creation will join human beings in the beatific vision.[49] Denis Edwards observes that Jesus' resurrection points to the final transfiguration of all things that has already begun in Jesus and is at work in the universe. He says, "The resurrection of Jesus is not only the culmination of the life and death of Jesus, but also the inner meaning of creation. The God who creates is the God who raises Jesus from the dead."[50] For Johnson, Jesus' resurrection discloses that "the evolving world of life, in all its endless permutations, will not be left behind but will likewise be transfigured by the resurrecting action of the Creator Spirit."[51] These reflections on the implications of Jesus' resurrection for the cosmos lead us to consider visions of cosmic fulfillment.

Visions of Fulfillment

Theological reflection on the resurrection of Jesus gives rise to the conviction that the evolving universe will not be set aside but will itself be transfigured. This theological affirmation is distinct from scientific scenarios about the future of the universe. Contemporary scientists predict that the universe as we know it will eventually end, though the manner of its ending is debated. One theory posits an end to the expansion of the universe and a giant contraction, leading to a collapse back to an extremely small, dense, and hot state. Another view, favored by many contemporary cosmologists, envisions the endless expansion of the universe, which will result in diminished energy and the inability to support life. Long before the demise of the universe, carbon-based life on earth will become extinct. Scientists predict that in about 5 billion years the sun will run out of hydrogen fuel, swell up and become a red giant, engulfing the orbits of Venus and Mars and burning up planet Earth in the process. In 40 to 50 billion years star formation will end in our galaxy and others.[52]

While engaging the theories of scientists, theological discussion of the transformation of the universe is based on trust in the fidelity of God to creation. It extends what God did in raising Jesus from the dead to the rest of humanity and to the universe. There is mystery here that must be acknowledged at the outset. The Second Vatican Council states in *Gaudium et Spes*, "We know neither the moment of the consummation of the earth and of man nor the way the universe will be transformed" (GS 39). We can briefly explore the discussion of cosmic fulfillment in the work of Karl Rahner and Denis Edwards.

We have seen that Rahner posits an active self-transcendence of creation that is made possible by the presence and pressure of God—"by the power of the absolute fullness of being."[53] Matter becomes *more*; it transcends itself to become spirit. Rahner describes the human being as "the existent in whom the basic tendency of matter to discover itself in spirit through self-transcendence reaches its definitive breakthrough."[54] God is both the origin and the goal of the dynamism of self-transcendence within creation, which in the human person reaches the level of self-consciousness and openness to the infinite. Rahner asserts that the incarnation of the Word of God is the key to the fulfillment of this dynamic movement. Rahner calls Christ "the initial beginning and definitive triumph of the movement of the world's self-transcendence into absolute closeness to the mystery of God."[55] Because of the incarnation, this movement into the mystery of God will ultimately succeed. Speaking in the patristic language of "divinization," Rahner depicts the incarnation as "the necessary and permanent beginning of the divinization of the world as a whole."[56] As the "absolute savior," Christ embodies both the definitive self-communication of God (true divinity) and the complete acceptance of God's self-communication (true humanity). Jesus is the person who fully lived out the acceptance of the grace bestowed on him by God.[57] In Christ, the outpouring of God's grace on the whole world is made irreversible and irrevocable. Reflecting on the ultimate fulfillment of humanity and the universe, Rahner says, "The world receives God, the infinite and ineffable mystery, in such a way that he himself becomes its innermost life."[58]

Edwards draws on Rahner as well as the thought of Eastern patristic theologians like Athanasius of Alexandria and Maximus the Confessor (ca. 580–662). Like Rahner, he appeals to the notion of salvation as divinization. Edwards speaks of the "deifying transformation" of the cosmos. Through the flesh assumed by the Word of God, God communicates divine life to all flesh in principle. God takes humankind and all of creation to God's self.[59] As noted above, Edwards wants to envision this deifying transformation of the universe in a noninterventionist way. This transformation "can be seen as the instantiation of the potentialities that God had placed in the natural world from the beginning, potentialities that have always been directed toward resurrection and new creation."[60] It is a fulfillment that results from an act of God working from within creation rather than intervening from outside of it. Edwards speculates that it may take place through secondary causes in the natural world that are not mapped by scientific theories.

Reflections on the Character of God

The effort of theologians to engage evolution and the universe story is a work in progress. Interpreting traditional doctrines like creation, providence, original sin, salvation, and eschatological fulfillment within an evolutionary perspective remains a distinct challenge for theology. There are a number of issues involved in this discussion; I will mention just one.[61]

This issue involves the perception of the character of God when the act of creation is understood as taking place through the evolutionary process. The costs entailed in evolution, mentioned above, give pause for reflection. The author of the book of Wisdom teaches, "God did not make death, nor does he rejoice in the destruction of the living. For he fashioned all things that they might have being; and the creatures of the world are wholesome, and there is not a destructive drug among them nor any domain of the nether world on earth, for justice is undying" (Wis 1:13-15). Turning to the New Testament, the gospel accounts of Jesus' proclamation of the reign of God vividly portray his ministry of healing and exorcism. In those actions, Jesus revealed the God who was acting to overcome the forces of sickness, suffering, and death. Edward Schillebeeckx's study of the New Testament leads him to speak of God as "Pure Positivity"—the source of life and goodness. All that comes from the "hands" of God is pure, unalloyed goodness. Likewise, Gutiérrez depicts the God of the Bible as the "God of life."

Is there a tension, or even a contrast, between a view of the God who creates by means of evolution and the depiction of God given in the Bible? If so, one theological strategy that might ameliorate this tension has been to speak of nature itself as "fallen" because of original sin. Gerald O'Collins alludes to the presence of this idea in John Milton's *Paradise Lost* (9. 782-4), where Milton speaks of the wound that nature suffered when the first human beings succumbed to the temptations of the serpent and initiated the history of sin.[62] Milton seems to be building on the idea of the cursing of the earth found in Genesis (3:17-19; 6:11-13). In this view, the evil introduced into creation by human sin produces a kind of "cosmic reflex" that leads to the struggle and loss that characterize the development of the universe. As we saw above, many contemporary theologians reject this idea, pointing out that the costs entailed in evolution were part of the cosmos long before the appearance of human beings and were intrinsically necessary to its development. Another theological strategy is to argue that, with regard to human beings, God did not make death *as we experience it*. In other words, it is not dying itself but our experience of death as alienating, as something to be feared, that is the result of sin and the distance from God that comes from sin. This strategy, however, does not resolve the problem of the suffering that usually accompanies human death, nor does it account for the suffering and death of nonhuman creatures.

In his treatment of creation, Thomas Aquinas taught that God's principal purpose in the work of ongoing creation is the common good of the entire universe. This requires that there should be some things that perish. In creating a dynamic universe in which things flourish and then decay, God is willing the good of the universe as a whole.[63] In dialogue with science, both Haught and Edwards argue that loss and death are necessary if God is to bring to fruition a cosmos that attains the level of development and the intensification of beauty that is found in our world. Haught asserts that this loss and suffering are essential to the dramatic character of life and of the cosmos as a whole. Once one appreciates the dramatic character of the universe, and the promised future to which it is heading, the suffering and loss within creation are more understandable.[64] Edwards is similar in saying that death is part of the price paid in a complex world with developed forms of life.[65] At the same time, all of these theologians affirm that God does actively oppose the *moral* evil committed by human beings, through which we inflict harm on one another and on the natural world.

These arguments notwithstanding, there remains some cognitive dissonance in trying to integrate the biblical God, particularly the God revealed in Jesus' life and ministry, with the dynamics of evolution. It is not easy to reconcile the God who, in Jesus, heals the sick in body and spirit with the God whose continuing creation includes massive extinction. Commenting on Jesus' ministry of healing and exorcism, Raymond Brown says, "When Jesus healed the sick or resuscitated the dead, he was breaking the Satanic power that manifested itself in illness and death."[66] Brown's biblical perspective envisions sickness and death as manifestations of the power of evil, rather than simply as natural occurrences that are intrinsic to the dynamics of evolution. Such a view makes it easier to speak of the God of life, or the God of Pure Positivity—the One who wills only life and who is on the move against all the forces that diminish life.

Haught, Edwards, and Johnson do, in fact, envision the God of evolution as the God of life. God's final word will be *life*—unending life for human beings and, in some mysterious way that we cannot imagine, for the cosmos as a whole. But the path to this life includes tremendous loss along the way. Johnson argues that the affliction that characterizes the natural world arises "from below" rather than being imposed from above "by direct divine will." It is a dimension of the free working of evolution, which "brought forth the kind of life that always entails death and, in its later development, pain and suffering."[67] She also underlines Christian belief in the faithful presence of God to all suffering and dying creatures, "an infinitely compassionate presence that accompanies them knowingly in their pain."[68] This enduring presence of God does not solve the problem of suffering but "it does make a supreme difference in what might come next."[69]

It is difficult to assess the assertion made by Haught and Edwards that the universe had to unfold in the way in which it did if it was to reach the level of development that it has attained. Such an assertion makes sense from a scientific point of view. Speaking theologically, however, it seems to limit the "options" available to God in the act of creating. The value of such theological speculation is not clear. How can a theologian know that this was "the only way" God could have created if the abundance of life on earth was eventually to appear? Perhaps one simply reaches the dead end of human thinking and language when facing what has traditionally been labeled "natural" or "physical" evil. Maybe Edwards says it best when he observes that "in any authentically *theological* approach to natural evil, we must stand with the Book of Job (38–42) before the mystery of God and God's creation, and acknowledge that there is a great deal that we do not know."[70] For the Christian, however, the affirmation that the God of Jesus Christ is the God of life—the God who raised Jesus from the dead and who desires the flourishing of life for all creatures—is a core conviction. Reconciling this affirmation with the reality of struggle, suffering, and loss within the evolutionary process remains an ongoing challenge for theology.

CHAPTER 8

Christ as Universal Savior

When Catholics and other Christians stand to recite the Creed of Nicea-Constantinople at the celebration of the Eucharist, they profess, "For us human beings (*di' hēmas tous anthrōpous*) and for our salvation he [One Lord Jesus Christ, the Only Begotten Son of God] came down from heaven, and by the Holy Spirit was incarnate of the Virgin Mary, and became human (*enanthrōpēsanta*)." Among other core faith convictions, these words express Christian belief in the universal significance of the person and saving work of Christ. In this sentence, the expression "for us human beings" has a broader scope than does the "we believe" (*pisteuomen*) that begins the creed. The "we" that initiates the profession of faith refers to the Christian faithful (the *Christifideles*)—those who profess the truths articulated in the creed. But the affirmation that the Son of God became incarnate "for us human beings and for our salvation" refers to all of humankind. It expresses the Christian belief that the life, death, and resurrection of Jesus have decisive significance for the salvation of all people, indeed (as we saw in the last chapter) for the salvation of the entire cosmos.

Christians make this profession of faith, however, in a religiously pluralistic world of which they comprise less than a third of the total population. With widespread access to communication across the world, the ease of global travel, and the burgeoning of immigration in many areas of the world, people of diverse religious traditions encounter one another with much greater frequency than in the past. In the United States—a nominally "Christian" country—the firsthand encounter with religious diversity is an everyday experience. We live, work, recreate, and collaborate in civic activities with people of a variety of religious traditions. In the Roman Catholic graduate school of theology in which I teach, Muslim students are sometimes enrolled in my courses in Christology. They engage the Christian tradition of the person and saving work of Jesus with great attention and respect, even though they do not share all of the beliefs about him that Christians profess.

An added (and very neuralgic) dimension of the context for discussion about the salvific significance of Christ is the ongoing tension that exists between people of different religious traditions. It sometimes seems as if the wars of religion that devastated Europe in the sixteenth and seventeenth centuries have returned to plague our world anew. One only has to recall 9/11 and the ongoing conflicts in Iraq, Afghanistan, Syria, and regions of Africa to recognize that religious fervor and intolerance can easily give rise to deadly violence. Thus the summons to meaningful dialogue between people of differing religious traditions that has been issued from many sides takes on new relevance. In his apostolic letter issued at the turn of the millennium, Pope John Paul II highlighted the importance of interreligious dialogue for the well-being of the world: "In the climate of increased cultural and religious pluralism which is expected to mark the society of the new millennium, it is obvious that this dialogue will be especially important in establishing a sure basis for peace and warding off the dread specter of those wars of religion which have so often bloodied human history. The name of the one God must become increasingly what it is: *a name of peace and a summons to peace.*"[1] Tragic events that have transpired since the publication of this letter serve only to confirm the urgent need to work toward greater understanding and respect between people of diverse religious traditions.

Beginning in the early church, the theological conversation about the universal salvific significance of Christ has been an ongoing one. The context for this conversation has shifted in the light of changing historical and cultural circumstances. For most of the history of the church, the salient issue was that of the possibility of salvation for those who do not believe in Christ or for Christians who are not members (in good standing) of the Catholic Church. Around the time of the Second Vatican Council, when agreement on that issue was settled, the question of the salvific value of other religious traditions came to the fore. Do these religious traditions and practices play a positive role in the salvation of "others"? As the conversation has developed in recent years, a further issue has been raised: Should Christians conceive of the pluralism of religious traditions in the world as positively willed by God, or as merely a *de facto* situation that is tolerated by God? As Jacques Dupuis articulates this third question, Christians now ask whether "the religious traditions have in the eternal plan of God for humankind a positive significance and are for their followers ways, means and channels of salvation willed and devised by God for their followers."[2] In this chapter, I will present a brief historical sketch of this theological conversation across the ages and then discuss the positions of two influential Catholic theologians.

Developments up to 1492

There is a clear missionary thrust in the Christian documents that comprise the New Testament. Matthew concludes his gospel with the commissioning of the eleven disciples by the risen Jesus: "Go, therefore, and make disciples of all nations, baptizing them in the name of the Father, and of the Son, and of the holy Spirit, teaching them to observe all that I have commanded you" (Matt 28:19-20a). When Paul writes to the Christians in Galatia and recounts his life-altering encounter with the risen Jesus, he claims that God was pleased to reveal God's Son to him so that Paul might proclaim Christ to the Gentiles (Gal 1:15-16). Throughout his letters, Paul gives witness to his deep conviction that the good news about the person and saving work of Jesus Christ is meant for all people. The rhetorical questions that he addresses to Christians at Rome evince the sense of urgency that impelled Paul in his apostolic labors: "But how can they call on him in whom they have not believed? And how can they believe in him of whom they have not heard? And how can they hear without someone to preach? And how can people preach unless they are sent?" (Rom 10:14-15).

In his presentation of the apostolic preaching of the early church, Luke depicts Peter as announcing the universal and exclusive role of Jesus in salvation: "There is no salvation through anyone else, nor is there any other name under heaven given to the human race by which we are to be saved" (Acts 4:12). But there are also statements that Luke attributes to apostles that add nuance to this absolute claim.[3] In Peter's speech at the house of Cornelius, after hearing that an angel had inspired Cornelius to send for him, the apostle says, "In truth, I see that God shows no partiality. Rather, in every nation whoever fears him and acts uprightly is acceptable to him" (Acts 10:34-35). Further along in this story, the Spirit descends on Cornelius and his household as Peter is preaching but before they have been baptized (10:46). In Paul's speech at the Areopagus, the apostle expresses his esteem for religious traditions that have existed before and outside of Christ and the Christian message: "You Athenians, I see that in every respect you are very religious. For as I walked around looking carefully at your shrines, I even discovered an altar inscribed, 'To an unknown God.' What therefore you unknowingly worship I proclaim to you" (Acts 17:22-23).[4]

A New Testament text that has played a central role in the theological conversation about Christ as universal savior is First Timothy 2:4-6. This letter, probably written by an author who lived after Paul's death, counsels the Christian community to offer prayers for everyone, especially those who exercise civil authority (1 Tim 2:1-2). The author names God as "our savior who wills everyone to be saved and to come to knowledge of the truth" (2:4). Then, possibly quoting a primitive Christian creed, the author affirms the unique mediatorial role of Christ: "For there is one God. There is also one mediator between God and the human race, Christ Jesus, himself human, who gave himself as a ransom for all" (2:5-6). At the heart of the ongoing discussion about Christ and other religions is the challenge of holding these two beliefs in creative tension: the universal salvific will of God and the unique mediatorial role of Christ.

Early Christian theologians expressed optimism about the possibility of salvation for those who had lived before the Christian era. Writing about Jews who lived before Christ, Justin Martyr asserted that they were able to be saved through obedience to the Mosaic Law. Those who were faithful to the Torah "did those things which are universally, naturally and eternally good" and thus they "are pleasing to God."[5] They will be saved in the resurrection. Francis Sullivan points out that in this statement it appears that Justin extends the possibility of salvation not only to Jews but also to all who did what is "universally, naturally, and eternally good," that is, to those who obeyed the natural law.[6] With regard to Gentiles who lived before Christ, Justin claims that those who lived according to reason (*logos*) were really Christians.[7] They were enlightened by the same Logos who later became incarnate in Christ. Later in this period, Augustine of Hippo responds to a letter from a priest named Deogratias, who wants to know how to answer the question posed by non-Christians as to whether those who lived before Christ had been deprived of saving grace. Augustine answers by saying that Christ, the Word and Son of God, has been present and active in the world from the beginning of time. He maintains that "all those who believed in him and knew him and lived a good and devout life according to his commands, whenever and wherever they lived, undoubtedly were saved by him."[8]

Early Christian theologians were much less optimistic about salvation for Christians who became separated from the church. With regard to these believers, they applied the maxim, "Outside the church no salvation" (*extra ecclesiam nulla salus*). This saying was adduced by a number of Christian theologians writing prior to the fourth century, among them Origen of Alexandria and Cyprian of Carthage.[9] Cyprian, the revered North African bishop and martyr, famously asserted, "You cannot have God for your Father if you have not the church for your mother."[10] It is important to note that these theologians were not addressing this teaching to Jews and to people of Greco-Roman religions, who at the time were still the majority of the population in the Mediterranean world. It was originally aimed at other Christians who were at risk of being separated from the church by excommunication or who had already been separated by heresy or schism. Cyprian conceived of the church as a unity of love. Therefore, anyone who violated this unity was guilty of a sin against charity and, in his mind, could not be saved. This famous teaching, then, was originally directed against dissident Christians; it was an admonition expressed out of pastoral concern for the unity of the church.

After Christianity became the official religion of the empire in the fourth century, however, Christian theologians did begin to address similar warnings to Jews and to followers of Greco-Roman religions. These theologians assume that the Gospel has been proclaimed everywhere and that everyone has had ample opportunity and good reason to accept it.[11] Ambrose of Milan says, "If someone does not believe in Christ he defrauds himself of this universal benefit, just as if someone were to shut out the rays of the sun by closing his window."[12] Augustine also issues a negative judgment on those who do not believe in Christ. As we saw in chapter 3, because Augustine was convinced of the efficacy of God's will, he struggled to interpret the New Testament teaching about God's universal salvific will. He argued that "everyone" (*pantas anthrōpous*) in 1 Timothy 2:4 might refer to "the human race in all its varieties of rank and circumstances," not to every person who ever lived.[13] Or, Augustine suggested, the passage could also be interpreted to mean that no one is saved unless God wills it.[14] But it could not mean literally that God wills all to be saved, because, if God so willed, then all would be saved. Especially in his later writings against the Pelagians, Augustine argued that the condemnation of unbaptized infants and of people who had never heard of Christ was justified because of original sin. He concluded that everyone deserves to be condemned because of the sin of Adam, in which all share. So the fact that anyone at all is saved is due to the undeserved, gracious mercy of God. Writing against the Pelagian Julian of Eclanum, he says, "In those He condemns we see what is due to all, so that those He delivers may thence learn what due penalty was relaxed in their regard and what undue grace was given them."[15]

Fulgentius of Ruspe (468–533), a North African bishop and theological disciple of Augustine, authored a particularly stark expression of the principle *extra ecclesiam nulla salus*. Fulgentius wrote, "Most firmly hold and by no means doubt, that not only all pagans, but also all Jews, and all heretics and schismatics who die outside the Catholic Church, will go to the eternal fire that was prepared for the devil and his angels."[16] This extreme statement was influential because it was later incorporated into a decree issued by the Council of Florence in 1442. This council was called to facilitate reunion between the Roman Church and separated Eastern Christian churches, though it failed in its efforts to restore unity. Among these Eastern churches were Coptic churches in Egypt, whose members were called Jacobites. The council crafted a decree in the form of a profession of faith, to which the Coptic Christians were obliged to give their assent. The first sentence of this profession of faith echoes the statement of Fulgentius quoted above. Further along, it again quotes Fulgentius in asserting, "And no one can be saved, no matter how much he has given in alms, even if he sheds his blood for the name of Christ, unless he remains in the bosom and unity of the Catholic Church.[17]

Why did Christian theologians and the magisterium of the church maintain such a negative judgment about the possibility of salvation for those who were not members of the Catholic Church? Sullivan points out that for Catholic Christians at this time the world was practically identical with Christian Europe.[18] They believed that the Gospel had been proclaimed everywhere and that everyone had been given ample opportunity to hear and respond to it. Christian thinkers were certainly aware of Jews and Muslims. Muslims, however, were viewed as a political and military threat and thus perceived as the enemy. Christian theologians conceived of Jews as guilty of sinful unbelief. As Sullivan puts it, "The medieval mind could not conceive how they [Jewish people] could be innocent in their rejection of Christ, since Christianity seemed to have been so abundantly proved to be the true religion, even by the fact that the great mass of society had accepted it."[19] Limitations in understanding of human psychology led Christian theologians to conclude that those who had heard the message of the Gospel and not accepted it must be guilty of a sinful rejection of divine truth.

From Columbus to Vatican II

Fifty years after the promulgation of the Decree for the Jacobites, Columbus sailed to America. When news of his discoveries reached theologians in Europe, they were confronted with the problem of justifying the belief that no one could be saved outside of the church with the realization that a multitude of peoples who had lived after Christ had never had an opportunity to hear the Gospel. This dilemma impacted upon Christian belief in the absolute goodness of God. As all-good, God could not unjustly condemn anyone. Augustine's notion that the guilty participation of all people in the sin of Adam justified such a condemnation was no longer accepted. So theologians were challenged to address the issue of the possibility of salvation for the many people who had never heard the Gospel. In so doing, they also came to reconsider the assumption that all those who had heard the Gospel and not accepted it were guilty of sin in rejecting the teaching of Christianity.

The Decree on Justification issued by the Council of Trent (1547) taught that the transition from the state of original sin to the state of grace "cannot take place without the bath of regeneration [baptism] or the desire for it (*eius voto*)."[20] In its reference to a desire for baptism, the council echoed the teaching of Thomas Aquinas, who in his *Summa Theologiae* had addressed the situation of a person who explicitly desired baptism but died before receiving it. He said that in such a case "God, whose power is not tied to visible sacraments, sanctifies a person inwardly."[21] Aquinas went further and argued that such a desire need not be explicit. Appealing to the story of Cornelius in Acts 10, he said that the desire could be implicit, presumably expressed through one's faith and charity.[22]

These issues were explored in the sixteenth and seventeenth centuries by Dominican theologians at the University of Salamanca in Spain and by Jesuits at the Roman College. For example, Francisco Suarez (1548–1619) argued for the sufficiency of an implicit faith in Christ, based on a person's faith in God and sincere repentance for sin. He thought that such implicit faith entails an implicit desire for baptism.[23] Juan De Lugo (1583–1660) also upheld the sufficiency of an implicit faith in Christ, but he went further in extending this possibility not only to those who had never heard of Christ but also to those who knew of Christ and did not believe in him or had a faith judged by the church as heterodox. These included Jews and Muslims. De Lugo argued that such people may have "invincible ignorance" of the true faith.[24] He recognized that a person might hear the message of Christ, diligently inquire about it, and yet remain unconvinced of its truth. Such a person would not be guilty of sinful unbelief; his or her ignorance would be invincible and inculpable.

In the nineteenth century, Pope Pius IX issued two statements that echoed this notion of invincible and inculpable ignorance. In an allocution to bishops who had gathered at Rome for the promulgation of the dogma of the Immaculate Conception (1854), the pope repeated the principle that "no one can be saved outside of the apostolic Roman Catholic Church." But he proceeded to affirm that "those who labor in ignorance of the true religion, if that ignorance be invincible, will never be charged with any guilt on this account before the eyes of the Lord."[25]

Nine years later, in a letter addressed to the bishops of Italy, the pope said, "It is known to Us and to you that those who labor in invincible ignorance concerning our most holy religion and who, assiduously observing the natural law and its precepts which God has inscribed in the hearts of all, and being ready to obey God, live an honest and upright life can, through the working of the divine light and grace, attain eternal life."[26] Here the pope teaches that such people (including non-Christians) will be saved not merely by their own efforts but "through the working of divine light and grace." This teaching acknowledges that divine grace is present and operative outside of the realm of explicit Christian faith and church membership.

In the middle of the twentieth century, a controversy arose in the United States because of a strict interpretation of the maxim *extra ecclesiam nulla salus* taught by Leonard Feeney and his followers. Feeney held that only members of the Roman Catholic Church can be saved, the only exception being someone who is preparing to enter the Roman Church but who dies unexpectedly. Feeney went so far as to accuse Archbishop Richard Cushing of Boston of heresy for teaching that non-Catholics could be saved.[27] In a letter to Cushing from the Holy Office (1949), the Vatican responded to the controversy by affirming that no one who knows that the Roman Catholic Church has been divinely established by Christ and who refuses to join will be saved.[28] Nevertheless, it went on to teach that it is not always required that a person be incorporated in reality (*reapse*) as a member of the church, though it is required that one belong to it at least in desire and longing (*voto et desiderio*). This desire need not be explicit. It can be an implicit desire, that is, a desire that "is contained in the good disposition of soul by which a person wants his or her will to be conformed to God's will."[29] This mid-twentieth-century authoritative teaching reveals the development in thinking among theologians and the magisterium that had taken place since the end of the fifteenth century, and it prepared the way for further developments at the Second Vatican Council.

The Teaching of Vatican II

The conviction that the saving grace of God in Christ is present and operative outside of the church was expressed with greater clarity at Vatican II. With regard to the salvation of individual non-Christians, three passages are especially important. In the second chapter of *Lumen Gentium*, the Dogmatic Constitution on the Church, the council taught that all people "are called to belong to the new people of God" (LG 13). It distinguished those who "belong" (*pertinet*) to this new people from those who are "related" (*ordinantur*) to it. Those who belong are all the Catholic faithful and others who believe in Christ. All others are said to be related to the people of God. The constitution enumerates five groups of people who are so related: Jews; Muslims; "those who in shadows and images seek the unknown God"; those who sincerely seek God; and those who without blame on their part have never arrived at an explicit knowledge of God (LG 16). The constitution acknowledges the special connection of the Jewish people with the church, recalling Paul's words about their enduring covenant relationship with God (see Rom 11:17-36). The Abrahamic faith of Muslims is also given special recognition. The mention of "those who in shadows and images seek the unknown God" seems to refer to members of other religious traditions like Hinduism and Buddhism. Here the constitution cites Paul's Areopagus speech in Acts 17. The last two groups include those who do not practice any particular religion. The council envisions all of these people as included in God's plan of salvation and thus as recipients of the offer of grace.[30] Because all are recipients of the offer of grace, all stand in some relation to the church. Since faith is necessary for salvation, God's offer of grace must make possible an act of faith, even if the content of that faith is implicit and rudimentary. In *Ad Gentes Divinitus*, the Decree on the Church's Missionary Activity, the council affirmed that "in ways known to himself God can lead those who, through no fault of their own, are ignorant of the Gospel to that faith without which it is impossible to please him" (AG 7). Here the council cites Hebrews 11:6 ("But without faith it is impossible to please him, for anyone who approaches God must believe that he exists and that he rewards those who seek him")—a verse that Thomas Aquinas interpreted as expressing in kernel form what Christians believe about the existence and providence of God.[31]

In *Gaudium et Spes*, the Pastoral Constitution on the Church in the Modern World, the bishops affirmed the limitless extent of God's gracious activity in the world (GS 22). Pope John Paul II loved this beautiful passage and often made reference to it in his writings. After lauding the gracious self-offering of Christ in his death and meditating on the way in which Christian believers are made partners in his paschal mystery, the constitution teaches, "All this holds true not for Christians only but also for all men [and women] of good will in whose hearts grace is active invisibly." The bishops affirm that the Holy Spirit "offers to all the possibility of being made partners, in a way known to God, in the paschal mystery." Here the council does not speculate about the way in which the Spirit makes this offer; it simply attributes this action to the mysterious saving designs of God. It does acknowledge, however, that the Holy Spirit is present and at work in a salvific way beyond the bounds of the church, even beyond the bounds of Christian belief.

In other conciliar texts, Vatican II began to probe beyond the issue of the salvation of individuals to the question of the value of other religious traditions. These statements were cautious but critically influential for subsequent theological reflection. In *Ad Gentes Divinitus*, the council says that "those elements of truth and grace which are found among peoples" are "a secret presence of God" (AG 9). It teaches that Christian missionary work purifies these positive elements of "evil associations" and restores them to Christ. The decree exhorts Christian missionaries to become familiar with the national and religious traditions of the people to whom they have been sent and to "uncover with gladness those seeds of the Word which lie hidden among them" (AG 11). The notion of "seeds of the Word" is present among early Christian theologians like Justin Martyr and Clement of Alexandria, who argued that the Word of God (the *Logos*) had been sowing seeds of truth and goodness throughout the universe before the Word became incarnate in Jesus.

Of particular significance is *Nostra Aetate*, the relatively brief Declaration on the Relationship of the Church to Non-Christian Religions. This conciliar document, the subject of tumultuous debate during the years of the council,[32] was originally conceived of as focusing on the church's relations with Judaism. Its scope, however, was expanded to include other religious traditions as well. Besides offering a substantial reflection on relations with the Jewish people, it makes specific mention of Hinduism, Buddhism, and Islam. One section in particular has become a fertile text for subsequent theological reflection. While affirming the ongoing duty of Christians to proclaim Christ to the world, the council teaches that the Catholic Church "rejects nothing of what is true and holy" in other religious traditions. The church maintains "a high regard for the manner of life and conduct, the precepts and doctrines which, although differing in many ways from her own teaching, nevertheless often reflect a ray of that truth which enlightens all men [and women]" (NA 2). The declaration proceeds to say that members of the church should collaborate with people of other religious traditions, preserving and promoting the spiritual and moral goods found among them. This conciliar acknowledgment of truth and holiness in other religious traditions—and not merely in people of other religious traditions—was an important advance. The council maintained the view that the truth and holiness found in these traditions finds its fulfillment in Christ and his Gospel. Still, as Richard Gaillardetz and Catherine Clifford observe, in its affirmation of all that is true and holy in other religions "Vatican II marks the commitment of the Catholic Church to live in a religiously pluralist world with an attitude of humility, respect and mutual esteem."[33]

Church Teaching Since Vatican II

In the years since Vatican II, the official teaching of the church about the relationship between the saving work of Christ and other religious traditions has been a back-and-forth affair. One significant influence in this ongoing conversation was the teaching of John Paul II about the presence and action of the Holy Spirit beyond the bounds of the church. In *Dominum et Vivificantem*, his 1986 encyclical on the Holy Spirit, the pope speaks of the universal activity of the Holy Spirit before the time of Christ and today outside of the church.[34] In his 1990 encyclical on mission, *Redemptoris Missio*, writing in reference to the salvation of individual non-Christians, John Paul acknowledges that "today, as in the past, many people do not have an opportunity to know or accept the gospel revelation or to enter the Church." With a reference to *Gaudium et Spes* 22, he goes on to say, "For such people salvation in Christ is accessible by virtue of a grace which, while having a mysterious relationship to the Church, does not make them formally part of the Church but enlightens them in a way which is accommodated to their spiritual and material situation." This grace "comes from Christ" and is "communicated by the Holy Spirit."[35] So for John Paul, the salvific grace of God is always the grace of Christ, though the Spirit makes this grace available to people outside the sphere of Christian faith and practice.

This encyclical is not entirely clear about whether Christians should speak about the saving value of other religious traditions themselves. The pope does affirm that the universal presence and activity of the Spirit affect not only individuals "but also society and history, peoples, cultures and religions."[36] In the context of a discussion about interreligious dialogue, John Paul says that God "does not fail to make himself present in many ways, not only to individuals but also to entire peoples through their spiritual riches, of which their religions are the main and essential expression, even when they contain 'gaps, insufficiencies and errors.'"[37] With regard to the role of other religious traditions in salvation, the pope makes reference to what *Lumen Gentium* said about Mary's role in mediating grace. After including the term "Mediatrix" in a list of titles under which the church invokes Mary, the council had taught that "the unique mediation of the Redeemer does not exclude but rather gives rise to a manifold cooperation which is but a sharing in this one source" (LG 62). John Paul II applies this same principle to the relationship between "Christ's one, universal mediation" and other religious ways. He writes, "Although participated forms of mediation of different kinds and degrees are not excluded, they acquire meaning and value *only* from Christ's own mediation, and they cannot be understood as parallel or complementary to his."[38]

Soon after the publication of this encyclical, the Pontifical Council for Interreligious Dialogue and the Congregation for the Evangelization of Peoples jointly issued an extended reflection on interreligious dialogue titled *Dialogue and Proclamation*. It included a section on a Christian approach to other religious traditions. This reflection said that all who are saved share, though differently, in the same mystery of salvation in Jesus Christ through the Spirit. For non-Christians, this takes place through the invisible action of the Spirit of Christ. It then says, "Concretely, it will be in the sincere practice of what is good in their own religious tradition and by following the dictates of their conscience that the members of other religious traditions respond positively to God's invitation and receive salvation in Christ, even while they do not recognize or acknowledge him as their savior."[39] Thus, while the salvation that these people receive remains "salvation in Christ," their positive response to it is expressed through the practice of what is good in their own religious traditions and by their fidelity to conscience. Jacques Dupuis argues that in this statement "a door seems to be timidly opened" for the recognition on the part of the church of a participated mediation of religious traditions in the salvation of their members.[40]

Dominus Iesus, the declaration issued by the Congregation for the Doctrine of the Faith in 2000, was much more cautious. Crafted in the wake of an investigation into the work of Jacques Dupuis and in light of ongoing discussions about interreligious dialogue with bishops from Asia, the declaration reaffirmed church teaching about the uniqueness and universality of Christ's saving work in the strongest possible way. The congregation acknowledges what is said in *Nostra Aetate* about all that is true and holy in other religions. Nevertheless, it vigorously reaffirms the missionary mandate to proclaim the Gospel of Christ to the world. It opposes the idea that the revelation of God in Jesus Christ is limited, incomplete, or imperfect.[41] Thus it rejects the notion that the revelation of God in Christ is complemented by the revelation found in other religious traditions. The declaration insists that the words and deeds of Jesus are those with the Divine Person of the Word as their subject. Thus they have definitive significance. It also makes a sharp distinction between the inspired writings of the Bible and the sacred writings of other religions, while still noting that such writings often reflect a ray of divine truth.[42] The declaration does cite the passage from *Redemptoris Missio* about "participated mediation." It invites theologians "to explore if and in what way the historical figures and positive elements of these [non-Christian] religions may fall within the divine plan of salvation."[43]

Karl Rahner

In chapter 5, we saw that Karl Rahner developed a theology of grace that made a significant impact on Catholic thought. Rahner sees grace primarily as God's self-communication, God's gift of Self. He argues that, in light of divine revelation, one can conclude that

God's desire to give of God's self is the ultimate reason for creation. Envisioning God's designs in this way, Rahner takes the New Testament affirmation of God's universal salvific will (1 Tim 2:4) to be of binding dogmatic significance. God's self-communication is present in the life of every person, at least as an offer.[44] God draws close to the life of every person. God desires a salvific relationship with every person. For Rahner, this self-communication of God is always made in view of Christ and because of Christ; grace is always "Christic."[45] While Rahner strongly affirms the presence of divine grace at work everywhere in the world, he wants to maintain the centrality of Christ in God's plan of salvation.

Rahner argues that the primary way in which a person accepts the offer of grace is through genuine love of neighbor.[46] For a Christian, this love of neighbor is rooted in and empowered by a living relationship to God through Christ in the Spirit. For a person of another religious tradition, or of no religious tradition, love of neighbor is also a graced way of being. Rahner would say that the source of such grace is Christ, even for those who do not explicitly know of or believe in Christ.

What role does another religious tradition play in this graced way of life? In an essay based on a lecture given in 1961 (before the start of the Second Vatican Council), Rahner presented four theses to inform a Catholic dogmatic approach to other religious traditions. Among them was the affirmation that other traditions contain not only elements of a "natural" knowledge of God but "also supernatural elements arising out of the grace which is given to men as a gratuitous gift on account of Christ."[47] In his later *Foundations of Christian Faith*, Rahner argued that when a person of another religious tradition attains salvation through faith, hope, and love, his or her religion cannot be understood as playing no role, or only a negative role, in this experience of salvation. Such a view would entail "understanding this event of salvation in this person in a completely ahistorical and asocial way."[48] So Rahner would affirm that if a Muslim has accepted God's offer of grace, Muslim tradition and practice must play a positive role in that free acceptance of grace. In a lecture given in 1975 at an international meeting of missiologists, Rahner asserted that for persons of other traditions, revelation and faith occur "*concretely* and *on the whole* only by the mediation of those categorial, institutional, and verbal realities which we know as non-Christian religions."[49] Thus, these religions can serve as mediations of salvific acts. He closes this lecture by affirming that God's grace is manifested in other religions, "making them ways of salvation by which human beings approach God and his Christ."[50]

With his conviction that grace is Christic, Rahner takes up the question of how to speak of Christ's presence in other religions.[51] To address this issue, he turns to the universal presence and activity of the Holy Spirit. Christ is present and active in the lives of non-Christian believers and in other religious traditions in and through the Spirit. From a Trinitarian standpoint, the Spirit is the Spirit who proceeds from the Father and the Son and thus is the Spirit of Christ. Rahner relates the Spirit to Jesus of Nazareth by means of an appeal to final causality. He argues that the incarnation, cross, and resurrection of Jesus are the final cause of God's universal self-communication in and through the Holy Spirit. God's self-communication to all people in the Spirit "is oriented to begin with towards a historical event in which this communication and its acceptance become irreversible despite the fact that they are free, and also become historically tangible in this eschatological triumph."[52] Thus for Rahner the Spirit who is communicated to all people is oriented toward and flows from the saving event that took place in the life, death, and resurrection of Jesus Christ.

Jacques Dupuis

The Belgian Jesuit Jacques Dupuis (1923–2004) built on the work of Rahner, though he sought to give a fuller elaboration of the way in which Christians envision the action of God's grace in other religions and the significance of religious pluralism in God's plan of salvation. His experience of living and teaching in both India and Rome informed his consideration of these questions. In particular, he explored the question whether one can affirm, from a Christian standpoint, that other religious traditions "have in the eternal plan of God for humankind a positive significance and are for their followers ways, means, and channels of salvation willed and devised by God for their followers."[53] The Vatican Congregation for the Doctrine of the Faith investigated his book *Toward a Christian Theology of Religious Pluralism* (1997), and it acknowledged the intention of Dupuis "to

remain within the limits of orthodoxy in his study of questions hith-
erto largely unexplored." The congregation issued an official "notification" meant to clarify the Church's teaching on Christ as universal
savior.[54] Dupuis continued to refine his thought in his later work
Christianity and the Religions (2001) and in a number of essays. He
wanted to affirm Jesus Christ as universal savior and still maintain
the salvific significance of other religious traditions for their followers.

Drawing on Irenaeus and other patristic theologians, Dupuis asserts that God has manifested God's self from the very beginning
of human history through God's Word and Spirit, whom Irenaeus
likened to God's "hands" in the work of creation and redemption.[55]
A pivotal gospel verse for Dupuis is John 1:9, where the Johannine
Prologue reads, "The true light, which enlightens everyone, was
coming into the world." The text proceeds to say that "he was in
the world" and that "to those who did accept him he gave power to
become children of God" (1:10a, 12). Appealing to a number of New
Testament exegetes, especially Xavier Léon-Dufour, Dupuis argues
that this text refers not to the incarnation of the Word in Jesus but
to the illuminating action of the Word before Christ.[56] With Léon-
Dufour, Dupuis maintains that the text also suggests a revealing action of the Word as such after the incarnation. Through this action of
the Logos as such, people are empowered to become children of God.

Dupuis describes the significance of the Christ event (which includes the incarnation, life, death, and resurrection of Jesus) this way:
"God's self-revelation and self-gift to human beings in Jesus Christ is
the center of history and the key for interpreting the entire process of
salvation. Jesus Christ is constitutive of salvation; he is truly the Savior of the world."[57] He affirms that this event "seals a bond of union
between Divinity and humankind that can never be broken, and it
constitutes the privileged channel through which God has chosen to
share the divine life with human beings."[58] The constitutive significance of Jesus for the salvation of all is based on his personal identity
as the Son/Word of God. Dupuis says that through the incarnation
"the Word of God has inserted himself personally, once and for all,
in the human reality and in the history of the world."[59]

While affirming the centrality of the Christ event for the salvation
of the world, Dupuis cites the teaching of the Council of Chalcedon
(451) about the abiding distinction of the divine and human natures

in Christ. The two natures remain distinct in their personal union. Thus the divine nature cannot be reduced to the dimension of the human. "This means that, while the human action of Jesus is truly the action of the Word, the divine action of the Word remains nevertheless distinct from his human action."[60] For Dupuis, this distinct divine action of the Word continues after the incarnation, indeed, after the resurrection of Jesus. He maintains that the activity of the Word "goes beyond the limits which mark the working presence of the humanity of Jesus even in his glorified state, just as the person of the Word goes beyond the human being Jesus Christ."[61] The Christ event does not exhaust the power and scope of the activity of the divine Word. Thus, Dupuis can conclude, "It is possible, therefore, to speak of an enduring enlightening and saving action of the Word of God as such, distinct from his saving activity through the risen existence of Jesus."[62] One dimension of this enduring activity of the Word of God is that the Word sows "seeds" of truth and goodness in the religious traditions.

Dupuis makes a similar argument about the Spirit of God. He appeals to the passage from *Redemptoris Missio* 28 mentioned above about the Spirit's universal presence and activity, affecting peoples, cultures, and religions. He stresses that the Spirit has been universally present before and after the Christ event. While noting that in some places the New Testament refers to the "Spirit of Christ" (e.g., Rom 8:9), Dupuis asks, "Is the action of the Spirit henceforth circumscribed by the action of the risen Christ, and in this sense limited?"[63] He answers this question in the negative, stressing that while we should not separate the Spirit from Christ, neither can the Spirit be reduced to a function of Jesus Christ.

From this analysis, Dupuis concludes that when Vatican II, in its Decree on the Missionary Activity of the Church, says that elements of truth and grace are present in human cultures and religions (AG 9), this is due to the combined action of God's Word and God's Spirit. The action of the Divine Persons impresses saving values on other religious traditions. Dupuis argues that in God's one plan for humanity, salvation reaches people in their concrete lives in three "complementary and convergent ways": (1) through the event of Jesus Christ, which has "lasting actuality and universal efficacy" notwithstanding its historical particularity; (2) through the universal operative presence of the Word of God, "whose action is not restricted by the human existence assumed by him in the mystery of the incarnation"; (3) through the universal action of the Spirit of God, "which is neither limited nor exhausted by its outpouring through the risen and glorified Christ."[64]

In light of this analysis, Dupuis concludes that religious pluralism in the world can be envisioned as willed by God. The plurality of religions is the result of the abundant richness and diversity of God's self-manifestation to humankind. In *Gaudium et Spes* 22, Vatican II taught that the Holy Spirit offers to all people the possibility of being made partners in Christ's paschal mystery. The Spirit does this "in a way known to God." Dupuis asks whether this way known to God "may not be the religions of the world as 'paths' initiated by God in pursuit of human beings."[65]

Reflections

The doctrine of the church develops. Perhaps nowhere is this more limpidly clear than with regard to the topic we have explored in this chapter. The Catholic Church has moved from a stance of pessimism about the possibility of salvation for those who are not members to a position that highlights the universal salvific will of God. Exploration of this issue makes it clear that theological development is always affected by historical and cultural circumstances. The discovery of the Americas catalyzed renewed theological reflection on the possibility of salvation for those who had never heard the Gospel, eventually leading to papal recognition that God's saving grace is present and operative outside of the Christian realm. The encounter with people of other religions in a world grown smaller has led to the church's recognition of truth and grace in their traditions and religious practice. It appears to me that at the heart of this development has been a shift in the image of God: from a view of God as One ready to condemn humanity because of sin to a vision of God as One who is passionate about salvation—whose deepest desire is to give of God's self to every human being and to effect a relationship of life and love.

The work of Jacques Dupuis has been highly influential in this discussion during the past twenty-five years. Dupuis labored to construct a Christian theology of religious pluralism that affirmed the constitutive role of Jesus Christ in God's one economy of salvation while at the same time acknowledging other religious traditions as ways of salvation for their followers, paths that are willed by God. Dupuis's tireless efforts to construct a balanced approach to this issue deserve the greatest respect. At the same time, I find one dimension of his argumentation to be problematic. It is not clear to me how the glorified humanity of the risen Christ could "limit" or "restrict" the revelatory and salvific activity of the Word. In an essay on this topic, Dupuis himself criticizes the work of another theologian (Carlo Molari) for failing to recognize the transformative effects of the resurrection. Dupuis says, "He fails to recognize that, due to the real transformation it has undergone through the mystery of his resurrection and glorification, the human being of Jesus has become 'transhistorical' or 'metahistorical,' and can thus exercise an efficacy that goes beyond the normal limits of time and space."[66] Thus, when Dupuis proposes that the activity of the Word "goes beyond the limits which mark the working presence of the glorified Jesus even in his glorified state," it is difficult to conceive what those limits might be, at least in terms of the extent of his activity. Certainly the humanity of Jesus remains human in its union with the divine Word. But as risen and glorified, its presence is effective everywhere. If the risen Jesus can exercise an efficacy beyond the normal limits of time and space, it seems more theologically appropriate to posit the ongoing revelatory and salvific activity of the Word as taking place through the humanity of the risen Christ. This includes the activity of the Word in the lives of people of other religious traditions and in their traditions themselves. Dupuis rightly insists on distinguishing, but never separating, the divinity and humanity of Christ. I think that the more adequate way in which to do that is to speak of the divine Word acting through the risen humanity of Jesus for the salvation of all people.

There is, I believe, a further reason why it is not helpful "to speak of an enduring enlightening and saving action of the Word of God as such, distinct from his saving activity through the risen existence of Jesus."[67] After the death and resurrection of Jesus, the Word of God is the Word who has suffered. In classical Christology, the unity of the person of Christ makes it legitimate to say that on the cross the Word/Son of God really suffered, though in his human nature and not his divine nature.[68] In a way known only to God, this experience impinges upon the Person of the Word. It makes a difference to God. I believe, then, that it makes better theological sense to affirm that after the death and resurrection of Jesus the saving action of the Word is always the work of the Word who in the human nature united in his person has experienced the depths of human suffering. This conviction makes a significant difference in the way in which we conceive of God's redemptive presence in the lives of people, especially those who suffer the most.

I find Rahner's views on the universal salvific significance of Christ and the presence of Christ in other religions to be coherent and illuminating. He envisions a world of grace in which God's self-communication is present and operative everywhere. This self-communication of God through the Spirit is oriented to the incarnation, through which God gives of Self in a definitive and fully personal way in Jesus. Thus Rahner preserves the constitutive role of Christ in God's saving designs, arguing that grace is oriented to and flows from Christ. Like Dupuis, Rahner acknowledges the presence and activity of the Holy Spirit in other religious traditions and ways, though for him this Spirit is always the Spirit of Christ. He does not suggest that the action of the Spirit would be limited by the humanity of the risen Christ. Because of the presence and activity of the Spirit, these other religions can be acknowledged and affirmed as ways of salvation for their followers. In making this statement, Rahner seems to have anticipated what *Dialogue and Proclamation* said when it taught that it is "in the sincere practice of what is good in their own religious tradition and by following the dictates of their conscience that the members of other religious traditions respond positively to God's invitation and receive salvation in Christ."[69]

CHAPTER 9

Reflections on a Tradition

n this study we have explored the origins and development of the Christian tradition about the saving work of Christ. It has been evident that this tradition is an exceedingly rich one, containing a wealth of images for and perspectives on the mystery of salvation. In this concluding chapter, I will not attempt to formulate a soteriological theory or craft a Christian narrative of salvation. Instead, I will simply enumerate a few critical principles that I believe are essential for any Christian account of salvation. I will also briefly explore one soteriological model that I think is relevant for contemporary Christians and for the world in which we live.

Inherent Diversity

Throughout this exploration of Christian soteriologies, we have taken note of the diversity of images, metaphors, and theories that theologians have employed to depict the saving action of God on behalf of humanity and the cosmos. This diversity is rooted in the Hebrew Scriptures and the New Testament, both of which witness to a pluriformity of ways to talk about what it means to experience salvation from God. In the introduction I cited the observation by Elizabeth Johnson that in telling the story of the crucified and risen Jesus, early Christians utilized financial, legal, cultic, personal, medical, and familial categories.[1] Arland Hultgren grouped the diverse New Testament witness to salvation into four types, two of which he named "theopractic" and the other two "christopractic." In addition, Hultgren identified four points of commonality among these

187

38–47

soteriological perspectives. Edward Schillebeeckx enumerated a lengthy list of concepts that "give us a good idea of the New Testament understanding of what redemption through Christ Jesus is from and what it is for."[2] His exploration of these concepts led him to suggest four "structural elements" that he found present in all of the New Testament theologies of salvation. John Galvin observed that a study of patristic soteriology reveals that theologians of the early church developed "a wide variety of themes and images, each of which contributed something to the overall picture."[3] Michael Slusser attributed this diversity within patristic soteriology to the polyvalence of the biblical testimony to salvation, and he named early Christian soteriology "polyphonic" rather than "eclectic."[4] Commenting on Anselm's theory of satisfaction from a feminist perspective, Lisa Sowle Cahill emphasized the importance of incorporating a plurality of symbols and images into Christian soteriology, since no single image or theory can exhaust the mystery of salvation in Christ. In particular, Cahill argued for the need to balance soteriologies that focus on the cross and suffering with those that highlight other themes, such as recapitulation, divinization, the inauguration of the reign of God, and resurrection.[5]

In chapter 4 I referred to the observation offered by Brian McDermott about "how close the correlation is between the theology of salvation developed in a particular era and the operative theories of human relations, particularly regarding the rupture of relationship and its restoration."[6] The truth of McDermott's insight has, I believe, been borne out in our exploration of the soteriological tradition. When biblical and patristic authors employed the category of ransom to depict Christ's saving work, they were appealing to the knowledge their audiences had of the ransoming of slaves and prisoners of war. Anselm's theory of satisfaction was relevant for a feudal society in which the maintenance of the honor of a superior was viewed as essential for the preservation of the public order. Calvin's theory of penal substitution fit in with the categories of the French criminal justice system. The three-tiered understanding of liberation proposed by Gustavo Gutiérrez resonates with the experience of impoverished peoples across the globe, who know firsthand the ways in which injustice can rupture human relationships and who yearn for liberation from oppressive conditions. The category of mutuality in relationship illuminates the ways in which many feminist theologians interpret the saving effects of Jesus' ministry, death, and resurrection. The mutuality that Jesus embodied and empowered in others serves as an antidote to the rupture in relationships caused by patriarchal systems.

It seems clear, then, that Christian soteriology must continue to encompass a diversity of images and metaphors for salvation, as well as a plurality of narratives that build on these images and metaphors. The experience of salvation from God in Christ is always richer and more encompassing than any particular formulation of this experience. Gerald O'Collins points out that no metaphor for redemption is even minimally adequate to the reality of redemption in Christ.[7] The saving grace of Christ touches every aspect of the human person, every dimension of human existence, and every "corner" of the universe. Thus even the most astute soteriologies will be but partial representations of this grace. At the same time, this soteriological diversity does not entail an unbounded pluralism. The biblical testimony to God's saving work in Christ, though diverse in itself, remains normative for later theologies of salvation. As I observed at the end of chapter 4, difficulties arise when the operative images and theories of human relations on which a soteriology is built obscure, rather than illumine, this biblical testimony to God's saving action. The points of commonality among New Testament soteriologies enumerated by Hultgren and the four structural elements offered by Schillebeeckx, while somewhat general, do serve as helpful touchstones for evaluating the appropriateness of a soteriology. The five principles that I will now discuss are related to the observations of Hultgren and Schillebeeckx; they can, I believe, also shed some light on essential elements in Christian soteriology.

Integrating All of the Aspects of Christ's Existence

Throughout this study, we have made mention of the important question posed by John Galvin about the aspects of Christ's existence—or "moments" in the Jesus story—that authors view as salvific. Christian Eberhart argues that "according to the New Testament, Christ's entire mission and life have salvific value."[8] In expounding the doctrine of recapitulation, Irenaeus of Lyons portrays all the aspects of Christ's existence as integral to his saving work as the New

Adam—from the incarnation to the resurrection. Anselm's theory of satisfaction, on the other hand, focuses on the incarnation and death of Christ, paying scant attention to his public ministry and resurrection. Aquinas rectifies this to some degree, through his treatment of the life and ministry of Jesus in the *Summa Theologiae* and his incorporation of the resurrection of Jesus into his soteriology. Schillebeeckx, whose Christology "from below" does not emphasize the doctrine of the incarnation, strongly insists that the shape and content of Jesus' public ministry should be elucidated in Christian soteriology. Otherwise, the character of God as "Pure Positivity" and as the loving opponent of evil will be missed. Opposing the tendency to glorify the cross and to attribute Jesus' death to the action of God, he argues that the death of Jesus should be interpreted as the consequence of his unwavering commitment to his mission. Like Schillebeeckx, feminist and liberationist theologians criticize the tendency in Christian soteriology to overlook Jesus' proclamation of the reign of God. This omission leads to a distorted depiction of his saving work and of the nature of the salvation he offers. Finally, we saw that theologians who address the mystery of Christ within an evolutionary view of the world connect all four aspects of Christ's existence to the well-being of the cosmos.

It seems clear that Elizabeth Johnson is right when she argues that "the whole life of Jesus is important for soteriology." Johnson asserts that "even while the climax is Jesus' faithful love to the point of death and resurrection, the repair of the world is signaled in his entire life as salvific."[9] Christian belief that in the person of Jesus we encounter the Word made flesh implies the conviction that God has acted to save the human family and the cosmos from within our own experience. Through the incarnation, God has entered into radical solidarity with us. The gospel accounts of the public ministry of Jesus disclose that his mission was to offer salvation from God. This is what his proclamation of the reign of God entailed. In word and deed, and through his encounters with all kinds of people, he made God's loving rule present in their lives. In so doing, he revealed the God of life, the God whose glory is the well-being of beloved daughters and sons. I am convinced that the death of Jesus should be envisioned as the outcome of his fidelity to the mission he received from the God he called "Abba."[10] He did not "come to die" as such. He "came" to offer salvation from God, though the way in which he integrated his death into his mission of service gave it a salvific significance it would not otherwise have had. Gerald O'Collins argues that "Christ's resurrection from the dead was the decisive moment in the drama of human salvation."[11] Whether or not it is the "decisive" moment, it is certainly an integral dimension of God's saving work in Christ. Aquinas was right in supplementing Anselm by incorporating the resurrection into his soteriology. The raising of Jesus from the dead disclosed that the God of life is, in fact, the loving opponent of evil and the proponent of all that is good. Echoing the "victory" motif found in the New Testament and early Christian soteriology, the believer can assert that the final word in the history of the cosmos belongs to this God of life. Christian soteriology, then, must integrate all of the aspects of Christ's existence into its account of his saving work.

The Initiative for Salvation Comes from God

The Christian doctrine of salvation affirms that the entire saving work of Christ originates from a loving God. God's love is the source of the Christ event and of all of the benefits that flow from it. This principle is evident from our survey of the Judeo-Christian tradition. Commenting on the tradition of sacrifice in the Hebrew Scriptures, Christian Eberhart pointed out that sacrifices that atone for sins are means given by God for expiating sin; they are not a human means of appeasing an angry God.[12] The first two points of commonality among New Testament soteriologies identified by Hultgren affirm that redemption is always grounded in the purposes of God and, correlatively, that the saving work of Christ is not depicted in the New Testament as Christ performing an act on behalf of humanity over against God.[13] Anselm's theory of satisfaction, though misconstrued in later preaching as a theology of appeasement, is actually motivated by the conviction that the redemptive work of Christ is grounded in the divine intention to effect salvation for humanity. Peter Abelard, of course, accentuated the conviction that God's love is the source of salvation, a love that is not only revealed in Christ but also communicated to human beings through Christ. Karl Rahner's appeal to sacramental causality as an illuminating category for soteriology is grounded in his insistence that the entire Christ event has its origin in the loving initiative of God. This is the God who "is possessed from the beginning of gratuitous mercy and, despite the world's sin, shares himself with the world, so overcoming its sin."[14]

We have encountered moments in the tradition that obscure this fundamental soteriological principle. Frances Young pointed out that some of the sermons of John Chrysostom speak of Christ's death as a sacrifice that had the power to propitiate the Father.[15] O'Collins notes two passages in Aquinas's *Summa Theologiae* wherein he uses the language of appeasement in describing the effects of Christ's death. While these passages are not representative of Aquinas's soteriology as a whole, O'Collins suggests that they did open the way to a view of Christ as the penal substitute propitiating the divine anger.[16] And in its statement on the Mass as sacrifice, the Council of Trent blended the language of sacrifice, propitiation, and appeasement to refer to Christ's redemptive act and to the celebration of the Eucharist. Such language is problematic because it connotes the idea of Christ performing an act of reparation *over against* God on behalf of humanity. It can obscure the gracious initiative of God in the work of salvation.

Those who propose a soteriology of penal substitution also attempt to ground the saving work of Christ in the love of God. John Calvin argues that, even though sinners are subject to the wrath of God, God "still finds something in us which in kindness he can love."[17] Christ undergoes the punishment of sin as God's chosen substitute for sinners. Similarly, Hans Urs von Balthasar maintains that Jesus, the Word made flesh, takes our place in bearing the consequences of sin and thus atones for the sin of the world. In Jesus' passion, the Father hands over the Son and unleashes upon the Son the divine wrath against sin. Balthasar insists that the entire redemptive process has its origin in God's merciful love.[18] Despite these claims, however, it appears that soteriologies of penal substitution obscure, rather than illumine, the loving initiative of God in salvation. The notion that Jesus (the Word/Son) absorbed the divine wrath so that this wrath would not be unleashed on humanity conveys the idea of a punishing God. The New Testament and the best of the Christian theological tradition emphasize that God was in Christ reconciling the world to God's self (2 Cor 5:19). It is not God who is reconciled to humanity but humanity that is reconciled to God through God's gracious action.

It is our resistance to God that must be changed.[19] Theories of penal substitution can easily convey the opposite impression.

The initiative of God in the saving work of Christ does not make human beings passive spectators in the process of salvation. Gisbert Greshake and Walter Kasper pointed out that Anselm's soteriology preserves the importance of human freedom in the order of salvation. As Kasper put it, God's righteousness in the covenant opens up a living space for humanity where human beings can be not only recipients of divine goodness but also God's free partner.[20] Here the fundamental principle often articulated by Rahner applies: dependence on God and human freedom vary in direct, not in inverse, proportion. Thus God's saving grace in Christ engages human freedom; rather than annulling our freedom, it frees our freedom. Or, as feminist theologians like to say, God's power to save is a power-with rather than a power-over; it is an empowering force. Thus the saving work of Christ—while motivated and fueled by God's passionate love for humanity—is a reality in which human beings participate in freedom.

Salvation *of* the World

The Christian conception of salvation is a comprehensive one, embracing the corporeal, spiritual, individual, communal, structural, and cosmic dimensions of reality. This has been clear in our survey of the tradition. Our brief exploration of the psalms in chapter 1 revealed the many references to personal and corporate salvation in individual and communal laments and in psalms of thanksgiving. The exodus tradition in the Hebrew Scriptures reflects a communal experience and interpretation of salvation; it is the whole people of God who are liberated and called to live in covenant relationship with God. The gospel accounts of Jesus' ministry show that the presence of the reign of God in him affects the whole person. For Jesus "the liberating power of the rule of God concerns the body as well as the soul."[21] Irenaeus of Lyons and Augustine of Hippo, among other theologians of the early church, upheld Christian belief in the intrinsic goodness and salvation of the world against a variety of forms of dualism. In their defense of belief in the incarnation, they argued that the world of flesh and spirit was the fitting realm for the Word of God to embrace in becoming human. In his construal of salvation as liberation,

Gustavo Gutiérrez proposed a three-tiered view of liberation that integrates the personal, communal, and the structural. In his words, "Salvation—the communion of men with God and the communion of men among themselves—is something which embraces all human reality, transforms it, and leads to its fullness in Christ."[22]

Our exploration of the contemporary theological dialogue with science in chapter 7 manifested the critical importance of Christian belief in the future of creation. The cosmos is a drama, a dynamic history of which humanity is a part. Everything in this cosmic drama is interrelated. Johnson summarizes this insight when she observes that we evolved relationally and exist symbiotically; our existence depends on interaction with the rest of the natural world.[23] Thus human salvation and the salvation of the entire cosmos are intrinsically connected. We saw that theologians who dialogue with contemporary science interpret the incarnation, public ministry, death, and resurrection of Jesus in ways that link his work, and God's presence in him, not only with humanity but also with the entire cosmos. For example, the notion of "deep incarnation" bonds God not merely with human flesh but with matter for all time. The death of Jesus represents the solidarity of God with the "groaning" of all of creation. These thinkers proceed to argue that the resurrection of Jesus points to the final transfiguration of the entire cosmos, what Denis Edwards names the "deifying transformation" of the cosmos.[24] Thus, the fundamental Christian conviction that the redemptive work of Christ extends to all of creation assumes special importance in light of the contemporary dialogue between theology and science.

Facing the Reality of Evil and Sin

As we saw in the introduction to this study, the Christian tradition of soteriology assumes that humanity and the rest of the world need to be saved *from* hostile powers and destructive ways of relating that are contrary to the will of God. Thus in imaging and conceptualizing Christ's saving work, Christian theology confronts the reality of evil, especially moral evil, perpetrated by human beings, which causes suffering for other human beings and creation itself. Schillebeeckx listed "victory over alienating powers" as one of the soteriological concepts found in the New Testament. This "victory" theme was further developed by early Christian theologians, who depicted Christ as God's champion confronting the enemies of the human race (including sin, death, the devil, and ignorance) and winning the palm of victory. This same commitment to address the power of evil is evident in Anselm's argument, when he asserts that God's saving work in Christ must integrate the demands of justice and mercy. For Anselm, sin (moral evil committed culpably), disturbs the order of creation, and this order must be restored. Commenting on Anselm, O'Collins argued that "God cannot treat an evil past and the lasting damage done by sin as if they were not there."[25] Balthasar, too, argued that the full demands of divine justice must be taken into account in Christian soteriology, though his manner of accounting for this is problematic. Liberationist and feminist theologies accentuate the terrible harm that results from injustice in the world, and they highlight the need for the restoration of justice in the divine work of salvation.

Christian soteriology, then, must address the reality of what Schillebeeckx calls the "barbarous excess" of evil and suffering in human history and in our contemporary world. In this endeavor, the place for narrative proposed by Schillebeeckx, Johnson, and others comes into play. Theologians need to listen to real-life stories of suffering, especially the stories of those who live on the "underside" of the world, if they are to articulate what Christ saves us *from* and what Christ saves us *for*. Balthasar is right in asserting that salvation in Christ has a "theodramatic" character. There is an "overcoming" dimension (a theme we also saw in Schillebeeckx) to Christ's saving work that is essential to the tradition. God, in Christ, acts to overcome all that stands in opposition to God's saving, life-giving grace, including the many obstacles to this grace that each of us erects in our own lives. This is why biblical and patristic writers often employ "battle" language in their soteriologies.

As we saw in chapter 7, it is especially challenging to deal theologically with the reality of what in the tradition has been called "natural" or "physical" evil. The costs entailed in the process of evolution are high, and they include the experience of struggle, pain, and death faced by all creatures. One of the "enemies" of the human race that patristic theologians saw Christ conquering was "death." In a hymnic tribute to the saving work of Christ, Paul of Tarsus proclaimed that "the last enemy to be destroyed [by Christ] is death"

(1 Cor 15:26). And yet the death of individual creatures and of entire species appears to be intrinsically necessary for the evolutionary development of the universe. We saw that contemporary theologians like Haught, Edwards, and Johnson deal with natural evil by connecting the "groaning" of creation with the death of Jesus. They interpret the cross "as a sign that divine compassion encompasses the natural world, bearing the cost of new life throughout the endless millennia of dying entailed by evolution."[26] And they argue that the resurrection of Jesus signals the eventual transfiguration of the entire cosmos. From this perspective, God's overcoming of the loss and death entailed in evolution is a process that spans the length of cosmic history. Language about "overcoming" the suffering and death that have been intrinsic to God's creative activity (by means of the evolutionary process) is paradoxical. Perhaps the terminology of "overcoming" does not apply to natural evil; language that is more "developmental" may be needed. As Edwards observes, with regard to the place of natural evil in creation and redemption, "there is a great deal that we do not know."[27]

Salvation in Christ and the Human Search for Meaning and Liberation

In the introduction, I said that soteriology is more than just a theoretical discipline. It is inextricably connected with the human quest for well-being and must always be related to the struggles of ordinary people throughout the world, particularly those who suffer the most. Schillebeeckx accentuated this principle in his theology as he endeavored to formulate a soteriology within the matrix of the human search for meaning and liberation. He suggested that Christian talk about salvation only makes sense if people have fragmentary experiences of salvation in their lives here and now, and he described a number of dimensions of that experience of salvation in life.[28] Liberationist and feminist theologians also insist on connecting talk about salvation from God with the concerns of those who exist on the "underside" of human history. Jon Sobrino makes this connection when he asserts that any statement about Jesus Christ will have something to say about Christ's crucified people, and any statement about the crucified people of the world will shed light on Christ.[29] Gutiérrez argues that theology is not just an activity of reflecting on the world; it also attempts to be part of the process of the transformation of the world.[30] Rosemary Radford Ruether defines the critical principle of feminist theology as the promotion of the full humanity of women; its corollary is that whatever denies, diminishes, or distorts women's full humanity "is, therefore, appraised as not redemptive."[31]

It seems clear, then, that an essential characteristic of Christian soteriology is its intrinsic connection with praxis on behalf of the well-being of others, especially the most vulnerable people of our world. While soteriology is a theological discipline and not a pastoral or political program, its content emerges from and flows back into the experience of salvation from God in Christ. Thus talk about how God redeems the world and what the benefits of this redemptive action are should be related to a commitment to make this salvation present (at least in a "fragmentary" way) for people in real life. This is the sacramental dimension of soteriology. Salvation remains grace, an unmerited gift from God, the fullness of which will only be experienced with the complete realization of the reign of God. Nevertheless, as Gutiérrez suggests, salvation in Christ is not only gift but also demand. Salvation is a participatory reality that engages human freedom and initiative. In an increasingly secularized world, where "salvation talk" sounds odd to many people, the Christian proclamation of salvation in Christ will be credible only if Christians manifest a courageous commitment to the flourishing of every human being and of creation itself. In other words, Christian believers should be recognized as people who engage in "salvific" activity on behalf of others. Christian soteriology must continue to highlight this intrinsic connection between the experience and proclamation of salvation and the human quest for meaning and for liberation from all that deprives people of life.

A Contemporary Soteriological Model: Communion

Throughout this study, the theme of *communion* and its theological "cousin," *solidarity*, has surfaced again and again. Exploring the foundational notion of covenant in the Hebrew Scriptures, we saw that salvation for Israel meant living in communion with the living God. Abraham Heschel stated it succinctly: the foundation of the community of Israel was "coexistence with God."[32] In their analysis of sacrifice in ancient Israel, Eberhart and Bernhard Anderson also adduced the theme of communion. Sacrifice in general was a means of drawing near to God; atonement sacrifices represented ways of "healing the breach of the covenant relationship and reuniting the people in communion with God."[33] One of the key New Testament concepts of salvation identified by Schillebeeckx was, "being redeemed for community." New Testament authors emphasize that communion with Christ also entails communion with other believers (e.g., 1 Cor 10:16-17). Our study of soteriologies in the early church revealed that the idea of salvation as communion with God was central to the themes of recapitulation and divinization. Because in Christ the Word of God entered into communion with humanity, he was able to restore the communion between humanity and God that had been ruptured by sin. A key assumption in the argument of Anselm is that humanity was created to live in communion with God, a vocation the fulfillment of which was imperiled by sin.

Karl Rahner argued that, in its essence, salvation is "the strictly supernatural and direct presence of God in himself afforded by grace."[34] Balthasar's meditations on the mystery of Holy Saturday moved him to envision Christ's descent to the dead as an act of solidarity undertaken by the crucified One: "the sinner who wants to be 'damned' apart from God, finds God again in his loneliness, but God in the absolute weakness of love who unfathomably in the period of nontime enters into solidarity with those damning themselves."[35] Schillebeeckx repeatedly speaks of communion and solidarity in his soteriology, interpreting what happened on Calvary as an experience of communion between Jesus and God. He argues that Jesus' "belonging to God in an 'anti-godly' situation seems to effect our salvation."[36] Gutiérrez conceives of salvation as the communion of human beings with God and the communion of human beings with one another. Sin is a breach of that communion. And, like Schillebeeckx, Gutiérrez says that the message of the cross is one of "communion in suffering and in hope, in the abandonment of loneliness and in trusting self-surrender in death as in life."[37] Johnson argued that Jesus' death on the cross signifies and effects God's solidarity with suffering people and with a "groaning" creation. She asserts that the memory of Jesus' ministry, death, and resurrection impels Christians to active solidarity with people who are suffering.

The theme of communion was pivotal for the Second Vatican Council, especially in its teaching on the nature and mission of the church. In the first chapter of *Lumen Gentium*, the Dogmatic Constitution on the Church, the council describes the church as "in the nature of a sacrament—a sign and instrument, that is, of communion with God and of unity among all men" (LG 1). This same constitution acknowledges that God has willed to make human beings holy "not as individuals without any bond or link between them, but rather to make them into a people who might acknowledge him and serve him in holiness." It affirms that the church has been established by Christ as "a communion of life, love and truth" (LG 9). *Gaudium et Spes*, the Pastoral Constitution on the Church in the Modern World, envisions "a certain parallel" between the union existing among the Persons of the Trinity and the union of the daughters and sons of God. Created in the image and likeness of the Triune God, a human being "can fully discover his true self only in a sincere giving of himself" (GS 24). This pastoral constitution affirms that the risen Christ, through the gift of the Spirit, established a new communion among the members of his body, a bond that gives rise to mutual service and solidarity (GS 32). Rooted in this teaching of the council, John Paul II offered an incisive observation on the eve of the new millennium: "To make the church the home and school of communion: that is the challenge facing us in the new millennium" (*Novo Millennio Ineunte*, 43).

The Orthodox theologian John Zizioulas and the Catholic thinker Timothy Radcliffe offer compelling reflections on the theme of communion. For Zizioulas, there is an intrinsic connection between *being*, *person*, and *communion*. What it means to be a (divine or human) "person" is inextricably linked with communion. The processions of the Divine Persons within the Trinity—the begetting of the Son and the bringing forth of the Spirit—are expressive of "the ecstatic character of God" whose being "is identical with an act of communion."[38] Zizioulas argues that without the concept of communion it would not be possible to speak of the being of God: God is a personal communion of life and love.[39] The Triune God is the revelation of true personhood because in God, being and communion coincide. This is what authentic personhood entails. In his words, "there is no true being without communion" and true being is personal.[40] Adducing the patristic theme of salvation as divinization, Zizioulas argues that divinization means a participation in God's personal existence. "The goal of salvation is that the personal life which is realized in God should also be realized on the level of human existence."[41] He asserts that "the person cannot exist without communion."[42] The gift of the Holy Spirit, who is the Giver of life, "opens up our existence to become relational."[43] The celebration of the Eucharist "incarnates and realizes our communion within the very life and communion of the Trinity, in a way that preserves the eschatological character of truth while making it an integral part of history."[44] In the Eucharist, Christians celebrate and enact the reality of salvation as communion with God and with others.

Radcliffe reflects on the concept of communion against the backdrop of the polarization that he views as a pervasive and destructive force in the church and in wider society. This polarization is evident in the ways in which people talk to and about one another. He points out that human unity is founded on our ability to talk to one another; language is a breakthrough into a new kind of communion.[45] Radcliffe asserts that "our human vocation is to go on searching for new and deeper ways of belonging together, new ways of speaking, which realize our capacity for communion more profoundly."[46] Reflecting on the passion of Jesus, he asserts that Jesus "bore in his body all the violence that human beings turn against one another, all the breakdown of communication, all the hatred we have ever had for each other."[47] The resurrection of Jesus inaugurates the victory of communion over all that separates us from one another. Christians remember and proclaim this truth every time they celebrate the Eucharist, which is the sacrament of pure communion in Christ. Radcliffe says, "There is no universal language of pure communion except Christ, and we do not yet know fully how to speak the Word that he is."[48] He insists that human beings "are called to a communion in which we can share all that we are, indeed become all that we are meant to be."[49]

From a Christian perspective, the call to live in communion with God and others pertains to the life of every person. Communion is made possible and realized through ever-deepening expressions of solidarity with others. Authentic communion embraces difference, grounded as it is in mutual respect and active concern for the well-being of the other. One can envision the saving work of Jesus in terms of the restoration of the possibility of communion. Through his solidarity with humanity in his life and death, he overcame the obstacles to communion between human beings and God and among human beings. This was evident in his earthly ministry to those who were on the margins of society, like the leper who came to him pleading for healing, and the sinners and tax collectors with whom he shared table fellowship. Jesus lived in intimate communion with the God he addressed as "Abba," even through the darkness of Gethsemane and Calvary. The Christian can confess that Jesus' solidarity with us into the very depths of death, and his continuing to belong to God in the anti-godly event of his crucifixion, had transformative effects for human history and for creation itself. Radcliffe is right in naming the resurrection of Jesus the "victory of communion" over all that separates us from God and one another. The grace that God offers humanity through the crucified and risen Christ is the grace of communion—the gift of an intimate, life-giving relationship with God and the gift and call of creating ever-stronger communion within the church and among all people.

The Little Girl in the Pink Dress

I began this book by recalling an encounter with a little Haitian girl who lives in Cité du Soleil—a meeting marked by smiles but devoid of words. I asked what salvation might mean for her as she struggles to survive life in one of the worst slums in one of the poorest countries in the world. When faced with the plight of this child, and of the millions of children who exist in similar situations, the Christian must avoid triumphalistic rhetoric about salvation. Though we believe that the reign of God has been inaugurated through the ministry, death, and resurrection of Jesus, the world order that human beings have manufactured is a far cry from the realization of God's reign.

But perhaps the model of salvation as communion has some relevance. The experience of salvation for this little girl would mean, first of all, the provision of at least the basic necessities of life, which would enable her to survive physically and psychologically and to develop as a human being. Salvation would also entail the ever-deepening realization throughout her life that God is close to her, holding her up and inviting her into a relationship marked by God's tenacious fidelity to her. The gift of salvation from God would encompass the experience of communion with others who have also experienced God's love in Christ and who celebrate that divine love in communal prayer, especially the Eucharist. Through her communion with God and others she would grow in her awareness of her own personal dignity and be given the opportunity to learn and develop her gifts. As she matures, she would be empowered to serve others in striving to create more humane living and working conditions. When she suffered failure in herself or her efforts, she would not be driven to despair because of her trust in God's abiding compassion. Her belief in the resurrection of Jesus would give her hope that the bonds of communion with God and others that she forged in life would not be severed by death. This belief would also assure that no sincere effort to make life better for herself and others, however small, will ever be lost. Rather, it will be raised up and transfigured.

The understanding of salvation as communion also means that I, and others who live in privileged situations, are called to live in solidarity with the little girl in the pink dress. Her salvation and mine are interconnected. Zizioulas is correct when he asserts that the gift of the Spirit of Christ opens up our existence to become relational. I am related to this child of God, and her well-being in this life and beyond is my concern. Salvation for her includes the compassionate solidarity of Christians and of many others who know and love God. Such solidarity entails more than sympathetic feelings; it is realized and expressed in active concern for her flourishing and that of many people living in similar situations of deprivation. My communion with her, even if expressed only through prayer and sharing of resources with those who serve the people of Haiti, strengthens my communion with God and the church. And her communion with me, nameless and from a distance, has salvific effects in my life. Together, we must hold on to the hand of a saving God.

Notes

Introduction—pages ix–xxiv

1. Gerald O'Collins, *Jesus Our Redeemer: A Christian Approach to Salvation* (New York: Oxford University Press, 2007), vi.

2. "Preface IV of Easter," in *The Roman Missal, Third Edition* (Collegeville, MN: Liturgical Press, 2011), 417.

3. Denis Edwards, *What Are They Saying about Salvation?* (New York: Paulist Press, 1986), 3–6.

4. See Denis Edwards, *How God Acts: Creation, Redemption, and Special Divine Action* (Minneapolis, MN: Fortress Press, 2010).

5. I am indebted to John Galvin for this definition of Christology, offered and analyzed in an unpublished lecture. Galvin's excellent work on Christology and soteriology has deeply influenced my own thinking and will be cited throughout this book. See especially his essay "Jesus Christ," in *Systematic Theology: Roman Catholic Perspectives*, ed. John Galvin and Francis Schüssler Fiorenza, vol. 1 (Minneapolis, MN: Fortress Press, 1991), 249–324. Galvin presents a concise and lucid overview of Christian soteriology on pp. 275–81.

6. Ibid., 252–53.

7. Elizabeth Johnson, "Jesus and Salvation," *Proceedings of the Catholic Theological Society of America* 49 (1994): 3.

8. Thomas Marsh, "Soteriology Today," *Irish Theological Quarterly* 46 (1979): 146.

9. This teaching about Christ as the unique and universal savior was reaffirmed in a particularly forceful way in the Declaration of the Congregation for the Doctrine of the Faith *Dominus Iesus: On the Unicity and Salvific Universality of Jesus Christ and the Church* (2000). See http://www.vatican.va/roman_curia/congregations/cfaith/documents/rc_con_cfaith_doc_20000806_dominus-iesus_en.html, accessed June 27, 2014.

10. Gerald O'Collins, *Christology: A Biblical, Historical, and Systematic Study of Jesus*, 2nd ed. (New York: Oxford University Press, 2009), 297.

11. See, for example, O'Collins, *Jesus Our Redeemer*, 2–3.

12. Ibid., 3.

13. Johnson, "Jesus and Salvation," 3–4.

14. Galvin, "Jesus Christ," 275. In making this point, Galvin cites an article by Cornelius Mayer, "Von der satisfactio zur liberatio? Zur Problematik eines neuen Ansatzes in der Soteriologie," *Zeitschrift für Katholische Theologie* 96 (1974): 405–14.

15. Marsh, "Soteriology Today," 151.

16. "Preface for the Epiphany of the Lord," in *Roman Missal*, 396.

17. Marsh, "Soteriology Today," 150. Paul Tillich employs the term "estrangement," which bears similarities to the notion of alienation. Tillich describes estrangement as "the personal act of turning away from that to which one belongs." Jesus is the one in whom the "New Being" overcomes this estrangement. See Paul Tillich, *Systematic Theology*, vol. 2 (Chicago: University of Chicago Press, 1957), 46, 126.

18. Melanchthon used this language in his *Loci Communes* (1521): "This is to know Christ, [namely], to know his benefits." In his discussion of the soteriology of the New Testament, Arland Hultgren borrows from this phrase for the title of his book. See *Christ and His Benefits: Christology and Redemption in the New Testament* (Philadelphia: Fortress Press, 1987).

19. Brian McDermott, *Word Become Flesh: Dimensions of Christology* (Collegeville, MN: Liturgical Press, 1993), 213.

20. It seems clear that the third edition of the *Roman Missal* accentuates the concept of sacrifice in the theology of Eucharist that is expressed in its prayers.

Chapter 1: The Saving God of Israel—pages 1–23

1. Suitbert H. Siedl, "Salvation," in *Sacramentum Verbi: An Encyclopedia of Biblical Theology*, vol. 3 (New York: Herder & Herder, 1970), 807.

2. John L. McKenzie, "Aspects of Old Testament Thought," in *The New Jerome Biblical Commentary*, ed. Raymond E. Brown, Joseph A. Fitzmyer, and Roland E. Murphy (Englewood Cliffs, NJ: Prentice-Hall, 1990), 1308.

3. Johannes B. Bauer, "Redemption," in *Sacramentum Verbi: An Encyclopedia of Biblical Theology*, vol. 2 (New York: Herder & Herder, 1970), 739. Bauer alludes to Isaiah 43:3, where Deutero-Isaiah, speaking in God's name says, "I give Egypt as your ransom, Ethiopia and Seba in return for you." Bauer suggests, however, that this expression is rhetorical.

4. Christian A. Eberhart, *The Sacrifice of Jesus: Understanding Atonement Biblically* (Minneapolis, MN: Fortress Press, 2011), 86.

5. Robin Ryan, *God and the Mystery of Human Suffering: A Theological Conversation across the Ages* (Mahwah, NJ: Paulist Press, 2011), 31.

6. K. A. Kitchen, "Exodus, The," in *The Anchor Bible Dictionary*, vol. 2, ed. David Noel Freedman (New York: Doubleday, 1992), 701.

7. Gerald O'Collins, "Salvation," in *The Anchor Bible Dictionary*, vol. 5, ed. David Noel Freedman (New York: Doubleday, 1992), 908.

8. Kitchen, "Exodus, The," 701.

9. Ibid., 704.

10. George Mendenhall and Gary Herion, "Covenant," in *The Anchor Bible Dictionary*, vol. 1, ed. David Noel Freedman (New York: Doubleday, 1992), 1186.

11. Kitchen, "Exodus, The," 706.

12. Nahum Sarna, "Exodus, Book of," *The Anchor Bible Dictionary*, vol. 2, ed. David Noel Freedman (New York: Doubleday, 1992), 698.

13. Bernhard Anderson, *Understanding the Old Testament*, 4th ed. (Englewood Cliffs, NY: Prentice-Hall, 1986), 79.

14. Walter Brueggemann, "The Book of Exodus," in *The New Interpreter's Bible: A Commentary in Twelve Volumes*, vol. 1 (Nashville, TN: Abingdon Press, 1994), 736.

15. Ibid., 737.

16. Ibid., 839–40.

17. Anderson, *Understanding the Old Testament*, 483.

18. Ibid., 484.

19. Ibid., 10.

20. Ibid., 91–92. Anderson identifies the material in Exodus 19–24 as belonging to the Old Epic tradition, i.e., the weaving together of the Yahwist and Elohist sources that form part of the Pentateuch.

21. Brueggemann, "The Book of Exodus," 834.

22. Anderson, *Understanding the Old Testament*, 92.

23. Brueggemann, "The Book of Exodus," 834–35.

24. Mendenhall and Herion, "Covenant," 1179.

25. Anderson, *Understanding the Old Testament*, 98–99.

26. Ibid., 93.

27. Mendenhall and Herion, "Covenant," 1184.

28. Anderson, *Understanding the Old Testament*, 93.

29. Leslie Hoppe, "The Deuteronomistic History," Reading Guide in *The Catholic Study Bible*, ed. Donald Senior and John J. Collins, 2nd ed. (Oxford: Oxford University Press, 2006), 180. Mendenhall and Herion identify the biblical pacts with Noah, Abraham, and David as "divine charters" rather than covenants, strictly speaking. They reflect written grants of rights by a sovereign. In these agreements, it is God, not human beings, who is bound by an oath. Mendenhall and Herion argue that these charters are, in effect, ideological legitimizations of the existing status quo. See Mendenhall and Herion, "Covenant," 1188.

30. Anderson, *Understanding the Old Testament*, 421.

31. In his reflections on Jeremiah, Richard Clifford emphasizes that the new covenant does not replace the old. It involves a renewal of the old covenant, just as the Sinai covenant was renewed after the incident of the golden calf (Exod 32–34). Clifford extends this idea to Christian understanding of the new covenant in Christ, which does not invalidate the covenant with the Jewish people. See Richard Clifford, "The Major Prophets, Baruch and Lamentations," Reading Guide, *Catholic Study Bible*, Senior and Collins, 306–7.

32. Mendenhall and Herion, "Covenant," 1179.

33. Quoted by Anderson, *Understanding the Old Testament*, 107. Anderson cites Abraham Heschel, *God in Search of Man: A Philosophy of Judaism* (New York: Farrar, Straus and Giroux, 1995). Anderson also refers to his own essay, "Coexistence with God: Heschel's Exposition of Biblical Theology," in *Abraham Joshua Heschel: Exploring His Life and Thought*, ed. John C. Merkle (New York: MacMillan, 1985), 47–65.

34. Anderson, *Understanding the Old Testament*, 107.

35. René Girard, *Violence and the Sacred*, trans. Patrick Gregory (Baltimore, MD: Johns Hopkins University Press, 1977); *Things Hidden Since the Foundation of the World*, trans. Stephen Bann and Michael Metleer (Stanford, CA: Stanford University Press, 1987). For illuminating excerpts from Girard's writings, see *The Girard Reader*, ed. James Williams (New York: Crossroad, 1996).

36. For a brief summary of Girard's arguments, see Eberhart, *The Sacrifice of Jesus*, 19–21.

37. As his thought developed, Girard acknowledged the validity of sacrificial terminology to refer to an interior attitude of offering one's life completely to God. This development is underlined by students of Girard. See the comments by James Williams in *The Girard Reader*, 70.

38. Gary A. Anderson, "Sacrifice and Sacrificial Offerings," *The Anchor Bible Dictionary*, vol. 5, ed. David Noel Freedman (New York: Doubleday, 1992), 872.

39. See the helpful summaries of these various sacrifices in Lawrence Boadt, "The Pentateuch," Reading Guide, *Catholic Study Bible*, Senior and Collins, 128–29; Eberhart, *The Sacrifice of Jesus*, 61–90.

40. Eberhart, *The Sacrifice of Jesus*, 90–91.

41. Boadt, "The Pentateuch," *The Catholic Study Bible*, 131.

42. Eberhart, *The Sacrifice of Jesus*, 71.

43. Ibid.

44. Ibid., 96 (emphasis in the original).

45. For an alternative interpretation, see T. V. Farris, *Mighty to Save: A Study in Old Testament Soteriology* (Nashville, TN: Broadman Press, 1993). Farris argues that these sacrifices involve the death of a substitute, the innocent for the guilty (157). God is angry with the sinner, not just with the sin. Sacrifices are made to satisfy the perfect holiness of God, who can neither

condone nor tolerate the utter abhorrence of sin (155). I do not find Farris's interpretation of the Old Testament evidence to be compelling.

46. Eberhart, *The Sacrifice of Jesus*, 97.

47. Anderson, *Understanding the Old Testament*, 463.

48. John Collins, "That You May Live Long in the Land: Salvation in the Old Testament," *Chicago Studies* 22 (1983): 27.

49. Ibid., 34.

50. Dianne Bergant, "Salvation," in *The Collegeville Pastoral Dictionary of Biblical Theology*, ed. Carroll Stuhlmueller (Collegeville, MN: Liturgical Press, 1996), 868.

51. See Collins, "That You May Live Long in the Land," 29.

52. Bergant, "Salvation," 868.

53. McKenzie, "Aspects of Old Testament Thought," 1309.

54. The books of the Maccabees and the book of Wisdom are not contained in the canon of the Jewish Bible.

55. Collins, "That You May Live Long in the Land," 33–34.

56. See Leslie Hoppe, "Messiah," in Stuhlmueller, *Collegeville Pastoral Dictionary of Biblical Theology*, 615–20; Marinus de Jonge, "Messiah," in *The Anchor Bible Dictionary*, vol. 4, ed. David Noel Freedman (New York: Doubleday, 1992), 777–88; McKenzie, "Aspects of Old Testament Thought," 1310–12.

57. McKenzie, "Aspects of Old Testament Thought," 1310.

58. Ibid., 1311.

59. See Hoppe, "Messiah," 617–18.

60. Quoted by de Jonge, "Messiah," 783.

61. Ibid., 787. De Jonge writes, "An investigation of Jewish writings around the beginning of the common era reveals that the term 'Messiah' was by no means generally used as a designation for God's representative or intermediary at the beginning of a new age of peace for Israel and the nations. The expectations of a radical and definitive change brought about by God did not necessarily include a task for (human or angelic) agents of divine deliverance, and the fact that God's agents were anointed need not be stressed."

62. In this section, I draw on comments found in my book *God and the Mystery of Human Suffering*, 31–34.

63. Daniel Harrington, *Why Do We Suffer: A Scriptural Approach to the Human Condition* (Franklin, WI: Sheed & Ward, 2000), 59–60.

64. Clifford, "The Major Prophets, Baruch and Lamentations," 291.

65. See de Jonge, "Messiah," 782–83; Hoppe, "Messiah," 615–20.

66. De Jonge, "Messiah," 783.

67. Ibid.

68. Leslie Hoppe notes that, because the interpretation of the messianic beliefs of the Qumran community is based on isolated passages from a number of documents, "there is no consensus on the exact contours of Qumran

messianism." He affirms, however, that "the people of Qumran believed that they were living in the eschatological age that would witness the victory of God's people over the powers of darkness." See Hoppe, "Messiah," 617.

69. See McKenzie, "Aspects of Old Testament Thought," 1310, 1312; Hoppe, "Messiah," 615–16.

70. Hoppe, "Messiah," 615.

71. McKenzie, "Aspects of Old Testament Thought," 1310.

72. Carroll Stuhlmueller, *Psalms 2: A Biblical-Theological Commentary*, Old Testament Message, vol. 22 (Wilmington, DE: Michael Glazier, 1983), 186. See also A. A. Anderson, *Psalms (73–150)*, The New Century Bible Commentary (Grand Rapids, MI: Eerdmans, 1981; London: Marshall, Morgan & Scott, 1972), 893.

73. Stuhlmueller, *Psalms 2*, 185.

Chapter 2: Salvation in the New Testament—pages 24–49

1. Edward Schillebeeckx, *Christ: The Experience of Jesus as Lord*, trans. John Bowden (New York: Crossroad, 1983), 19.

2. Christian Eberhart, *The Sacrifice of Jesus: Understanding Atonement Biblically* (Minneapolis, MN: Fortress Press, 2011), 133. Among many others, see also Herman Emiel-Mertens, *Not the Cross, But the Crucified: An Essay in Soteriology* (Louvain: Peeters Press, 1990), 39.

3. In my interpretation of this passage, I draw on Luke Timothy Johnson, *The Gospel of Luke*, ed. Daniel J. Harrington, Sacra Pagina Series (Collegeville, MN: Liturgical Press, 1991), 77–82; and Eugene LaVerdiere, *Luke*, ed. Wilfrid Harrington and Donald Senior, New Testament Message Series (Wilmington DE: Michael Glazier, 1980), 65–68.

4. LaVerdiere, *Luke*, 67; instead of "vengeance," the *New American Bible* translates this part of the verse as "a day of *vindication* by our God." The *New Revised Standard Version* has "the day of *vengeance*."

5. Johnson, *Gospel of Luke*, 81.

6. Ibid.

7. LaVerdiere, *Luke*, 68.

8. See Terrence Tilley, *The Disciples' Jesus: Christology as Reconciling Practice* (Maryknoll, NY: Orbis Books, 2008), 137–43.

9. N. T. Wright, *Jesus and the Victory of God* (Minneapolis, MN: Fortress Press, 1996), 199–203.

10. Robin Ryan, *God and the Mystery of Human Suffering: A Theological Conversation across the Ages* (Mahwah, NJ: Paulist Press, 2011), 52.

11. Gerald O'Collins, *Jesus Our Redeemer: A Christian Approach to Salvation* (New York: Oxford University Press, 2007), 95.

12. John Meier, "Jesus," in *The New Jerome Biblical Commentary*, ed. Raymond E. Brown, Joseph A. Fitzmyer, and Roland E. Murphy (Englewood Cliffs, NJ: Prentice-Hall, 1990), 1320.

13. O'Collins, *Jesus Our Redeemer*, 97.

14. John Meier, *A Marginal Jew: Rethinking the Historical Jesus*, vol. 2: *Mentor, Message, and Miracles* (New York: Doubleday, 1994), 300.

15. Meier, *A Marginal Jew*, vol. 2, *Mentor, Message, and Miracles*, 450.

16. Raymond E. Brown, *An Introduction to New Testament Christology* (New York: Paulist Press, 1994), 66n88.

17. Ryan, *God and the Mystery of Human Suffering*, 57.

18. O'Collins, *Jesus Our Redeemer*, 101.

19. This statement assumes that, while Jesus had a consciousness of his unique relationship with his Father and of his own salvific mission, there were limitations to his knowledge that were part of his being human. As truly human as well as divine, Jesus had a real human history.

20. Emiel-Mertens says that the earthly Jesus could not possibly have spoken these words, as his listeners would not have understood what he meant. See Emiel-Mertens, *Not the Cross, But the Crucified*, 50. O'Collins argues that, even if the Christian community or the evangelist added the words "to give his life as a ransom for the many," there was a basis in Jesus' life for this saying; see *Jesus Our Redeemer*, 104.

21. See John Meier, "Jesus," 1326.

22. John Galvin, "Jesus Christ," in *Systematic Theology: Roman Catholic Perspectives*, ed. John Galvin and Francis Schüssler Fiorenza, vol. 1 (Minneapolis, MN: Fortress Press, 1991), 294–95. Galvin builds on the work of Heinz Schürmann, *Gottes Reich—Jesu Geschick* (Leipzig: St. Benno, 1983), 183–251. See also John Galvin, "Jesus' Approach to Death: An Examination of Some Recent Studies," *Theological Studies* 41 (1980): 713–44.

23. John Meier, "The Eucharist at the Last Supper: Did It Happen?," *Theology Digest* 42 (1995): 335–51.

24. Ibid., 350.

25. O'Collins, *Jesus Our Redeemer*, 99–106. See also Gerald O'Collins, *Christology: A Biblical, Historical, and Systematic Study of Jesus*, 2nd ed. (Oxford: Oxford University Press, 2009), 67–81.

26. O'Collins, *Jesus Our Redeemer*, 104.

27. Ibid., 102.

28. For example, in his treatment of soteriology, Emiel-Mertens argues that it is "rather doubtful" that Jesus himself assigned to his death a salvific meaning. See *Not the Cross, But the Crucified*, 49. See also the discussion of various viewpoints on this question in Galvin, "Jesus Christ," 296–97.

29. Ibid., 297.

30. See my discussion of the resurrection in *God and the Mystery of Human Suffering*, 61–64. See also Galvin, "Jesus Christ," 297–314.

31. See Wolfhart Pannenberg, *Jesus: God and Man*, trans. Lewis Wilkins and Duane Priebe (Philadelphia: Westminster Press, 1968/1977), 69.

32. Ryan, *God and the Mystery of Human Suffering*, 63.

33. O'Collins, *Christology*, 107.

34. Joseph A. Fitzmyer, *Romans: A New Translation with Introduction and Commentary*, Anchor Bible, vol. 33 (New York: Doubleday, 1992), 389. Fitzmyer also points out that both effects of Christ's saving work—the removal of human trespasses and justification—are to be ascribed to the death *and* the resurrection.

35. Arland Hultgren, *Christ and His Benefits: Christology and Redemption in the New Testament* (Philadelphia: Fortress Press, 1987), 176.

36. Ibid., 176–77.

37. Ibid., 45–164.

38. Ibid., 42.

39. Ibid.

40. Ibid., 47–68.

41. Ibid., 48–49.

42. Ibid., 67.

43. Ibid., 69–89.

44. Ibid., 88.

45. Ibid., 91–143.

46. Hultgren argues that all of these New Testament authors assume Christ to have been preexistent; ibid., 136.

47. Hultgren observes that in Ephesians and 1 Peter, Christ is depicted as the one who manifests God's purposes and nature in the world. In Colossians, the Pastoral Letters, Hebrews, and Revelation, there is a further move "to assert an ontological unity—even if a distinction remains—between God and Christ" (137).

48. Hultgren finds some divergence among these authors regarding the universality of final salvation, a question in which he is particularly interested. While he observes that no author makes a clear statement on the matter, he concludes that universal final salvation is implied in Colossians, Ephesians, the Pastorals, and Revelation (140–41). He focuses, for example, on Revelation 22:1-5, where the seer has a vision of the river of life-giving water beside which stands the tree of life, the leaves of which "serve as medicine for the nations" (133–35). Hultgren draws on the exegesis of this passage given by Mathias Rissi and Elizabeth Schüssler Fiorenza. See Mathias Rissi, *The Future of the World: An Exegesis Study of Revelation 19:11–22:15*, Studies in Biblical Theology 23 (London: SCM Press, 1972), 80; and Elizabeth Schüssler Fiorenza, *The Book of Revelation: Justice and Judgment* (Philadelphia: Fortress Press, 1985), 52.

49. Hultgren, *Christ and His Benefits*, 145–64. Hultgren follows many biblical scholars in assuming that the Gospel of John was written by an author who then revised his text; after this, it was supplemented by an editor. Both the author and the editor were anonymous (145). He also accepts the view of Raymond Brown that the letters of John were written by a single author who was someone other than the fourth evangelist and who wrote after the exit of secessionists from the Johannine community (156).

50. Ibid., 151.

51. Ibid., 174–77.

52. Ibid., 175.

53. Ibid., 176.

54. Ibid., 177.

55. Schillebeeckx, *Christ: The Experience of Jesus as Lord*, 477.

56. Ibid., 478.

57. See J. Paul Sampley, "The Second Letter to the Corinthians: Introduction, Commentary, and Reflections," in *The New Interpreter's Bible: A Commentary in Twelve Volumes*, vol. 11 (Nashville, TN: Abingdon Press, 2000), 95.

58. Schillebeeckx, *Christ: The Experience of Jesus as Lord*, 483.

59. Ibid., 484.

60. Joseph Fitzmyer suggests that the better translation of *hilastērion* is "means of expiation"; see Joseph A. Fitzmyer, "Pauline Theology," in Brown, Fitzmyer, and Murphy, *New Jerome Biblical Commentary*, 1399.

61. Fitzmyer, *Romans*, 350. N. T. Wright comments that the use of *hilastērion* denotes that "Jesus is the place where the holy God and sinful Israel meet, in such a way that Israel, rather than being judged, receives atonement." See "The Letter to the Romans: Introduction, Commentary and Reflections," in *The New Interpreter's Bible: A Commentary in Twelve Volumes*, vol. 10 (Nashville, TN: Abingdon Press, 2002), 474.

62. Schillebeeckx, *Christ: The Experience of Jesus as Lord*, 488–89.

63. Ibid., 489 (emphasis in the original).

64. Ibid., 154.

65. Fitzmyer, "Pauline Theology," 1397.

66. Raymond E. Brown, *The Gospel According to John*, Anchor Bible, vol. 26A (New York: Doubleday, 1970), 644.

67. Schillebeeckx, *Christ: The Experience of Jesus as Lord*, 491.

68. Ibid., 494–95.

69. Ibid., 501–6. Schillebeeckx discusses several of these texts, including *1 Enoch*, the *Book of Jubilees*, the *Testaments of the Twelve Patriarchs*, the *Life of Adam and Eve*, and some of the Qumran writings.

70. Schillebeeckx, *Christ: The Experience of Jesus as Lord*, 508.

71. Ibid., 512.

72. Ibid., 514.

73. Ibid., 639.

74. See the discussion by Schillebeeckx in *Christ: The Experience of Jesus as Lord*, 29–64. Schillebeeckx's treatment of this issue was criticized by Louis Dupré. Dupré thought that Schillebeeckx's account of the relationship between experience and interpretation resulted in a relativizing of the authority of the New Testament. See "Experience and Interpretation: A Philosophical Reflection on Schillebeeckx's *Jesus* and *Christ*," *Theological Studies* 43 (1982): 30–51.

Chapter 3: Perspectives on Salvation in Early Christian Thought—
pages 50–70

1. Gerard Ettlinger, *Jesus, Christ and Savior*, Message of the Fathers of the Church Series, ed. Thomas Halton, vol. 2 (Wilmington, DE: Michael Glazier, 1987), 13.

2. H. E. W. Turner, *The Patristic Doctrine of Redemption: A Study of the Development of Doctrine During the First Five Centuries* (London: A. R. Mowbray & Co./New York: Morehouse-Gorham, 1952), 13.

3. Ettlinger, *Jesus, Christ and Savior*, 12.

4. Michael Slusser, "Primitive Christian Soteriological Themes," *Theological Studies* 44 (1983): 555–69, at 557.

5. Ibid.

6. See John Galvin, "Jesus Christ," in *Systematic Theology: Roman Catholic Perspectives*, ed. John Galvin and Francis Schüssler Fiorenza, vol. 1 (Minneapolis, MN: Fortress Press, 1991), 275.

7. Robin Ryan, *God and the Mystery of Human Suffering: A Theological Conversation across the Ages* (Mahwah, NJ: Paulist Press, 2011), 96.

8. Irenaeus of Lyons, *Against Heresies*, 4.20.1, in *Ante-Nicene Fathers*, Second Series, vol. 1: *The Apostolic Fathers, Justin Martyr, Irenaeus*, ed. Alexander Roberts and James Donaldson, rev. and arr. by A. Cleveland Coxe (Peabody, MA: Hendrickson, 1995), 487–88.

9. Ibid., 4.33.2, p. 507.

10. Ibid., 5.2.2, p. 528.

11. Augustine, *Confessions*, trans. Henry Chadwick (Oxford: Oxford University Press, 1991), 7.12.18. See the discussion in Ryan, *God and the Mystery of Human Suffering*, 85–87.

12. Augustine, *On the Gift of Perseverance* (67), in Ettlinger, *Jesus, Christ and Savior*, 151.

13. Slusser, "Primitive Christian Soteriological Themes," 558.

14. Ibid.

15. Melito of Sardis, *On Passover* (66), in Ettlinger, *Jesus, Christ and Savior*, 72.

16. Irenaeus of Lyons, *Against Heresies*, 3.18.6, pp. 447–48.

17. Clement of Alexandria, *Exhortation to the Heathens*, 11.111.3, in Ettlinger, *Jesus, Christ and Savior*, 76.

18. Gregory of Nazianzus, *Oration 30 (Fourth Theological Oration)* 6, in Ettlinger, *Jesus, Christ and Savior*, 120.

19. Ambrose, *On the Holy Spirit*, 1.9.108, in Ettlinger, *Jesus, Christ and Savior*, 148.

20. Gustaf Aulén, *Christus Victor: An Historical Study of the Three Main Types of the Idea of the Atonement* (New York: Macmillan, 1969). The book is based on a series of lectures delivered by Aulén at the University of Uppsala in 1930.

21. Slusser, "Primitive Christian Soteriological Themes," 559.

22. In his typology of patristic soteriology, H. E. W. Turner unites the themes of victory and recapitulation. See Turner, *The Patristic Doctrine of Redemption*, 47.

23. Irenaeus of Lyons, *Against Heresies*, 3.18.1, p. 446.

24. Ibid., 3.18.7, p. 448.

25. Turner, *The Patristic Doctrine of Redemption*, 63–68.

26. J. N. D. Kelly, *Early Christian Doctrines*, rev. ed. (San Francisco: Harper & Row, 1978), 173–74.

27. Ibid., 174.

28. See Galvin, "Jesus Christ," 276.

29. Irenaeus of Lyons, *Against Heresies*, 3.18.6, pp. 447–48.

30. Slusser treats the themes of Christ as revealer and as exemplar separately in his examination of patristic soteriology. See Slusser, "Primitive Christian Soteriological Themes," 565–67.

31. See Kelly, *Early Christian Doctrines*, 163–66.

32. *First Letter of Clement*, 59.2.3, in *Early Christian Fathers*, ed. Cyril Richardson (New York: Simon & Schuster, 1996), 70.

33. Justin Martyr, *First Apology* 21–22, in Ettlinger, *Jesus, Christ and Savior*, 47.

34. Irenaeus of Lyons, *Against Heresies*, 5.1.1, p. 526.

35. Clement of Alexandria, *Christ the Educator* (*Paidagōgos*), 1.7.7 (53), trans. Simon Wood, *Fathers of the Church*, vol. 23 (New York: Fathers of the Church, Inc., 1954), 49.

36. Slusser, "Primitive Christian Soteriological Themes," 563.

37. Hans Urs von Balthasar argues that this idea of the exchange is the basic intuition common to all of the patristic soteriological models. See *Theodrama: Theological Dramatic Theory*, vol. 4, *The Action*, trans. Graham Harrison (San Francisco: Ignatius Press, 1994), 244.

38. *The Roman Missal*, 3rd ed. (New Jersey: Catholic Book Publishing Corp., 2011), 381.

39. Irenaeus of Lyons, *Against Heresies* 5, preface, p. 526.

40. Ibid., 3.19.1, p. 448.

41. Athanasius of Alexandria, *Letter to Adelphius* 4, in Ettlinger, *Jesus, Christ and Savior*, 97.

42. Gregory of Nazianzus, *Oration* 29 (*Third Theological Oration*) 19, in Ettlinger, *Jesus, Christ and Savior*, 119–20.

43. Gerald Bonner, "Augustine's Conception of Deification," *Journal of Theological Studies*, n.s., 37 (1986): 369–86.

44. J. N. D. Kelly argues that deification is only a secondary motif in the thought of Augustine. See Kelly, *Early Christian Doctrines*, 391. Presumably, Bonner would disagree with Kelly's assessment.

45. Bonner, "Augustine's Conception of Deification," 381.

46. Augustine, *City of God*, trans. Marcus Dods (New York: Modern Library, 1950), 21.15, pp. 785–86.

47. Ibid.

48. Bonner quotes a passage from *On the Trinity,* 14.17.24, in Bonner, "Augustine's Conception of Deification," 381.

49. Bonner, "Augustine's Conception of Deification," 385.

50. Frances Young, *Sacrifice and the Death of Christ* (Philadelphia: Westminster Press, 1975), 90.

51. *First Letter of Clement,* 7.4-5, p. 47.

52. Athanasius, *On the Incarnation* 9, in *St. Athanasius on the Incarnation: The Treatise Incarnatione Verbi Dei,* trans. A Religious of C.S.M.V. (Crestwood, NY: St. Vladimir's Orthodox Theological Seminary), 35.

53. Ibid., 19, p. 49.

54. Ambrose, *On the Sacrament of the Lord's Becoming Flesh,* 6.56, in Ettlinger, *Jesus, Christ and Savior,* 144.

55. Young, *Sacrifice and the Death of Christ,* 73.

56. John Chrysostom, *Homilies on Hebrews* 29, in Young, *Sacrifice and the Death of Christ,* 73.

57. Augustine, *On the Trinity,* 13.11.15, in Ettlinger, *Jesus, Christ and Savior,* 155.

58. Ibid.

59. Augustine, *City of God,* 10.6, p. 309.

60. Augustine, *The Enchiridion on Faith, Hope, and Love,* chap. 41, ed. Henry Paolucci (Washington, DC: Regnery Gateway, 1961), 52.

61. John Cavadini, "An Augustinian Spirituality of the Cross," in *The Cross in Christian Tradition: From Paul to Bonaventure,* ed. Elizabeth A. Dreyer (Mahwah, NJ: Paulist Press, 2000), 169–91.

62. Augustine, *City of God,* 10.24, p. 329.

63. Augustine, *On the Trinity,* 4.17, in Cavadini, "An Augustinian Spirituality of the Cross," 179.

64. Cavadini, "An Augustinian Spirituality of the Cross," 184–85. Cavadini is quoting *City of God,* 10.24.

65. Augustine, *City of God,* 10.6, in Cavadini, "An Augustinian Spirituality of the Cross," 185.

66. Gregory of Nyssa, *Address on Religious Instruction* (*Logos Katēchētikos; Oratio Catechetica*) 23, in *Christology of the Later Fathers,* ed. Edward R. Hardy (Philadelphia: Westminster Press, 1954), 299.

67. Ibid.

68. Ibid., 24, in Hardy, *Christology of the Later Fathers,* 301.

69. Ibid., 26, in Hardy, *Christology of the Later Fathers,* 303.

70. See Randall Sachs, "Apocatastasis in Patristic Theology," *Theological Studies* 54 (1993): 617–40, at 634.

71. Augustine, *On the Trinity,* 13.12.16, in Ettlinger, *Jesus, Christ and Savior,* 155.

72. Ibid., 13.15.19, in Ettlinger, *Jesus, Christ and Savior*, 158.

73. Gregory of Nazianzus, *Oration 45* 22, in Ettlinger, *Jesus, Christ and Savior*, 124.

74. Ibid.

75. Ibid., 125.

76. Young, *Sacrifice and the Death of Christ*, 92.

77. Cavadini, "An Augustinian Spirituality of the Cross," 178–79.

78. Ibid., 179.

79. J. Patout Burns, "The Economy of Salvation: Two Patristic Traditions," *Theological Studies* 37 (1976): 598–619.

80. Ibid., 599.

81. Sachs cites *Stromateis* 7, 6.34.4, and 7, 16.102.5, in Sachs, "Apocastastasis in Patristic Theology," 618.

82. Sachs, "Apocatastasis in Patristic Theology," 621. Sachs cites *Contra Celsum* 7.72 among many other texts.

83. Sachs, "Apocatastasis in Patristic Theology," 625. There is some ambiguity in Origen about the salvation of the devil and the demons. Sachs points especially to Origen's *Letter to Friends in Alexandria*, in which Origen denies having taught the conversion and redemption of the demons.

84. Ibid., 637. See Gregory of Nyssa, *On the Making of Man*, 16.16-18, in *Nicene and Post-Nicene Fathers*, Second Series, vol. 5: *Gregory of Nyssa: Dogmatic Treatises, etc.*, ed. Philip Schaff and Henry Wace, trans. H. A. Wilson (Peabody, MA: Hendrickson Publishers, 1995), 406.

85. Gregory of Nyssa, *Address on Religious Instruction*, 26, in Hardy, *Christology of the Later Fathers*, 304.

86. See especially Augustine, *Enchiridion on Faith, Hope, and Love*, chap. 112, pp. 129–31; see also Augustine, *City of God*, 21.17-22, pp. 788–92.

87. Augustine, *City of God* 21.17, p. 788.

88. Augustine, *Enchiridion on Faith, Hope and Love*, chap. 99, pp. 115–16.

89. Ibid., chap. 103, pp. 119–22.

90. J. Neuner and J. Dupuis eds., *The Christian Faith in the Doctrinal Documents of the Catholic Church*, 6th ed. (New York: Alba House, 1996), n2301 (hereafter ND); H. Denzinger and A. Schönmetzer, *Enchiridion Symbolorum Definitionum et Declarationum de rebus fidei et morum*, 36th ed. (Freiburg im Breisgau: Herder, 1976), n411 (hereafter DS).

91. Sachs, "Apocatastasis in Patristic Theology," 639. Sachs appeals to the evaluation of these ecclesial condemnations given by Brian Daley, *The Hope of the Early Church* (New York: Cambridge University Press, 1991), 190.

92. Galvin, "Jesus Christ," 275.

93. Slusser, "Primitive Christian Soteriological Themes," 564.

94. See Elizabeth Johnson, "Jesus and Salvation," *Proceedings of the Catholic Theological Society of America* 49 (1994): 4.

Chapter 4: Medieval and Reformation Soteriologies—pages 71–100

1. Gerald O'Collins, *Jesus Our Redeemer: A Christian Approach to Salvation* (New York: Oxford University Press, 2007), 3.

2. See *Anselm of Canterbury: The Major Works*, ed. Brian Davies and G. R. Evans (Oxford: Oxford University Press, 2008), 260–356.

3. Coloman Viola, "Saint Anselm et Abelard: auteurs de deux theologies?," in *Anselm and Abelard: Investigations and Juxtapositions*, ed. G. E. M. Gasper and H. Kohlenberger (Toronto: Pontifical Institute of Medieval Studies, 2006), 131.

4. Anselm of Canterbury, "Meditation on Human Redemption," in *The Prayers and Meditations of Saint Anselm, with the Proslogion*, ed. Benedicta Ward (London: Penguin Books, 1973), 230–37.

5. Anselm, *Cur Deus Homo*, "Commendation of the Work to Pope Urban II," in *Anselm of Canterbury: The Major Works*, 261.

6. Ibid., 261–62.

7. See R. W. Southern, *Saint Anselm: A Portrait in a Landscape* (Cambridge: Cambridge University Press, 1990), 202–3.

8. Ibid., 197–202.

9. Ibid., 198.

10. Ibid., 199.

11. Southern writes, "Even if the argument can be stated without any feudal imagery, it is nevertheless also true that Anselm's thoughts about God and the universe were colored by the social arrangements with which he was familiar" (221–22). Eugene Fairweather says, "To suggest that his formulation [the idea of satisfaction made to the divine honor] is dependent on (of all things) feudal notions of honor is quite gratuitous, even though his social environment may have contributed to the form of expression that he adopts." See *A Scholastic Miscellany: Anselm to Ockham*, ed. Eugene R. Fairweather (Philadelphia: Westminster Press, 1956), 56n40.

12. Fairweather emphasizes the influence of the church's penitential system on Anselm's thought; see *A Scholastic Miscellany*, 56n40.

13. See John Galvin, "Jesus Christ," in *Systematic Theology: Roman Catholic Perspectives*, ed. John Galvin and Francis Schüssler Fiorenza, vol. 1 (Minneapolis, MN: Fortress Press, 1991), 277.

14. Southern, *Saint Anselm*, 204; Southern notes that this argument is found in the *Sententiae* of Ralph of Laon, who was the brother of Anselm of Laon, the leading theologian of that school.

15. Anselm, *Cur Deus Homo*, 1.7, in Davies and Evans, *Anselm of Canterbury: The Major Works*, 272.

16. Ibid.

17. Anselm, *Meditation on Human Redemption*, lines 61–64, in *The Prayers and Meditations of Saint Anselm*, 231.

18. Southern, *Saint Anselm*, 205.

19. Klaus Kienzler, "Anselm von Canterbury (1033–1109): Theologie wird Wissenschaft," in Gasper and Kohlenberger, *Anselm and Abelard*, 29.

20. Anselm, *Cur Deus Homo*, 1.15, in Davies and Evans, *Anselm of Canterbury: The Major Works*, 288.

21. Ibid.

22. Southern, *Saint Anselm*, 226.

23. Anselm, *Cur Deus Homo*, 2.6, in Davies and Evans, *Anselm of Canterbury: The Major Works*, 319–20.

24. Ibid., 1.24, p. 310.

25. Ibid., 1.19, p. 302.

26. Southern, *Saint Anselm*, 214.

27. Anselm, *Cur Deus Homo*, 2.20, in Davies and Evans, *Anselm of Canterbury: The Major Works*, 354.

28. Ibid., 2.5, p. 319.

29. Ibid.

30. Ibid.

31. Ibid., 318.

32. Ibid.

33. Ibid., 2.11, p. 329.

34. Ibid., 1.9, p. 279.

35. Ibid., 276.

36. Ibid., 277.

37. Ibid., 278–79.

38. Ibid., 2.14, p. 335.

39. Gustaf Aulén, *Christus Victor: An Historical Study of the Three Main Types of the Idea of the Atonement*, trans. A. G. Herbert (New York: MacMillan, 1969), 84–92.

40. Hans Küng, *On Being a Christian*, trans. Edward Quinn (New York: Doubleday, 1976), 421–24.

41. Gerald O'Collins, *Christology: A Biblical, Historical, and Systematic Study of Jesus*, 2nd ed. (Oxford, Oxford University Press, 2009), 204–5.

42. Ibid.

43. See Gisbert Greshake, "Erlösung und Freiheit: Zür Neuinterpretation der Erlösungslehre Anselms von Canterbury," *Theologische Quartalschrift* 153 (1973): 323–45. A condensed version of this article can be found in "Redemption and Freedom," *Theology Digest* 21 (1977): 61–65.

44. Walter Kasper, *Jesus the Christ*, trans. V. Green (London: Burns & Oates/New York: Paulist Press, 1976), 219–21.

45. O'Collins, *Christology*, 204.

46. O'Collins, *Jesus Our Redeemer*, 173.

47. Ibid.

48. Lisa Sowle Cahill, "Quaestio Disputata, The Atonement Paradigm: Does It Still Have Explanatory Value?," *Theological Studies* 68 (2007): 418–32, at 422.

49. One of the purported errors of Abelard that was condemned at the Council of Sens (1141) was the proposition that Christ did not assume flesh in order to liberate us from the yoke of the devil: ("*Quod Christus non assumpsit carnem, ut nos a iugo diaboli liberaret*"), DS 723.

50. See Viola, "Saint Anselm et Abelard," 125–32.

51. Richard Weingart, *The Logic of Divine Love: A Critical Analysis of the Soteriology of Peter Abailard* (Oxford: Clarendon Press, 1970).

52. See Peter Abelard, *Commentary on the Epistle to the Romans*, trans. Steven R. Cartwright, The Fathers of the Church, Medieval Continuation, vol. 12 (Washington, DC: Catholic University of America Press, 2011).

53. Steven Cartwright, introduction to Abelard, *Commentary on the Epistle to the Romans*, 6.

54. Abelard, *Commentary on the Epistle to the Romans*, 3.26, p. 164.

55. Ibid., 165.

56. Most scholars conclude that Abelard is criticizing Anselm's theory of satisfaction, though he does not mention him by name. Weingart thinks it probable that Abelard had direct acquaintance with *Cur Deus Homo*. He notes that there is textual evidence that suggests that Abelard read some of Anselm's other writings. See Weingart, *The Logic of Divine Love*, 89.

57. Abelard, *Commentary on the Epistle to the Romans*, 3.26, p. 167.

58. Weingart, *The Logic of Divine Love*, 90–91.

59. Abelard, *Commentary on the Epistle to the Romans*, 3.26, pp. 167–68.

60. Ibid., 168.

61. Ibid., 5.6, p. 206.

62. Ibid., 5.7-8, p. 206.

63. See, for example, Cartwright, introduction to Abelard, *Commentary on the Epistle to the Romans*, 50.

64. Abelard, *Commentary on the Epistle to the Romans*, 4.25, p. 204.

65. Ibid., 5.21, p. 228.

66. Ibid., 8.32, p. 281.

67. Ibid., 14.9, p. 359.

68. Cartwright gives a list of modern interpreters who view Abelard as "primarily, if not exclusively, an exemplarist." See Cartwright, introduction to ibid., 44–45.

69. Ibid., 44. Cartwright cites William of Saint Thierry, *Disputatio adversus Petrum Abaelardum, disp. 7*.

70. Paul Tillich, *Systematic Theology*, vol. 2, *Existence and the Christ* (Chicago: University of Chicago Press, 1957), 172.

71. Cartwright, introduction to Abelard, *Commentary on the Epistle to the Romans*, 51. Here Cartwright cites M. T. Clancy, *Abelard: A Medieval Life* (Oxford: Blackwell, 1997), 274.

72. Cartwright, introduction to Abelard, *Commentary on the Epistle to the Romans*, 51.

73. Abelard, *Commentary on the Epistle to the Romans*, 3.26, p. 167.

74. Weingart, *The Logic of Divine Love*, 90.

75. Ibid., 202.

76. Ibid., 128.

77. Ibid., 204.

78. O'Collins, *Jesus Our Redeemer*, 181.

79. Ibid., 182.

80. Yves Congar, *A History of Theology*, trans. Hunter Guthrie (Garden City, NY: Doubleday, 1968), 120.

81. For an extensive treatment of the soteriology of Aquinas with a focus on the question of suffering, see W. Jerome Bracken, *Why Suffering in Redemption? A New Interpretation of the Theology of the Passion in the Summa Theologica, 3, 46–49, By Thomas Aquinas* (January 1, 1978), *ETD Collection for Fordham University*. Paper AAI7814883.

82. O'Collins, *Christology*, 209.

83. Thomas Aquinas, *Summa Theologiae*, trans. Richard T. A. Murphy, vol. 54 (London: Blackfriars, 1965), III, q. 48, a. 2, p. 79.

84. Aquinas, *Summa Theologiae* III, q. 48, a. 4.

85. O'Collins, *Christology*, 210.

86. Thomas Aquinas, *Summa Theologiae*, trans. R. J. Hennessey, vol. 48 (London: Blackfriars, 1976), III, q. 1, a. 2, pp. 11–12.

87. See Augustine, *The Trinity*, 13.10, trans. Stephen McKenna, Fathers of the Church, vol. 45 (Washington, DC: CUA Press, 1963), 388–90.

88. Aquinas, *Summa Theologiae* III, q. 46, a. 2, ad. 2, p. 11.

89. Ibid.

90. Ibid., III, q. 46, a. 3, pp. 11–13.

91. Ibid., III, q. 46, a. 1, ad. 3, p. 7.

92. Ibid., III, q. 46, a. 3, p. 13.

93. Ibid., III, q. 1, a. 3, pp. 15–21. For a discussion of Aquinas's response, see Brian Davies, *The Thought of Thomas Aquinas* (Oxford: Clarendon Press, 1992), 321–22; see also O'Collins, *Christology*, 208, 211.

94. See Davies, *The Thought of Thomas Aquinas*, 321–22. Davies cites Rupert's work *De gloria et honore Filii hominis*.

95. Aquinas, *Summa Theologiae*, III, q. 3, a. 8, p. 113. See the discussion in O'Collins, *Christology*, 203–4.

96. Davies, *The Thought of Thomas Aquinas*, 321.

97. Aquinas, *Summa Theologiae* III, q. 48, a. 1, p. 77. On the grace of Christ as head of the church, see Thomas Aquinas, *Summa Theologiae*, trans. Liam Walsh, vol. 49 (London: Blackfriars, 1973), III, q. 8, pp. 3–82.

98. Ibid., III, q. 48, a. 1, p. 77.

99. Augustine, *City of God*, 10.6; trans. Marcus Dods (New York: Modern Library, 1950), 309.

100. Aquinas, *Summa Theologiae* III, q. 48, a. 3, p. 81.

101. Ibid., III, q. 48, a. 4, p. 85.

102. Aquinas, *Summa Contra Gentiles*, trans. Charles J. O'Neil (Notre Dame, IN: University of Notre Dame Press, 1957), 4.55.25, p. 244. See the discussion in Ryan, *God and the Mystery of Human Suffering*, 137–38.

103. Aquinas, *Summa Theologiae* III, q. 47, a. 3, ad. 3, p. 65.

104. Ibid., III, q. 47, a. 4, ad. 1, ad. 2, p. 67.

105. Ibid., III, q. 49, a. 4, ad. 3, p. 107.

106. Mary Ann Fatula, *Thomas Aquinas: Preacher and Friend* (Collegeville, MN: Liturgical Press, 1993), 68.

107. Thomas O'Meara, *Thomas Aquinas: Theologian* (Notre Dame, IN: University of Notre Dame Press, 1997), 135.

108. Thomas Aquinas, *Summa Theologiae*, trans. C. Thomas Moore, vol. 55 (London: Blackfriars, 1975), III, q. 56, a. 1, a. 2, pp. 67–75.

109. Ibid., III, q. 57, a. 6, p. 97.

110. Aquinas, *Summa Theologiae*, trans. David Bourke, vol. 56 (London: Blackfriars, 1975), III, q. 60, a. 6, p. 23.

111. Ibid., III, q. 62, a. 5, p. 69.

112. Ibid.

113. Ibid., III, q. 48, a. 3, p. 81.

114. Ibid., III, q. 49, a. 4, p. 107.

115. O'Collins, *Christology*, 210.

116. O'Meara, *Thomas Aquinas: Theologian*, 129.

117. Martin Luther, *Lectures on Galatians (1535)*, 2:20, in *Luther's Works*, vol. 26, ed. Jaroslav Pelikan (Saint Louis: Concordia Publishing House, 1963), 177. Luther originally delivered these lectures in the summer and fall of 1531; they were first published in 1535.

118. Ibid., 175.

119. Martin Luther, *Small Catechism*, 2.4; cited in Jaroslav Pelikan, *The Christian Tradition: A History of the Development of Doctrine*, vol. 4, Reformation of Church and Dogma (1300–1700) (Chicago: University of Chicago Press, 1984), 161.

120. Martin Luther, *The Bondage of the Will*, 18, in *Martin Luther: Selections from His Writings*, ed. John Dillenberger (Garden City, NY: Doubleday, 1961), 199.

121. Martin Luther, *Scholia on the Epistle to the Romans*, 2:15; cited in Pelikan, *The Christian Tradition*, 161.

122. Luther, *Lectures on Galatians (1535)*, 3:13, in Pelikan, *Luther's Works*, 284.

123. Aulén, *Christus Victor*, 101–22. Aulén claims that "Luther's teaching can only be rightly understood as a revival of the old classic theme of the atonement as taught by the fathers, but with a greater depth of treatment" (102). Pelikan, on the other hand, asserts that "as it has been a common oversimplification to reduce Luther's theology of the cross to a version of

the Anselmic theory of atonement through satisfaction, so it is also a form of reductionism to make the image of 'Christus Victor' exclusive—something he himself did not do." See Pelikan, *The Christian Tradition*, 163.

124. Luther, *Lectures on Galatians (1535)*, 3:13, in Pelikan, *Luther's Works*, 286–87.

125. Ibid., 2:16, p. 132.

126. Ibid., 2:20, p. 178.

127. Ibid., 3:13, p. 280.

128. Aulén, *Christus Victor*, 113.

129. Luther, *Lectures on Galatians (1535)*, 3:13, in *Luther's Works*, 277–78.

130. Ibid., 278.

131. John Calvin, *Institutes of the Christian Religion*, trans. Henry Beveridge (Grand Rapids, MI: Eerdmans, 1989), 2.16.3, p. 436.

132. Ibid.

133. Ibid., 2.16.5, p. 437.

134. Ibid.

135. Ibid.

136. Ibid., 2.16.7, p. 440.

137. See Brian McDermott, *Word Become Flesh: Dimensions of Christology* (Collegeville, MN: Liturgical Press, 1993), 225.

138. Calvin, *Institutes of the Christian Religion*, 2.16.5, pp. 438–39.

139. Ibid., 2.16.12, pp. 445–46.

140. Ibid., 2.16.11, p. 444.

141. Ibid., 2.16.10, p. 443.

142. Ibid.

143. Ibid., 2.16.11, p. 444.

144. Ibid., 2.16.13, pp. 446–47.

145. Ibid., 2.16.16, p. 450.

146. Ibid.

147. DS 1520–1583; J. Neuner and J. Dupuis, eds., *The Christian Faith in the Doctrinal Documents of the Catholic Church*, 6th ed. (New York: Alba House, 1996), nn1924–1983. Quotations from the Council of Trent in this section are taken from the translation in *The Christian Faith in the Doctrinal Documents of the Catholic Church*.

148. See the discussion in O'Collins, *Jesus Our Redeemer*, 137–38.

149. DS 1529; ND 1932.

150. DS 1530; ND 1933.

151. O'Collins, *Jesus Our Redeemer*, 138.

152. DS 1738–1759; ND 1545–1563.

153. DS 1635–1661; ND 1512–1536.

154. See the discussion in David Power, *The Eucharistic Mystery: Revitalizing the Tradition* (New York: Crossroad, 1995), 257–63.

155. DS 1740; ND 1546.

156. DS 1743; ND 1548.

157. Ibid.

158. Ibid.

159. DS 1751, 1753; ND 1555, 1557.

160. Power, *The Eucharistic Mystery*, 258.

161. O'Collins, *Jesus Our Redeemer*, 138–39.

162. Ibid., 139.

163. Ibid.

164. McDermott, *Word Become Flesh*, 228.

165. O'Collins, *Jesus Our Redeemer*, 140.

Chapter 5: Three Twentieth-Century Theologians—pages 101–26

1. For two clear and helpful discussions of Karl Rahner's Christology and soteriology, see John Galvin, "Jesus Christ," in *Systematic Theology: Roman Catholic Perspectives*, ed. John Galvin and Francis Schüssler Fiorenza, vol. 1 (Minneapolis, MN: Fortress Press, 1991), 249–324, at 314–18; and Harvey Egan, *Karl Rahner: Mystic of Everyday Life* (New York: Crossroad, 1998), 129–50.

2. Karl Rahner, "Concerning the Relationship between Nature and Grace," in *Theological Investigations*, vol. 1, *God, Christ, Mary, and Grace*, trans. Cornelius Ernst (New York: Helicon Press, 1961), 310.

3. Ibid.

4. Karl Rahner, "The One Christ and the Universality of Salvation," in *Theological Investigations*, vol. 16, *Experience of the Spirit: Source of Theology*, trans. David Moreland (New York: Crossroad, 1979), 202.

5. See Galvin, "Jesus Christ," 316. Rahner famously names this offer of grace present in the life of every person the "supernatural existential." He argues that the presence of this offer, God's drawing near to every person, has effects on us. See *Foundations of Christian Faith*, trans. William Dych (New York: Seabury, 1978), 126–33. The German original of this work was published in 1976.

6. Karl Rahner, "The Christian Understanding of Redemption," in *Theological Investigations*, vol. 21, *Science and Christian Faith*, trans. Hugh M. Riley (New York: Crossroad, 1988), 244–47.

7. Karl Rahner, "Christology in an Evolutionary View," in *Theological Investigations*, vol. 5, *Later Writings*, trans. Karl-H. Kruger (London: Darton, Longman & Todd/New York: Seabury Press, 1966), 185.

8. In *Foundations of Christian Faith*, Rahner articulates this idea in these words: "Because in the Incarnation the Logos creates the human reality by assuming it, and assumes it by emptying *himself*, for this reason there applies here, and indeed in the most radical and specific and unique way, the axiom

for understanding every relationship between God and creatures, namely, that closeness and distance, or being at God's disposal and being autonomous, do not vary for creatures in inverse, but rather in direct proportion" (226).

9. See Galvin, "Jesus Christ," 317.

10. See Aquinas, *Summa Theologiae* III, q. 9, a. 2.

11. See Rahner, "Dogmatic Reflections on the Knowledge and Self-Consciousness of Christ," in *Theological Investigations*, vol. 5, 205–8; see also Rahner, *Foundations of Christian Faith*, 249.

12. Rahner, *Foundations of Christian Faith*, 249.

13. Ibid.

14. Ibid.

15. Ibid., 248.

16. Ibid., 250.

17. Ibid., 247–49.

18. Ibid., 248.

19. Ibid., 254.

20. Ibid., 248.

21. Ibid., 248–49.

22. Ibid., 272.

23. Karl Rahner, *Prayers and Meditations: An Anthology of the Spiritual Writings of Karl Rahner*, ed. John Griffiths (New York: Seabury Press, 1980), 101.

24. Karl Rahner, "Dogmatic Questions on Easter," in *Theological Investigations*, vol. 4, *More Recent Writings*, trans. Kevin Smyth (Baltimore: Helicon Press/London: Darton, Longman & Todd, 1966), 128.

25. Rahner, *Foundations of Christian Faith*, 266.

26. Ibid.

27. Ibid., 267.

28. Rahner, "The One Christ and the Universality of Salvation," in *Theological Investigations*, vol. 16, 200.

29. Rahner, "Reconciliation and Vicarious Representation," in *Theological Investigations*, vol. 21, 257–60.

30. Ibid., 259.

31. Ibid.

32. Ibid.

33. Rahner, *Foundations of Christian Faith*, 283.

34. Rahner, "The One Christ and the Universality of Salvation," in *Theological Investigations*, vol. 16, 207.

35. Rahner, *Foundations of Christian Faith*, 284.

36. Rahner, "The One Christ and the Universality of Salvation," in *Theological Investigations*, vol. 16, 212; see also *Foundations of Christian Faith*, 284.

37. Rahner, *Foundations of Christian Faith*, 284.

38. Ibid., 435.

39. Ibid.

40. Ibid., 309.

41. For helpful introductions to Balthasar's theological project see Aidan Nichols, Introduction to *Mysterium Paschale: The Mystery of Easter*, trans. Aidan Nichols (San Francisco: Ignatius Press, 1990), 1–10; and Medard Kehl, "Hans Urs von Balthasar: A Theological Portrait," in *The Von Balthasar Reader*, ed. Medard Kehl and Werner Löser (New York: Crossroad, 1982), 3–54.

42. Hans Urs von Balthasar, *The Glory of the Lord: A Theological Aesthetics*, vol. 1, *Seeing the Form*, trans. E. Leiva-Merikakis (Edinburgh: T & T Clark, 1982), 310.

43. Ibid., 188–89.

44. See especially, *Theodrama: Theological Dramatic Theory*, vol. 4, *The Action*, trans. Graham Harrison (San Francisco: Ignatius Press, 1994).

45. Ibid., 189.

46. Ibid., 190.

47. Ibid., 338.

48. Ibid., 190.

49. Ibid., 257. Balthasar criticizes Anselm on several counts: his replacement of the patristic notion of "exchange" with a variant of the ransom motif; his lack of attention to Jesus' role as the bearer of sin; his restriction of Christ's saving work to his death, with little attention given to his life and ministry.

50. Ibid., 323.

51. Ibid., 327.

52. Balthasar, *Mysterium Paschale*, 28.

53. Balthasar, *Theodrama*, vol. 4, *The Action*, 247.

54. Balthasar, *Mysterium Paschale*, 49.

55. Balthasar, *Theodrama*, vol. 4, *The Action*, 247. Here Balthasar quotes from Gregory of Nyssa, *The Catechetical Oration*, 32.

56. Balthsar, *Theodrama*, vol. 4, *The Action*, 498.

57. Ibid., 450.

58. Balthasar, *The Von Balthasar Reader*, 120. This passage is taken from "Warum ich noch ein Christ bin" in Balthasar and Joseph Ratzinger, *Zwei Plädoyers* (Münchener Akademie-Schriften 57; Munich: Kösel, 1971), 24–30. The English translation of this work is *Two Say Why: Why I Am Still a Christian, by Hans Urs Von Balthasar and Why I Am Still in the Church, by Joseph Ratzinger*, trans. John Griffiths (London: Search Press/Chicago: Franciscan Herald Press, 1973). Balthasar's statement can be found on p. 27 of the English translation.

59. Balthasar, *The Von Balthasar Reader*, 123. This passage is taken from *Pneuma und Institution* (*Skizzen zur Theologie IV*), 49–51.

60. Balthasar, *Mysterium Paschale*, 91.

61. Ibid., 90.

62. Ibid., 117.

63. Ibid., 101.

64. Ibid., 104.

65. Balthasar, *Theodrama*, vol. 4, *The Action*, 345. Here Balthasar appeals to the theology of Karl Barth, about which Balthasar was an expert. He cites *Church Dogmatics* 2.1, p. 396.

66. On this point (and several others), Balthasar's soteriology resembles that of Jürgen Moltmann in *The Crucified God* and *The Trinity and the Kingdom*. Balthasar is critical of Moltmann's interpretation of the cross (see *Theodrama*, vol. 4, 322), arguing that Moltmann lumps together the internal divine process (the inner life of the Trinity) with the process of salvation history. Nevertheless, Balthasar's account of Calvary bears remarkable similarities to that of Moltmann.

67. Balthasar, *Mysterium Paschale*, 107–12.

68. Ibid., 111.

69. Balthasar, *Theodrama*, vol. 4, *The Action*, 500.

70. Ibid., 495.

71. Ibid., 348–49.

72. Balthasar said of von Speyr that "her work and mine is neither psychologically nor philosophically separable, two halves of a whole which, as center, has but one foundation." See *The Von Balthasar Reader*, 42.

73. Balthasar, *Mysterium Paschale*, 164. Here Balthasar appeals to a text from Thomas Aquinas in *De Anima*, 55.

74. Balthasar, *The Von Balthasar Reader*, 153. This passage is taken from *Pneuma und Institution* 401–4; 407–9.

75. Balthasar, *Mysterium Paschale*, 210.

76. Ibid., 205.

77. Ibid., 262.

78. In a recent publication Walter Kasper also proposes a soteriology of substitutionary atonement. See Walter Kasper, *Mercy: The Essence of the Gospel and the Key to Christian Life*, trans. William Madges (Mahwah, NJ: Paulist Press, 2014), 74–77.

79. Balthasar, *Theodrama*, vol. 4, *The Action*, 297. The quotation from Galot is taken from *La Rédemption, mystère d'alliance* (Paris-Bruges: Desclée de Brouwer, 1965), 268.

80. Balthasar, *Theodrama*, vol. 4, *The Action*, 241 (emphasis in the original).

81. Ibid., 243.

82. Balthasar, *Dare We Hope "That All Men Be Saved"?*, trans. David Kipp and Lothar Krauth (San Francisco: Ignatius Press, 1988).

83. Ibid., 211 (emphasis in the original).

84. Balthasar, *Theodrama*, vol. 4, *The Action*, 389.

85. Ibid., 395.

86. Ibid., 398.

87. Ibid., 483.

88. For a more complete treatment of Schillebeeckx's theology, see *The Praxis of Christian Experience: An Introduction to the Theology of Edward Schillebeeckx*, ed. Robert J. Schreiter and Mary Catherine Hilkert (San Francisco: Harper & Row, 1989). See also Ryan, *God and the Mystery of Human Suffering*, 215–40.

89. Edward Schillebeeckx, *Christ: The Experience of Jesus as Lord*, trans. John Bowden (New York: Crossroad, 1983), 477.

90. Robert Schreiter, "Edward Schillebeeckx: His Continuing Significance," in Schreiter and Hilkert, *The Praxis of Christian Experience*, 153.

91. Schillebeeckx, *Christ: The Experience of Jesus as Lord*, 791.

92. Ibid., 725.

93. Edward Schillebeeckx, *Church: The Human Story of God*, trans. John Bowden (New York: Crossroad, 1990), 5.

94. Schillebeeckx, *Christ: The Experience of Jesus as Lord*, 818.

95. Ibid., 698.

96. John Galvin, "Retelling the Story of Jesus," in Schreiter and Hilkert, *The Praxis of Christian Experience*, 54.

97. Schillebeeckx, *Christ: The Experience of Jesus as Lord*, 795.

98. Schillebeeckx, *Church: The Human Story of God*, 111–12.

99. Edward Schillebeeckx, *Jesus: An Experiment in Christology*, trans. Hubert Hoskins (New York: Crossroad, 1979), 179.

100. Schillebeeckx, *Church: The Human Story of God*, 116.

101. Schillebeeckx, *Jesus: An Experiment in Christology*, 256. See Ryan, *God and the Mystery of Human Suffering*, 225.

102. Ibid., 268.

103. Schillebeeckx, *Christ: The Experience of Jesus as Lord*, 794.

104. Schillebeeckx, *Church: The Human Story of God*, 124.

105. Schillebeeckx, *Jesus: An Experiment in Christology*, 301.

106. Edward Schillebeeckx, "The 'God of Jesus' and the 'Jesus of God,'" in *Concilium*, vol. 93 (New York: Herder & Herder, 1973), 126.

107. Ibid., 310.

108. In *Christ*, Schillebeeckx says, "Nor will the Christian blasphemously claim that God required the death of Jesus as compensation for what *we* make of our history. This sadistic interpretation of suffering is certainly alien to the most authentic tendencies of the great Christian tradition, at the very least" (728).

109. Schillebeeckx, *Church: The Human Story of God*, 120.

110. Schillebeeckx, *Christ: The Experience of Jesus as Lord*, 824. See, among other texts, Jürgen Moltmann, *The Trinity and the Kingdom: The Doctrine of God*, trans. Margaret Kohl (San Francisco: Harper & Row, 1981), 75–80.

111. Schillebeeckx, *Christ: The Experience of Jesus as Lord*, 825 (emphasis in the original). See Ryan, *God and the Mystery of Human Suffering*, 230.

112. Schillebeeckx, *Christ: The Experience of Jesus as Lord*, 799.

113. Schillebeeckx, *Jesus: An Experiment in Christology*, 641.

114. Schillebeeckx, *Christ: The Experience of Jesus as Lord*, 728.

115. Ibid., 729 (emphasis in the original).

116. Ibid., 730.

117. Schillebeeckx, *Jesus: An Experiment in Christology*, 652.

118. Schillebeeckx, *Church: The Human Story of God*, 126.

119. Ibid., 128.

120. Schillebeeckx, *Christ: The Experience of Jesus as Lord*, 466.

121. Ibid., 729.

122. Schillebeeckx, *Church: The Human Story of God*, 130.

123. Ibid., 134–39.

124. Ibid., 137.

125. Ibid., 136.

126. Ibid., 138.

127. Schillebeeckx, *Christ: The Experience of Jesus as Lord*, 806.

128. Schillebeeckx, *Church: The Human Story of God*, 131.

129. Ibid.

130. Ibid., 132.

131. Balthasar offers a lengthy critique of Rahner's soteriology in *Theodrama*, vol. 4, *The Action*, 273–84. On p. 362 of the same work, without mentioning Rahner by name, Balthasar writes, "So we should not say that the Cross is nothing other than the ('quasi-sacramental') manifestation of God's reconciliation with the world, a reconciliation that is constant, homogeneous and always part of the given; rather we should say that God, desiring to reconcile the world to himself (and hence himself to the world) acts dramatically in the Son's Cross and Resurrection." It seems clear to me that Balthasar's mention of "the ('quasi-sacramental') manifestation of God's reconciliation with the world" is a reference to Rahner's soteriology.

132. In *Christ*, Schillebeeckx speaks of "the critical barrenness of theological speculations which neglect the circumstances of Jesus' death and consider that death in and of itself, almost detached from the specific Jesus of Nazareth, then going on to ascribe to that death various world-embracing, universal saving meanings" (794). It is not clear which "theological speculations" Schillebeeckx is criticizing here. As shown in my discussion of Rahner's soteriology, he does not ignore the circumstances that led to Jesus' death, but he devotes much less attention to them than Schillebeeckx. It is clear however, that Schillebeeckx's approach to the death of Jesus and to death in general is quite distinct from that of Rahner, as expressed, for example, in the latter's theology of death, found in his *On the Theology of Death* and in later essays on the topic.

133. See Rahner, "Reconciliation and Vicarious Representation," in *Theological Investigations*, vol. 21, 265–66. In *Church: The Human Story of God*, Schillebeeckx writes, "Many existing theories of redemption through Jesus Christ deprive Jesus, his message and career of their subversive power, and even worse, sacralize violence to be a reality within God. God is said to call for a bloody sacrifice which stills or calms his sense of justice. First sin must be avenged and only then is reconciliation possible. The rejection of Jesus by God is said then to reconcile us with God. That goes against the whole proclamation and career of Jesus. Jesus refuses to heal human violence in our history through 'divine force'" (125).

134. Balthasar, *Theodrama*, vol. 4, *The Action*, 271. Balthasar includes Schillebeeckx among those theologians who, in his view, reduce the notion of solidarity to the social and psychological level, ignoring the importance of "Jesus' communion with our (sinful) nature" (267). Balthasar is critical of "a liberal Christology that puts the emphasis on Jesus' solidarity—expressed in his life and teaching—with the poor, sinners, and the marginalized and sees the Cross as nothing more than the ultimate consequence of this 'social' solidarity" (268). He thinks that such Christologies fail to do justice to the principle of the "exchange" (*commercium*), which was so important for biblical and patristic soteriology.

Chapter 6: Liberationist and Feminist Views of Salvation—pages 127–47

1. It should be noted that feminist theologians draw on a number of types and methods of theology and are not limited to those of liberationist theology. As just one example, in her soteriology Mary Grey appeals to some of the insights of process theology, in addition to those of liberationist theology. See Mary Grey, *Feminism, Redemption, and the Christian Tradition* (Mystic, CT: Twenty-Third Publications, 1990).

2. See Elizabeth Johnson, *Consider Jesus: Waves of Renewal in Christology* (New York: Crossroad, 1990), 102.

3. Jon Sobrino, *Christ the Liberator: A View from the Victims*, trans. Paul Burns (Maryknoll, NY: Orbis Books, 2001), 221.

4. Ibid., 222.

5. Gustavo Gutiérrez, *We Drink from Our Own Wells: The Spiritual Journey of a People*, trans. Matthew O'Connell (Maryknoll, NY: Orbis Books, 1984), 114–15. See Ryan, *God and the Mystery of Human Suffering: A Theological Conversation across the Ages* (New York: Paulist Press, 2011), 247.

6. Gustavo Gutiérrez, in Daniel Hartnett, "Remembering the Poor: An Interview with Gustavo Gutiérrez," *America* 188, no. 3 (February 3, 2003): 13.

7. Ibid.

8. Rosemary Radford Ruether, *Sexism and God-Talk: Toward a Feminist Theology* (Boston: Beacon, 1983), 18–19.

9. Gustavo Gutiérrez, *A Theology of Liberation*, trans. Caridad Inda and John Eagleson (Maryknoll, NY: Orbis Books, 1973), 15.

10. Ibid., 13.

11. Elizabeth Johnson, *Friends of God and Prophets: A Feminist Theological Reading of the Communion of Saints* (New York: Continuum, 1998), 35.

12. Johnson, *Consider Jesus*, 99.

13. Gutiérrez, *A Theology of Liberation*, 35. See Ryan, *God and the Mystery of Human Suffering*, 248.

14. Sobrino, *Christ the Liberator*, 226.

15. Ibid., 236 (emphasis in the original).

16. Elizabeth Johnson, *She Who Is: The Mystery of God in Feminist Theological Discourse* (New York: Crossroad, 1992), 151.

17. Ibid.

18. Ruether, *Sexism and God-Talk*, 116–19.

19. Cynthia Crysdale, *Embracing Travail: Retrieving the Cross Today* (New York: Continuum, 2001), 105.

20. Rita Nakashima Brock, "And a Little Child Will Lead Us: Christology and Child Abuse," in *Christianity, Patriarchy, and Abuse: A Feminist Critique*, ed. Joanne Carlson Brown and Carole R. Bohn (New York: Pilgrim Press, 1990), 42–61, at 52.

21. Ibid.

22. Elizabeth Schüssler Fiorenza, *Jesus: Miriam's Child, Sophia's Prophet; Critical Issues in Feminist Christology* (New York: Continuum, 1994), 106.

23. Johnson, *She Who Is*, 158.

24. Crysdale, *Embracing Travail*, 53.

25. Sobrino, *Christ the Liberator*, 305.

26. Johnson, *Consider Jesus*, 102.

27. Crysdale, *Embracing Travail*, 102–3.

28. Grey, *Feminism, Redemption, and the Christian Tradition*, 24.

29. Crysdale, *Embracing Travail*, 112.

30. Lisa Sowle Cahill, "Quaestio Disputata, The Atonement Paradigm: Does It Still Have Explanatory Value?," *Theological Studies* 68 (2007): 424.

31. Elizabeth Johnson, "Jesus and Salvation," *Proceedings of the Catholic Theological Society of America* 49 (1994): 7. Johnson cites the famous critique of Rahner's thought by his former student, J. B. Metz. Metz argued that Rahner's optimism of grace was so strong that the tragedies of history were not taken adequately into account in his system. See Johnson, 7–8; J. B. Metz, *Faith in History and Society*, trans. David Smith (New York: Seabury, 1980), 154–68.

32. In this section, I will be drawing on my discussion of Gutiérrez in *God and the Mystery of Human Suffering*, 241–68.

33. Gutiérrez, *A Theology of Liberation*, 36–37.

34. Ibid., 37.

35. Ibid., 149–87.

36. Ibid., 150–52.

37. Ibid., 151.

38. Ibid., 153.

39. Ibid.

40. Gustavo Gutiérrez, *The God of Life*, trans. Matthew J. O'Connell (Maryknoll, NY: Orbis Books, 1991), 85.

41. Ibid., 99.

42. Ibid., 102.

43. Gustavo Gutiérrez, *The Power of the Poor in History: Selected Writings*, trans. Robert R. Barr (Maryknoll, NY: Orbis Books, 1983), 15.

44. Gustavo Gutiérrez, *On Job: God-Talk and the Suffering of the Innocent*, trans. Matthew J. O'Connell (Maryknoll, NY: Orbis Books, 1987), 97.

45. Ibid., 99–100.

46. Ibid., 100.

47. Ibid.

48. Ibid.

49. Gustavo Gutiérrez, *The Truth Shall Make You Free: Confrontations*, trans. Matthew J. O'Connell (Maryknoll, NY: Orbis Books, 1990), 30.

50. Gutiérrez, *The God of Life*, 14.

51. Gutiérrez, *A Theology of Liberation*, 177 (emphasis in the original).

52. In this section, I will draw on my treatment of Johnson's theology in *God and the Mystery of Human Suffering*, 269–93.

53. Johnson, *She Who Is*, 247.

54. Ibid., 270.

55. Ibid., 253.

56. Ibid., 270.

57. Elizabeth Johnson, "Does God Play Dice? Divine Providence and Chance," *Theological Studies* 57 (1996): 3–18, at 17.

58. Johnson, *She Who Is*, 153.

59. Ibid., 168.

60. Johnson, "Jesus and Salvation," 11.

61. Johnson, *She Who Is*, 157.

62. Elizabeth Johnson, "Deep Incarnation: Prepare for Astonishment" (The Albertus Magnus Lecture, the Siena Center, Dominican University, River Forest, IL, November 19, 2009), 10. This lecture has been published by the university.

63. Johnson, "Jesus and Salvation," 14.

64. Johnson, *She Who Is*, 158.

65. Ibid.

66. Elizabeth Johnson, "And Their Eyes Were Opened: The Resurrection as Resource for Transforming Leadership," lecture given to the Joint Assembly of the Conference of Major Superiors of Men and the Leadership Confer-

ence of Women Religious, Anaheim, CA, August 1995. To my knowledge, this lecture has not been published.

67. Johnson, *She Who Is*, 159.

68. Johnson, "Jesus and Salvation," 15.

69. Elizabeth Johnson, *Quest for the Living God: Mapping Frontiers in the Theology of God* (New York: Continuum, 2008), 59.

70. Johnson, *She Who Is*, 159.

71. Johnson, *Friends of God and Prophets*, 177.

72. Johnson, "Jesus and Salvation," 10.

73. Ibid., 13–14.

74. Ibid., 9.

75. Ibid., 9–10.

76. Gerald O'Collins, *Jesus Our Redeemer: A Christian Approach to Salvation* (Oxford: Oxford University Press, 2007), 168.

77. Johnson, "Jesus and Salvation," 10.

78. Ibid., 11.

79. Ibid., 15.

80. Johnson, *Quest for the Living God*, 59.

Chapter 7: Christ and the Cosmos—pages 148–65

1. Elizabeth Johnson, *Quest for the Living God: Mapping Frontiers in the Theology of God* (New York: Continuum, 2008), 185.

2. In this section, I am dependent on the summaries provided by a number of theologians and scientists. See John Haught, *Making Sense of Evolution: Darwin, God, and the Drama of Life* (Louisville, KY: Westminster John Knox Press, 2010); Denis Edwards, *How God Acts: Creation, Redemption, and Special Divine Action* (Minneapolis, MN: Fortress Press, 2010), especially 1–14; John Polkinghorne, *Belief in God in an Age of Science* (New Haven, CT: Yale University Press, 1998); Elizabeth Johnson, *Ask the Beasts: Darwin and the God of Life* (London: Bloomsbury Press, 2014), especially chaps. 7 and 8; Elizabeth Johnson, *Quest for the Living God*, 181–201; Thomas Berry, *The Great Work: Our Way into the Future* (New York: Three Rivers Press, 1999). I have also benefited from the insights of Dr. Anthony Mahowald, an emeritus professor of biology from the University of Chicago, who has read my text and offered helpful comments for clarification.

3. Haught, *Making Sense of Evolution*, 56.

4. Edwards, *How God Acts*, 3.

5. John Haught places particular emphasis on the notion of the "drama" of the cosmos. See *Making Sense of Evolution*, especially 53–66.

6. Berry, *The Great Work*, 26.

7. Arthur Peacocke, "Theology and Science Today," in *Cosmos as Creation*, ed. Ted Peters (Nashville, TN: Abingdon, 1989), 28–43, at 32; cited

by Elizabeth Johnson, "Deep Incarnation: Prepare for Astonishment" (The Albertus Magnus Lecture, the Siena Center, Dominican University, River Forest, IL, November 19, 2009), 7. This lecture has been published by the university.

8. Johnson, "Deep Incarnation," 8.

9. Haught, *Making Sense of Evolution*, 58.

10. Holmes Rolston, *Science and Religion: A Critical Survey* (New York: Random House, 1987), 134; cited in Edwards, *How God Acts*, 12.

11. Johnson, *Ask the Beasts*, 184.

12. Edwards, *How God Acts*, 12.

13. Haught, *Making Sense of Evolution*, 85.

14. Pierre Teilhard de Chardin, "Christology and Evolution," in *Christianity and Evolution: Reflections on Science and Religion*, trans. René Hague (Orlando: Harcourt, 1971), 77.

15. Pierre Teilhard de Chardin, "Christ the Evolver" (1942), in *Christianity and Evolution*, 149 (emphasis in the original).

16. Berry, *The Great Work*, 26.

17. Thomas Berry, "The Wisdom of the Cross," in *The Christian Future and the Fate of the Earth*, ed. Mary Evelyn Tucker and John Grim (Maryknoll, NY: Orbis, 2009), 92. This chapter was originally a paper given by Berry in 1994 at a conference in Rome celebrating the three-hundredth anniversary of the birth of Saint Paul of the Cross.

18. See Thomas Aquinas, *Summa Theologiae* I, q. 47, a. 1. David Tracy also comments on this loss of a sense of nature as a manifestation of the divine in the modern world, noting, however, that indigenous traditions have preserved it. See David Tracy, "Evil, Suffering, Hope: The Search for New Forms of Contemporary Theodicy," *Proceedings of the Catholic Theological Society of America* 50 (1995): 19–20.

19. Berry, "Wonderworld as Wasteworld: The Earth in Deficit," *Cross Currents* 35 (1985): 408–22, at 415.

20. See also Tracy, "Evil, Suffering, Hope," 21.

21. Edwards, *How God Acts*, 81.

22. Thomas Aquinas, *Summa Theologiae* I, q. 8, a. 1.

23. Ibid., I, q. 22, a. 3.

24. Edwards, *How God Acts*, 61.

25. Johnson, *Quest for the Living God*, 193.

26. Ibid.

27. See Karl Rahner, *Hominisation: The Evolutionary Origin of Man as a Theological Problem, Quaestiones Disputatae*, vol. 13 (New York: Herder & Herder, 1965); *Foundations of Christian Faith*, trans. William Dych (New York: Seabury Press, 1978), 178–202; "Natural Science and Reasonable Faith," in *Theological Investigations*, vol. 21, *Science and Theology*, trans. Hugh M. Riley (New York: Crossroad, 1988), 16–55. Denis Edwards draws on Rahner's exposition in *How God Acts*, 39–45.

28. Rahner, "Natural Science and Reasonable Faith," 33.

29. Ibid., 36.

30. Edwards, *How God Acts*, 44.

31. See, among many others, Edwards, *How God Acts*, 30–33, 50–52, 63–66, 70–71; Haught, *Making Sense of Evolution*, 63–65; Johnson, *Ask the Beasts*, 154–80, 191; *Quest for the Living God*, 196–97.

32. Johnson, *Quest for the Living God*, 196.

33. Haught, *Making Sense of Evolution*, 65.

34. Ibid.

35. Edwards, *How God Acts*, 104.

36. Pierre Teilhard de Chardin, "Christianity and Evolution: Suggestions for a New Theology" (1945), *Christianity and Evolution*, 181.

37. Niels Gregersen, "The Cross of Christ in an Evolutionary World," *Dialog: A Journal of Theology* 40 (2001): 192–207. See also "*Cur deus caro*: Jesus and the Cosmos Story," *Theology and Science* 11 (2013): 370–93.

38. Gregersen, "*Cur deus caro*," 375.

39. Elizabeth Johnson, "An Earthy Christology," *America* 200, no. 12 (April 13, 2009): 30.

40. Johnson, *Ask the Beasts*, 200.

41. Johnson, "An Earthy Christology," 28.

42. Johnson, *Ask the Beasts*, 202.

43. Haught, *Making Sense of Evolution*, 93.

44. Ilia Delio, *The Unbearable Wholeness of Being* (Maryknoll, NY: Orbis Books, 2013), 88. Delio draws on the observations of Holmes Rolston in her discussion of the cruciform nature of evolution. See Holmes Rolston, "Kenosis and Nature," in *The Work of Love: Creation as Kenosis*, ed. John Polkinghorne (Grand Rapids, MI: Eerdmans, 2001), 58–60.

45. Johnson, "An Earthy Christology," 29.

46. Gerald O'Collins, *Christology: A Biblical, Historical, and Systematic Study of Jesus*, 2nd ed. (Oxford: Oxford University Press, 2009), 105.

47. Karl Rahner, "Dogmatic Questions on Easter," in *Theological Investigations*, vol. 4, *More Recent Writings*, trans. Kevin Smyth (London: Darton, Longman & Todd, 1966), 128.

48. Ambrose, *De excessu fratris sui*, bk. 1, in *Patrologia Latina*, 16:1354; cited by Johnson, "An Earthy Christology," 29.

49. Ambrose, *Epistle 35:13*, in *Patrologia Latina*, 16:1081A; cited in *Heaven and Earth Are Full of Your Glory*, statement of the U.S. Methodist-Catholic Dialogue, *Origins* 41, no. 47 (May 3, 2012): 767.

50. Edwards, *How God Acts*, 93.

51. Johnson, *Ask the Beasts*, 209.

52. See Edwards, *How God Acts*, 152; Johnson, *Ask the Beasts*, 219–20.

53. Rahner, *Foundations of Christian Faith*, 185.

54. Ibid., 181.

55. Ibid.

56. Ibid.

57. Ibid., 195.

58. Ibid., 190–91.

59. Edwards, *How God Acts*, 115.

60. Ibid., 105.

61. Another key theological issue, which limits of space prevent me from treating here, is that of how to speak of God's action in the world. The appeal to a "noninterventionist" account of divine action in the world is theologically attractive. Nevertheless, the language of God acting "from within" (rather than "from without") is still spatial language, used to depict the action of God, who is not spatial. And it is difficult to speak of the incarnation and resurrection of Jesus without connoting some sense of God "intervening" in the world. Gerald O'Collins argues that the course of events in the world "is not utterly fixed and rigidly uniform." O'Collins, who also avoids the language of "intervention," speaks of "special divine causality" whereby God acts in ways that are qualitatively distinct from the "ordinary" divine work in creating and sustaining the world. See *Jesus Our Redeemer: A Christian Approach to Salvation* (New York: Oxford University Press, 2007), 265–66; *Christology*, 112–18.

62. O'Collins, *Jesus Our Redeemer*, 263. In his book *Mercy*, Walter Kasper includes a section in which he expounds the Genesis stories of creation and fall (44–45). Commenting on Genesis 3, Kasper writes, "Alienation from God led to human alienation from nature and from other human beings. The earth now bears thorns and thistles and it has to be tilled with effort and the sweat of one's brow. New life can be born only in pain" (44). Kasper's main point in this section is that, despite sin, divine mercy "is factually palpable and effective from the very beginning" (44). It is not clear to me whether Kasper is simply expounding the narrative of Genesis, which connects "thorns and thistles" and toil and pain in nature with human sin, or whether this traditional view is one that he adopts as a theologian.

63. Thomas Aquinas, *Summa Theologiae* I, q. 49, a. 2. See Ryan, *God and the Mystery of Human Suffering: A Theological Conversation across the Ages* (Mahwah, NJ: Paulist Press, 2011), 128.

64. Haught, *Making Sense of Evolution*, 54.

65. Edwards, *How God Acts*, 11.

66. Raymond Brown, *Introduction to New Testament Christology* (New York: Paulist Press, 1994), 64–65.

67. Johnson, *Ask the Beasts*, 191.

68. Ibid., 210.

69. Ibid.

70. Denis Edwards, *The God of Evolution: A Trinitarian Theology* (Mahwah, NJ: Paulist Press, 1999), 36.

Chapter 8: Christ as Universal Savior—pages 166–86

1. John Paul II, *Novo Millennio Ineunte* (January 6, 2001), n55 (emphasis in the original). Jacques Dupuis cited this passage from the apostolic letter in his 2001 *Tablet* Open Day Lecture. See Jacques Dupuis, "Christianity and Other Religions: From Confrontation to Encounter," *The Tablet* (October 20, 2001): 4–7; (October 27, 2001): 8–10; (November 3, 2001): 8–11. In these lectures, Dupuis was commenting on his recently published book *Christianity and the Religions: From Confrontation to Dialogue*, trans. Phillip Berryman (London: Darton, Longman & Todd/Maryknoll, NY: Orbis Books, 2002). Dupuis's book was originally published as *Il cristianesimo e le religioni: Dallo scontro all'incontro* (Brescia: Edizioni Queriniana, 2001).

2. Jacques Dupuis, "Christianity and Other Religions: From Confrontation to Encounter 1," *The Tablet* (October 20, 2001): 6.

3. See Gerald O'Collins, *Christology: A Biblical, Historical, and Systematic Study of Jesus*, 2nd ed. (Oxford: Oxford University Press, 2009), 318–19.

4. Ibid., 318.

5. Justin Martyr, *Dialogue with Trypho* 45, in Francis A. Sullivan, *Salvation Outside the Church? Tracing the History of the Catholic Response* (New York: Paulist Press, 1992), 14–15. My discussion in this section is heavily dependent on Sullivan's excellent study of the question.

6. Sullivan, *Salvation Outside the Church?*, 15.

7. Justin Martyr, *First Apology* 46, in Sullivan, *Salvation Outside the Church?*, 15. Clement of Alexandria attributed the fragments of truth that existed in ancient philosophies to the divine Word, the source of all truth. See Sullivan, "Clement of Alexandria on Justification through Philosophy," in *In Many and Diverse Ways: In Honor of Jacques Dupuis*, ed. Daniel Kendall and Gerald O'Collins (Maryknoll, NY: Orbis Books, 2003), 101–13, at 112.

8. *Epistula* 102:11–15; *Corpus Scriptorum Ecclesiasticorum Latinorum* (CSEL), vol. 34, 2:553–58, in Sullivan, *Salvation Outside the Church?*, 29.

9. Origen of Alexandria, *Homiliae in Jesu Nave* 3:5; PG 12: 841–42, in Sullivan, *Salvation Outside the Church?*, 19–20. Cyprian of Carthage, *Epist. 4:4*; CSEL 3, 2:476–77, in Sullivan, *Salvation Outside the Church?*, 21.

10. Cyprian, *The Unity of the Catholic Church* 6, in Sullivan, *Salvation Outside the Church?*, 22.

11. Sullivan, *Salvation Outside the Church?*, 24.

12. Ambrose, *In Psalm.* 118 *Sermo* 8:57; PL 15:1318; Sullivan, *Salvation Outside the Church?*, 25.

13. Augustine, *Enchiridion on Faith, Hope, and Love*, 103, trans. J. F. Shaw (Washington, DC: Regnery Gateway, 1961), 120.

14. Ibid.

15. Augustine, *Contra Julianum* 4:8, in Sullivan, *Salvation Outside the Church?*, 39.

16. Fulgentius of Ruspe, *De fide, ad Petrum* 38 (79); PL 65:704; Sullivan, *Salvation Outside the Church?*, 43.

17. Council of Florence, *Decree for the Copts.* DS 1351; ND 810. The decree is quoting Fulgentius from *De fide liber ad Petrum*, 39 (80). Sullivan points out that the bishops at the Council of Florence would not have thought, as had Fulgentius, that all people who lacked Christian faith because they had not heard the Gospel would be condemned to the torments of hell for the guilt of original sin alone. By the fifteenth century, the church had come to view the penalty of original sin as the privation of the vision of God. This view, expressed by Anselm of Canterbury and adopted by Peter Abelard and Peter Lombard, was confirmed by Pope Innocent III in 1201, who taught that the punishment of original sin is the lack of the vision of God; the punishment of actual sin is "the torture of eternal hell." Sullivan adds, however, that the council would have judged Jews, Muslims, heretics, and schismatics as culpable either for refusing to accept the truth of the Christian faith or failing to remain true to it. See Sullivan, *Salvation Outside the Church?*, 45–46, 67. The teaching of Innocent III, expressed in a letter to Humbert, Archbishop of Arles, can be found in DS 780, ND 506.

18. Sullivan, *Salvation Outside the Church?*, 67–68.

19. Ibid., 68.

20. DS 1524; ND 1928.

21. Thomas Aquinas, *Summa Theologiae* III, q. 68, a. 2.

22. Ibid., III, q. 69, a. 4, ad. 2. Sullivan argues that when talking of an implicit desire for baptism, Aquinas presumably thought that "the dispositions of faith and charity which a person possesses conform his will to the will of God in his regard." See Sullivan, *Salvation Outside the Church?*, 59–60.

23. Francisco Suarez, *De fide theologica*, disp. 12, sect. 4, n22; ed. Vives, vol. 12 (Paris, 1858), 359, in Sullivan, *Salvation Outside the Church?*, 93–94.

24. Juan De Lugo, *De virtute fidei divinae*, disp. 12, nn50–51, in Sullivan, *Salvation Outside the Church?*, 95.

25. Pius IX, *Singulari quadam, Acta Pii IX*, I/1, 626, in Sullivan, *Salvation Outside the Church?*, 113.

26. Pius IX, *Quanto conficiamur moerore, Acta Pii IX*, I/3, 613, in Sullivan, *Salvation Outside the Church?*, 115. Sullivan argues that in this teaching, Pius IX was influenced by the theology of Giovanni Perrone (1794–1876) and that Perrone probably had a hand in preparing these documents for the pope (p. 116).

27. Sullivan, *Salvation Outside the Church?*, 135–36.

28. DS 3867; ND 854.

29. DS 3870; ND 855.

30. Sullivan, *Salvation Outside the Church?*, 155.

31. Thomas Aquinas, *Summa Theologiae* II-II, q. 2, a. 8, ad. 1.

32. Richard Gaillardetz and Catherine Clifford give a helpful overview of the development of this document in *Keys to the Council: Unlocking the Teaching of Vatican II* (Collegeville, MN: Liturgical Press, 2012), 180–87.

33. Ibid., 187.

34. John Paul II, *Dominum et Vivificantem* (On the Holy Spirit in the Life of the Church and the World), 53, http://www.vatican.va/holy_father/john _paul_ii/encyclicals/documents/hf_jp-ii_enc_18051986_dominum-et -vivificantem_en.html, accessed July 9, 2014.

35. John Paul II, *Redemptoris Missio* (On the Permanent Validity of the Church's Missionary Mandate), 10, http://www.vatican.va/holy_father/john _paul_ii/encyclicals/documents/hf_jp-ii_enc_07121990_redemptoris-missio _en.html, accessed July 9, 2014.

36. Ibid., 28.

37. Ibid., 55. The note to this text cites several documents here, including LG 16, NA 2, and AG 9.

38. Ibid., 5 (emphasis in the original).

39. Vatican Pontifical Council for Interreligious Dialogue and Congregation for the Evangelization of Peoples, *Dialogue and Proclamation* (Reflection and Orientations on Interreligious Dialogue and the Proclamation of the Gospel of Jesus Christ), 29, http://www.vatican.va/roman_curia /pontifical_councils/interelg/documents/rc_pc_interelg_doc_19051991 _dialogue-and-proclamatio_en.html, accessed July 9, 2014.

40. Dupuis, *Christianity and the Religions*, 72.

41. Vatican Congregation for the Doctrine of the Faith, *Dominus Iesus: On the Unicity and Salvific Universality of Jesus Christ and the Church*, 6, http://www.vatican.va/roman_curia/congregations/cfaith/documents /rc_con_cfaith_doc_20000806_dominus-iesus_en.html, accessed July 9, 2014. It should be noted that Vatican II's *Dei Verbum*, the Dogmatic Constitution on Divine Revelation, suggests that the revelation in Christ is incomplete, at least in the sense that more will be revealed at the Parousia. In n4, the Constitution says that "no new public revelation is to be expected before the glorious manifestation of our Lord, Jesus Christ (cf. 1 Tim 6:14 and Tit 2:13)." This statement implies that there will be a fuller revelation when the risen Christ is manifested to all.

42. *Dominus Iesus*, 8.

43. Ibid., 14.

44. Among many other places where Rahner makes this assertion, see *Foundations of Christian Faith*, trans. William Dych (New York: Seabury, 1978), 126–33; "Christianity and the Non-Christian Religions," *Theological Investigations*, vol. 5, *Later Writings*, trans. Karl-H. Kruger (London: Darton, Longman & Todd, 1966), 123; "On the Importance of the Non-Christian Religions for Salvation," *Theological Investigations*, vol. 18, *God and Revelation*, trans. Edward Quinn (New York: Crossroad, 1983), 291.

45. Rahner, "Christianity and the Non-Christian Religions," 121.

46. Rahner, *Foundations of Christian Faith*, 309–10.

47. Rahner, "Christianity and the Non-Christian Religions," 121.

48. Rahner, *Foundations of Christian Faith*, 314.

49. Rahner, "On the Importance of the Non-Christian Religions for Salvation," 293 (emphasis in the original).

50. Ibid., 295.

51. Rahner, *Foundations of Christian Faith*, 311–21.

52. Ibid., 318.

53. Jacques Dupuis, "Christianity and Other Religions: From Confrontation to Encounter 1," 7.

54. Jacques Dupuis, *Toward a Christian Theology of Religious Pluralism* (Maryknoll, NY: Orbis Books, 1997). For the CDF Notification, see http://www.vatican.va/roman_curia/congregations/cfaith/documents/rc_con_cfaith_doc_20010124_dupuis_en.html; accessed December 31, 2014.

55. Irenaeus of Lyons, *Against Heresies*, 4.20.1.

56. Dupuis, *Christianity and the Religions*, 142–43. Dupuis cites Xavier Léon-Dufour, *Lecture de l'Evangile selon Saint Jean*, vol. 1 (Paris: Seuil, 1988), 62–144. He also lists R. Schnackenburg, J. Dupont, A. Feuillet, and M.-E. Boismard as those who "can serve as witnesses for a universal action of the Logos before the incarnation and of the Logos as such after the incarnation, according to the Prologue of John" (143). Dupuis admits that Raymond Brown argues that in this verse the Prologue is making a direct and explicit reference to Jesus Christ as the Word incarnate. See Brown, *The Gospel According to John*, The Anchor Bible, vol. 29 (Garden City, NY: Doubleday, 1966), 27–30. Francis J. Moloney also interprets this part of the Prologue as referring to the incarnate Word. See *The Gospel of John*, ed. Daniel J. Harrington, Sacra Pagina Series (Collegeville, MN: Liturgical Press, 1998), 37. It is interesting to note that Francis Sullivan cites a text from Francisco Suarez in which Suarez appeals to John 1:9 in arguing that God offers to unbelievers to whom the Gospel has never been preached "a way by which they are enlightened and moved sufficiently for an act of faith, provided they put no obstacle in the way." See Sullivan, *Salvation Outside the Church?*, 93–94. The text from Suarez is from *De auxiliis gratiae*, lib. 4: *De auxilio sufficienti*, n17, ed. Vives, vol. 8, p. 318.

57. Dupuis, "Christianity and Other Religions: From Confrontation to Encounter 2," *The Tablet* (October 27, 2001): 9.

58. Dupuis, *Christianity and the Religions*, 166.

59. Dupuis, "Christianity and Other Religions: From Confrontation to Encounter 2," 9.

60. Jacques Dupuis, "Universality of the Word and Particularity of Jesus Christ," in *The Convergence of Theology: A Festschrift Honoring Gerald O'Collins, S. J.*, ed. Daniel Kendall and Stephen T. Davis (Mahwah, NJ: Paulist Press, 2001), 333.

61. Dupuis, *Christianity and the Religions*, 160.

62. Dupuis, "Christianity and Other Religions: From Confrontation to Encounter 2," 10.

63. Dupuis, "Christianity and Other Religions: From Confrontation to Encounter 3," *The Tablet* (November 3, 2001): 9.

64. Dupuis, "Universality of the Word and Particularity of Jesus Christ," 320. See also "Christianity and the Other Religions: From Confrontation to Encounter 3," 10.

65. Dupuis, *Christianity and the Religions*, 255.

66. Dupuis, "Universality of the Word and Particularity of Jesus Christ," 325.

67. Dupuis, "Christianity and Other Religions: From Confrontation to Encounter 2," 10.

68. The unity of the person of Christ was the major issue at the Council of Ephesus (431). See also Thomas Aquinas, *Summa Theologiae* III, q. 46, a. 12. Elsewhere I argue for the possibility that the suffering of creatures does impinge even upon the divine nature. See Robin Ryan, *God and the Mystery of Human Suffering: A Theological Conversation across the Ages* (Mahwah, NJ: Paulist Press, 2011), 310.

69. Vatican Pontifical Council for Interreligious Dialogue and Congregation for the Evangelization of Peoples, *Dialogue and Proclamation*, 29.

Chapter 9: Reflections on a Tradition—pages 187–202

1. Elizabeth Johnson, "Jesus and Salvation," *Proceedings of the Catholic Theological Society of America* 49 (1994): 3–4.

2. Edward Schillebeeckx, *Christ: The Experience of Jesus as Lord*, trans. John Bowden (New York: Crossroad, 1983), 477.

3. John Galvin, "Jesus Christ," in *Systematic Theology: Roman Catholic Perspectives*, ed. John Galvin and Francis Schüssler Fiorenza, vol. 1 (Minneapolis, MN: Fortress Press, 1991), 275.

4. Michael Slusser, "Primitive Christian Soteriological Themes," *Theological Studies* 44 (1983): 564.

5. Lisa Sowle Cahill, "Quaestio Disputata, The Atonement Paradigm: Does It Still Have Explanatory Value?," *Theological Studies* 68 (2007): 424.

6. Brian McDermott, *Word Become Flesh: Dimensions of Christology* (Collegeville, MN: Liturgical Press, 1993), 228.

7. Gerald O'Collins, *Jesus Our Redeemer: A Christian Approach to Salvation* (New York: Oxford University Press, 2007), 120n3.

8. Christian Eberhart, *The Sacrifice of Jesus: Understanding Atonement Biblically* (Minneapolis, MN: Fortress Press, 2011), 133.

9. Johnson, "Jesus and Salvation," 11.

10. See Robin Ryan, *God and the Mystery of Human Suffering: A Theological Conversation across the Ages* (Mahwah, NJ: Paulist Press, 2011), 297.

11. O'Collins, *Jesus Our Redeemer*, 108.

12. Eberhart, *The Sacrifice of Jesus*, 97.

13. Arland Hultgren, *Christ and His Benefits: Christology and Redemption in the New Testament* (Philadelphia: Fortress Press, 1987), 174–77.

14. Karl Rahner, "The One Christ and the Universality of Salvation," in *Theological Investigations*, vol. 16, *Experience of the Spirit: Source of Theology*, trans. David Moreland (New York: Crossroad, 1979), 207.

15. Frances Young, *Sacrifice and the Death of Christ* (Philadelphia: Westminster Press, 1975), 73.

16. Gerald O'Collins, *Christology: A Biblical, Historical, and Systematic Study of Jesus*, 2nd ed. (Oxford: Oxford University Press, 2009), 210; see Thomas Aquinas, *Summa Theologiae* III, q. 48, a. 3, and III, q. 49, a. 4.

17. John Calvin, *Institutes of the Christian Religion*, trans. Henry Beveridge (Grand Rapids, MI: Eerdmans, 1989), 2.16.3, p. 436.

18. Hans Urs von Balthasar, *Theodrama: Theological Dramatic Theory*, vol. 4, *The Action*, trans. Graham Harrison (San Francisco: Ignatius Press, 1994), 243.

19. See O'Collins, *Jesus Our Redeemer*, 140.

20. Walter Kasper, *Jesus the Christ*, trans. V. Green (London: Burns & Oates/New York: Paulist Press, 1976), 219–21.

21. Wolfgang Schrage, in Erhard Gerstenberger and Wolfgang Schrage, *Suffering*, trans. John E. Steely (Nashville, TN: Abingdon, 1980), 263–64. See Ryan, *God and the Mystery of Human Suffering*, 55–56.

22. Gustavo Gutiérrez, *A Theology of Liberation*, trans. Caridad Inda and John Eagleson (Maryknoll, NY: Orbis Books, 1973), 151.

23. Elizabeth Johnson, "Deep Incarnation: Prepare for Astonishment" (The Albertus Magnus Lecture, the Siena Center, Dominican University, River Forest, IL, November 19, 2009), 8. This lecture has been published by the university.

24. Denis Edwards, *How God Acts: Creation, Redemption, and Special Divine Action* (Minneapolis, MN: Fortress Press, 2010), 115.

25. O'Collins, *Jesus Our Redeemer*, 173.

26. Elizabeth Johnson, "An Earthy Christology," *America* 200, no. 12 (April 13, 2009): 28.

27. Denis Edwards, *The God of Evolution: A Trinitarian Theology* (New York: Paulist Press, 1999), 36.

28. Edward Schillebeeckx, *Church: The Human Story of God*, trans. John Bowden (New York: Crossroad, 1990), 132.

29. Jon Sobrino, *Christ the Liberator: A View from the Victims*, trans. Paul Burns (Maryknoll, NY: Orbis Books, 2001), 222.

30. Gutiérrez, *A Theology of Liberation*, 15.

31. Rosemary Radford Ruether, *Sexism and God-Talk: Toward a Feminist Theology* (Boston: Beacon, 1983), 18–19.

32. Abraham Heschel, quoted by Bernhard Anderson in *Understanding the Old Testament*, 4th ed. (Englewood Cliffs, NJ: Prentice-Hall, 1986), 107. See Abraham Heschel, *God in Search of Man: A Philosophy of Judaism* (New York: Farrar, Straus, and Giroux, 1995).

33. Anderson, *Understanding the Old Testament*, 463.

34. Rahner, "The One Christ and the Universality of Salvation," 200.

35. Hans Urs von Balthasar, *The Von Balthasar Reader*, ed. Medard Kehl and Werner Löser (New York: Crossroad, 1982), 153.

36. Edward Schillebeeckx, *Jesus: An Experiment in Christology*, trans. Hubert Hoskins (New York: Crossroad, 1979), 652.

37. Gustavo Gutiérrez, *On Job: God-Talk and the Suffering of the Innocent*, trans. Matthew J. O'Connell (Maryknoll, NY: Orbis Books, 1990), 100.

38. John D. Zizioulas, *Being as Communion: Studies in Personhood and the Church* (Crestwood, NY: St. Vladimir's Seminary Press, 1985), 44.

39. Ibid., 17.

40. Ibid., 18.

41. Ibid., 50.

42. Ibid., 18.

43. Ibid., 112.

44. Ibid., 114.

45. Timothy Radcliffe, *What Is the Point of Being Christian?* (London: Burns and Oates, 2005), 158. In this section, Radcliffe draws on the insights of Herbert McCabe. See Herbert McCabe, *Law, Love and Language* (London: Continuum, 2003).

46. Radcliffe, *What Is the Point of Being Christian?*, 159.

47. Ibid., 160.

48. Ibid., 161.

49. Ibid.

Index of Subjects

Index of Persons